LEVADAS
FOOTPATHS
of MADEIRA

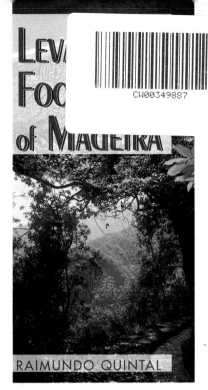

RAIMUNDO QUINTAL

THIRD EDITION

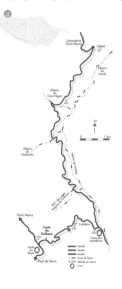

FRANCISCO RIBEIRO
EDITIONS

Title:	Levadas and Footpaths of Madeira
Edition/year	3rd. Edition/2002
Author	Raimundo Quintal
Photography	Marcial Fernandes (MF); Raimundo Quintal (RQ), António Ferro (AF), Adriano Ribeiro (AR), Juvenal Freitas (JF), Agostinho Spínola (AS), Francisco Maya (FM) e Colecção Perestrellos Photographos (Museu Vicentes)
Translation	Editorial Escudo de Oro, S.A.
Revision	James Graham Quinn
Publisher	Francisco Ribeiro & Filhos, Lda. Rua Nova de São Pedro, 27-29 • 9000-048 Funchal Tel.: 291.223930 Fax: 291.228427
Design	Meio, Serviços de Publicidade e Marketing, Lda.
Printed by	Editorial Escudo de Oro, S.A., Barcelona
Print run	6.000 ex.
Legal deposit	B.12259-2002
ISBN	972-9177-34-1 (972-9177-22-8 Portuguese Edition) (972-9177-17-1 French Edition) (972-9177-19-8 German Edition) (972-9177-25-2 Spanish Edition) (972-9177-26-0 Dutch Edition) (972-9177-27-9 Swedish Edition) (972-9177-28-7 Finish Edition)

Introduction

This is more than a simple guide book describing walks for the people of Madeira and visitors to the archipelago. This volume is aimed at helping readers to appreciate the beauty of these mountains, which emerged from the Atlantic during the Tertiary Period and became adorned with a rich carpet of trees to receive the first settlers in the 15th century.

As we describe the routes, we shall also urge visitors and locals alike to help preserve the magnificent natural and cultural heritage of Madeira and Porto Santo. Its geological formations, its flora, this or that solitary tree, a stretch of *levada* (irrigation channel), an ancient path, a staircase of *poios*, (terraces), a noble old mansion or a humble dwelling with its fine garden full of delightful forms and bright colours, all these elements form a powerful appeal to the senses, worthy of the highest praise.

The main objective of this volume is, therefore, to contribute, however modestly, to a new and urgently needed way of relating to nature. Our children and grandchildren have the sacred right to inherit an archipelago where we can feel the pleasure of living. Visitors should look at us with the respect due to a people who have, over the centuries, wisely built a magnificent humanised landscape without destroying the work of our Creator.

Schools and the media are honour-bound to play an important part in the work of providing people with ENVIRONMENTAL EDUCATION. For instance, instigating a change of habits, discouraging waste, helping us to realise that consumerism is not synonymous with the quality of life, urging a more fraternal relation with nature.

MF

MF

Numerous educators and journalists all over the world are committed to this crusade, and Madeira also has its role to play in this movement.

As a geography teacher, television producer, writer of articles and, more recently, as head of Environment and Education for Funchal City Council, I should like to take this opportunity of urging those who live here and those who visit our islands to adopt a healthy co-existence with nature. With these objectives in mind, I wrote the texts reproduced in this book, describing a Madeira within easy reach of all those who maintain the salutary custom of walking in search of pure air and spiritual peace.

RQ

The first edition was issued in 1994, and was quickly sold out, revealing the interest awakened by this modest work amongst those interested in visiting the natural beauty spots of these islands to find the perfect remedy for the stress of competitive, agitated urban life.

The second edition, year 1999, contained a chapter devoted to the history of the *levadas* (irrigation channels) and ten additional walks.

This third edition (2002) is updated and includes several new photographs.

My thanks to all at MEIO, which carried out the graphic work, and to Marcial Fernandes, author of most of the photographs in the book, for the dedication and expertise they lent to this project.

Geographical Situation

The Archipelago of Madeira lies in the North Atlantic, some 900 kilometres from continental Portugal and about 600 kilometres from the coast of Morocco. It is made up of the inhabited islands of Madeira and Porto Santo and by the uninhabited *Ilhas Desertas*, ("Desert Islands"). The Island of Madeira is the longest of all. It has a total area of 736.75 square kilometres and a maximum length of 57 kilometres, from east to west. It has a breadth of some 23 kilometres (from north to south). Its latitude is defined by parallels 32º 38´N and 32º 52´N and its longitudes are between 16º 39´W and 17º 16´W.

Porto Santo has an area of 42.17 square kilometres and lies 40 kilometres northeast of Madeira, between parallels 33º 00´N and 33º 07´N and meridians 16º 17´W and 16º 25´ W.

The Desertas form an arc southeast of Madeira in a prolongation of Ponta de São Lourenço. They lie between parallels 32º 24´N and 32º 35´N and meridians 16º 28´W and 16º 33´W. Deserta Grande, Bugio and Ilhéu Chão have a combined area of 14.23 square kilometres.

Ilhéu Chão lies 11 sea miles (20 kilometres) from Ponta de São Lourenço, and 19 miles (35 kilometres) from the port of Funchal. Funchal and Deserta Grande are separated by 22 sea miles (41 kilometres).

A channel with a maximum depth of 500 metres separates Ponta de São Lourenço from Ilhéu Chão. The characteristics of this channel and the geological structure of the islets show that the Desertas are intimately related to Madeira.

Since 23 May 1990, the Desertas have been designated an Area of Special Protection, and since 1992 have formed part of the Council of Europe's Biogenetic Reserves.

Situated 300 kilometres south-southwest from the Island of Madeira is the minuscule archipelago of the Selvagens. These islands with a total area of 3.62 square kilometres, lie between latitudes 30º 01′ N and 30º 09′N and longitudes 15º 56′ W and 16º 03′ W.

"Formed by two small groups of adjacent islands and islets: Selvagem Grande, with the islets of Palheiro de Terra and Palheiro do Mar constitute the northern group. These are separated by a deep channel some ten miles from the other group to the southwest consisting of Selvagem Pequena, Ilhéu de Fora and adjacent islets". ("Roteiro do Arquipélago da Madeira e Ilhas Selvagens", Hydrographic Institute). Because of the colonies of nesting seabirds this archipelago is of great ornithological interest and designated a Nature Reserve in October 1971.

Madeira, Porto Santo, the Desertas and the Selvagens are all Portuguese territories making up the Autonomous Region of Madeira. The region has its own government and legislative assembly. Administratively, the region is divided into 11 councils: ten on Madeira and one on Porto Santo.

Relief

From the earth's core burst out torrents of lava, ash and other pyroclastic materials, which gradually accumulated. The volcanic cones grew so much as to emerge from the ocean waters. With time, this phenomenon became consolidated. Madeira lies in an area where the ocean crust is about 130 million years old, around the turbulent Mid-Atlantic Ridge. A **"hot spot"** under the African Tectonic Plate seems to have been responsible for the rise of this magma from the depths. The elevation of this underwater structure to the surface of the Atlantic took over 100 million years. The phase of emergence, as an island rising from the water, began some 5.2 million years ago, the last eruptions occurring 25,000 years ago.

Central Mountain Range
MF

There are no historic records of volcanic manifestations, even secondary ones, on the islands and islets forming the Madeira and Selvagens archipelagos. Volcanic activity here is considered to be extinct, unlike in the Azores, younger and with active volcanoes. The volcanic craters of Madeira were profoundly corroded by erosive agents, and only two small craters are now conserved in good state, at Santo da Serra and Fanal.

This original volcanic action gave origin to the central mountainous massif formed, amongst others, by the following peaks: Ruivo

Paul da Serra

(1,862 m), Torres (1,851 m), Areeiro (1,818 m), Cidrão (1,802 m), Cedro (1,759 m), Casado (1,725 m), Grande (1,657 m) and Ferreiro (1,582 m).

By the end of the first phase, a small island had been formed, surrounded by coral reefs. Remains of the marine fauna responsible can still be found in the limestone bed at Lameiros, on the right bank of the São Vicente river.

After this initial phase, the volcanic chimneys began to produce less intense eruptions leaving behind a covering of volcanic ash, slag and bombs of basalt lava.

During this predominantly effusive volcanic period, new foci emerged to the west and east of the tiny original island. To the west, the Paul da Serra plateau (24 square kilometres) was formed, whilst to the east, the small high plateau platforms of Poiso and Santo da Serra and the São Lourenço Peninsula came into being.

The enormous tension in the interior of the volcanoes caused fractures, many of which were later filled by injections of magma, thus forming the spectacular networks of sills and dikes which can be seen in the central zone of the island and on some parts of the coastline.

Once the volcanoes had completed their work, it was the turn of torrential water from rainfall and snow to erode the rocks, whose degree of resistance varied substantially. As a result of this fierce battle between the natural elements, lasting millions of years, the landscape we now see, as beautiful as it is vast, was formed.

This journey through the geological history of the Island of Madeira would be incomplete without mention of Curral das Freiras, which many people consider to be a volcanic *caldeira* - wide crater - of the same type as those found in the Azores. This idea that the Curral is a gigantic flattened crater still enjoys widespread acceptance, but has been countered by the opinions of various geographers and geologists, such as Lyell (1854), Hartung (1864), Grabham (1948), Lautensach (1949), Orlando Ribeiro (1949) and Zbyszewski (1971). These scientists describe Curral das Freiras as "a deep (over 1,000 metres), elongated catchment basin with large vertical walls reaching a height of 600 metres, dominated by peaks rising to 1,700 metres. This gigantic depression is excavated into the pyroclastic materials of the original volcanic complex, easily eroded, prone to rockfalls, with the consequent falling back of the walls..." ("Geologia do Arquipélago da Madeira", Galopim de Carvalho and José Brandao).

The Curral das Freiras, then, is a great "cirque of erosion" formed by the powerful energies of the torrential waters which, over many thousands of years, opened up the Socorridos river valley to carry the materials collected down to the Atlantic.

To conclude this brief summary of the relief forms of the island, a reference to the coast. The coastline of Madeira is predominantly high and scarped. *Fajãs* - platforms - and pebbly beaches occupy narrow spaces between the cliffs and the sea. These *fajãs* are small flat areas at the base of the cliffs, formed by earth and rock from landslides. The northern coast is the highest and steepest of all, and access to the sea is therefore easier on the south coast.

Curral das Freiras

MF

ALTITUDE (m)
1600 - 1862
1200 - 1600
800 - 1200
400 - 800
0 - 400

The volcanic eruptions which brought Porto Santo into being ended over seven million years ago in the Miocene Period of the Tertiary Age. Porto Santo is older than Madeira!

The principal volcanic areas are found to the east and northeast. This is the zone where the highest altitudes are reached, as well as the deepest valleys, even though this is the oldest geomorphologic unit. At 517 metres, Pico do Facho is the highest of these peaks, followed by Branco (450 m), Gandaia (449 m) and Castelo (437 m).

The most important peaks in the west of the island are Espigão (270 m) and Ana Ferreira (283 m) - lower, despite their more recent formation, than the volcanic cones to the northeast.

Scrutiny of the altitudes of the two groups of volcanic cones makes it easy to deduce that Porto Santo is much lower than Madeira. Between Pico Castelo and Pico Ana Ferreira extends a depression where the airport was built. This almost flat area constitutes the third geomorphic unit of the tiny island.

The coasts to the east, north and west - high, steep and rugged - are in stark contrast with the extensive sandy beaches which occupy practically the whole of the southern coastline.

MF

East Coast of Porto Santo

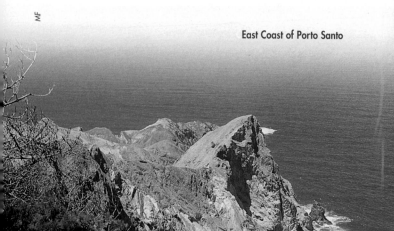

MF

Climate

The Azores anticyclone is one of the fundamental elements to understanding the characteristics of the climate not just of the Azores themselves, but also of Madeira, the Canaries and the western regions of the Iberian Peninsula. Its presence determines situations of atmospheric calm, clear skies or, at most, clouds of low vertical development without the capacity of generating rain. To put it even more simply, it is responsible for the good weather in summer and even in winter. Strangely enough, this is a case in which "those with the reputation do not enjoy the fruits", for the fact that it is called the Azores anticyclone does not, nevertheless, mean that the archipelago of the same name comes frequently under its influence. What is true is that the nucleus of high pressure is just displaced to the south of the Azores in winter, its centre whilst a little to the north, is in summer. If it is correct to speak of an annual average position, this would be to the southwest of the Azores. Madeira and the Canary Islands benefit much more, particularly in autumn and winter, from the influence of the anticyclone than do the Azores. Almost all the year round, the Azores are affected by the passing of frontal systems associated with centres of low pressure which cause cloudy weather and rainfall.

Due to its orography, the island of Madeira contains many microclimates. The central mountains, with altitudes over 1,200 metres and with an east-west orientation, creates a southern side which is sunny and protected from the action of the northerly winds, and a north side which is less exposed to the rays of the sun and swept by these humid winds.

Let us look now at some of the figures recorded by the National Institute of Meteorology and Geophysics over the 1961-1990 period at two stations on the south coast - Funchal and Lugar de Baixo - one on the north coast - Ponta Delgada - and one, finally, at Bica da Cana, on Paul da Serra, at an altitude of 1,560 metres.

The annual average temperature clearly shows the influence of geographic location and altitude:

- Lugar de Baixo: 19.4ºC
- Funchal: 18.7ºC
- Ponta Delgada: 17.9ºC
- Bica da Cana: 9.3ºC

LUGAR DE BAIXO
(ALTITUDE - 15m)

MONTH	TºC	Rainfall (mm)
J	16,9	109,3
F	16,6	83,2
M	17,7	70,0
A	17,4	35,4
M	18,5	21,5
J	20,2	14,4
J	21,9	2,1
A	22,9	4,4
S	22,9	34,3
O	21,5	85,2
N	19,6	91,8
D	17,7	103,8
YEAR	19,4	655,4

August is the hottest month of the year, with average temperatures as follows:

- Lugar de Baixo: 22.9ºC
- Funchal: 22.3ºC
- Ponta Delgada: 21.4ºC
- Bica da Cana: 14.9ºC

FUNCHAL
(ALTITUDE - 58m)

MONTH	TºC	Rainfall (mm)
J	16,1	102,7
F	15,9	87,2
M	16,3	63,6
A	16,5	38,9
M	17,7	18,9
J	19,4	11,9
J	21,1	2,5
A	22,3	3,1
S	22,3	36,7
O	20,9	75,0
N	18,8	100,8
D	16,9	99,9
YEAR	18,7	641,2

These figures indicate that summers are not excessively hot on Madeira. Temperatures are a little higher in Lugar de Baixo, which lies in a sheltered coastal plateau between Ribeira Brava and Ponta do Sol, than in Funchal. Whilst Ponta Delgada is less exposed to direct sunlight and is therefore cooler than the capital. The influence of altitude is clear in the case of Bica da Cana.

February is the month with the lowest average temperatures:

- Lugar de Baixo: 16.6ºC
- Funchal: 15.9ºC
- Ponta Delgada: 15.2ºC
- Bica da Cana: 5.8ºC

These temperatures show clearly that the winters are mild on the coast, whilst they are a little cooler on the coastal plateaux.
One of the most marked characteristics of winter in Madeira is the fact

PONTA DELGADA
(ALTITUDE - 136m)

MONTH	TºC	Rainfall (mm)
J	15,2	162,5
F	15,2	134,5
M	15,6	119,0
A	16,0	78,0
M	17,3	46,5
J	19,0	39,6
J	20,5	15,7
A	21,4	24,4
S	21,2	58,8
O	19,6	141,3
N	17,5	167,4
D	15,8	148,4
YEAR	17,9	1.136,1

that it is perfectly possible to swim in the sea, with water temperature of 17 or 18 degrees, and on the same day pass through mountains covered with a white mantle of hail or snow. It is also interesting to note that there is only a slight annual variation in temperatures in the coastal resorts. The average temperature of the hottest month is scarcely six degrees higher than that of the coolest. In the mountain areas, this difference is more accentuated, the difference in average temperature ranging from nine to ten degrees.

BICA DA CANA
(ALTITUDE - 1560m)

MONTH	T°C	Rainfall (mm)
J	5,8	448,4
F	5,8	370,4
M	6,5	299,9
A	6,4	217,1
M	8,5	133,7
J	10,9	92,6
J	14,5	25,4
A	14,9	42,2
S	13,1	156,5
O	10,6	318,8
N	8,1	422,9
D	6,3	438,6
YEAR	9,3	2.966,5

Between 1961 and 1990, the capital enjoyed an annual average of 2,165 hours of sunshine. December was the month with the least sunshine but even so an average of 140 hours sunshine were recorded, a daily average of 4.5 hours.

With regard to relative humidity, Funchal has an annual average of 71%, with the minimum in March-April (68%) and the maximum in June-July (73%).

The Lugar de Baixo station presents very similar figures to those recorded for Funchal, with annual average relative humidity of 70%. At Ponta Delgada, however, relative humidity is higher than in Funchal. This

PORTO SANTO (AIRPORT)
(ALTITUDE - 78m)

MONTH	T°C	Rainfall (mm)
J	15,6	58,6
F	15,4	45,1
M	15,7	45,3
A	16,3	24,1
M	17,6	11,9
J	19,4	8,5
J	21,1	3,1
A	22,3	4,6
S	22,1	23,1
O	20,5	48,2
N	18,3	54,5
D	16,4	59,4
YEAR	18,4	386,4

northern locality, more exposed to the prevailing winds, registers annual average relative humidity of 77%. Due to the altitude factor, Bica da Cana has a higher rate (78%), with a maximum in November (86%) and a minimum in July (61%).

The Funchal Observatory recorded annual average rainfall of 641 mm, scarcely 18 mm falling in the June-August period. Between 1961 and 1990, it rained on an average of 90 days per year, but only on an average of 20 days was the rainfall more than 10mm for day.

Lugar de Baixo recorded slightly higher rainfall than Funchal over the period, with an annual average of 655 mm, 21 mm of it between June and August.

Much higher figures were recorded for Ponta Delgada: average annual rainfall of 1,136 mm, 80 mm of it between June and August.

In Bica da Cana, average annual rainfall is 2,967 mm, with 160 mm between June and August, with 160 days of rain, hail or snow. Snow falls on an average of ten days per year, hail on around fifteen days.

The interaction of all these figures is what determines the characteristics of the climate. In Funchal and the localaties of the southern coastline, where the overwhelming majority of the population lives and where practically all tourist accommodation is located, the climate can be classified as "warm temperate" or "dry subtropical". The climate of Ponta Delgada is "wet temperate".

The climate of Porto Santo is determined by its subtropical latitude and the proximity of the northwest coast of Africa.

Mean annual air temperature over the 1961-1990 period was 18.4ºC. August was the hottest month, with an average temperature of 22.3ºC, February the coolest, with a mean annual temperature of 15.4ºC.

Seawater temperature is relatively high, varying throughout the year between 17ºC in February and 23ºC in September.

Annual average relative humidity over the 1961-1990 period was 75%, with a minimum of 72% in April and a maximum of 78% in January.

Atmospheric humidity in Porto Santo is higher than in Funchal, but precipitation is much lower (386 mm), hence the arid local landscape. The low altitudes of the island prevent the mountains from acting as condensation barriers to the prevailing sea winds from the northeast, and this explains why it rains so little in Porto Santo.

The result of the combination of all these data, is a hot, dry temperate or a dry subtropical climate.

MF

Porto Santo Beach

Dragon trees *(Dracaena drago)*

MF

Indigenous vegetation and rural landscape

aving taken a look at the geomorphologic and climatic features of the islands, we can now turn to a description of their vegetation, both indigenous and exotic, and agricultural landscape.

The indigenous plant associations of Madeira belong to the Macaronesian flora, of which the endemic species of the Selvagens, the Azores, the Canaries and the Cape Verde Islands also form part. We can define various levels of indigenous vegetation on Madeira, though the lower altitudes have become severely depleted.

RQ

Isoplexis sceptrum - a shrub of the *Laurisilva* (laurel woods)

Beside the sea and up to an altitude of 30 metres on the south coast, where the climate is hot and dry, dragon trees (*Dracaena draco*) should dominate a formation where bushes are more abundant than trees. The bushy plants include fish-stunning spurge *(Euphorbia piscatoria)*, globularia *(Globularia salicina)* and pride of Madeira *(Echium nervosum)* all of which are highly resistant to human activity and are frequently found even to-day.

When the first settlers came to the island, they found Canary laurel (*Apollonias barbujana*) wax myrtle (*Myrica faya*) and Canary holly (*Ilex canariensis*) growing abundantly in the fresher, more humid environment at an altitude of between 300 and 600 metres.

Further up to an altitude of around 1300 metres, where the highest relative humidity is found, there still remain some beautiful traces of the original hygrophilous forest - Laurisilva, or laurel woods - typical escamples include the til-tree (*Ocotea foetens*) and the Madeira mahogany (*Persea indica*) emerging amongst laurels (*Laurus azorica*) and lily-of-the-valley trees (*Clethra arborea*). Somewhat rarer is the Madeira cedar (*Juniperus cedrus*), once much sought-after for its excellent wood.

In the highest parts of the island, the vegetation cover is much poorer, though the tree heath (*Erica arborea*), the Madeira billberry (*Vaccinium padifolium*) and the rowan (*Sorbus maderensis*) are well-equipped to withstand the cold and wind.

As a result of human activity much of the island's forests have been cut and burnt, particularly at the lower altitudes, to establish agriculture and pastures for livestock.

Large areas of forest were cut down to produce wood for the sugar industry, or to extract high-quality timber, sent in enor-

The Laurisilva,
a World Heritage Site

Madeira Geranium
(Geranium maderense)

mous quantities to the capital.

Though it is true that much of the island's forest heritage has been destroyed over more than 550 years of human settlement, nonetheless worthy of note is the work carried out on this island of steep orography and poor soil. Near the sea, particularly in the south, tropical and subtropical crops are grown: bananas, sugarcane, custardapple, papaya, passionfruit, vines, etc. thrive. The most important crop by far is the banana, whilst sugarcane production is on the point of extinction.

In the north, cooler and more humid, the vine dominates the areas near the sea, whilst other crops include maize, potatoes, sweet potatoes, beans, cabbages, wheat, etc. Up to altitudes of 600-700 metres, we find conditions suited to the cultivation of such trees as the loquat, the orange and the lemon. The vine still appears here, along with the crops mentioned earlier. Nevertheless, vines are little-grown above altitudes of 300-400 metres, as the weather is unfavourable at harvest time.

At the highest cultivated level, in no case over an altitude of 1000 metres, we find fruit trees typical of western Europe: Sweet chestnut, walnut, cherry and apple.

And we cannot end this brief description of the vegetation which cloaks the slopes and valleys of Madeira without mentioning that many hectares formerly covered by Laurisilva are now occupied by eucalyptus, acacia, pine and Douglas pine. *Eucalyptus globulus* and various species of *Acacia* find conditions favourable here for growth and rapid propagation, their invasive nature causing problems to the functioning of natural systems.

On Madeira, houses in the country stand in isolation, dotting the farmlands or distributed in an orderly fashion in areas where plots

MF

Madeira rowan
(Sorbus maderensis)

of agricultural land are found bordering the roads and old paths. An exception to this rule are the tiny populations of Falca de Baixo, Falca de Cima, Lombo do Urzal and Serra de Água, in the northern district of Boaventura and in the southern district of Jardim do Mar. Nevertheless, these and other small centres of population clustering around a church or chapel are not sufficient to alter the general model, that of a dispersed population whose dwellings make up one of the typical features of the rural landscape of the island.

The climate of Porto Santo to-day is similar to that experienced by the first settlers, the vegetation growing in balance with the more arid conditions and capable of with-standing drought and highly saline soils. The dominant species of the original vegetation were dragon trees (*Dracaena draco*) and juniper (*Juniperus phoenicea*), as well as olive trees (*Olea europea ssp. maderensis*), ironwood (*Sideroxylon marmulano*), heath (*Erica scoparia*), shrubby bitter sweet *(Maytennus umbellata),* pride of Madeira (*Echium nervosum*) and numerous small plants with dainty flowers.

The need for wood and fuel, the extraction of dragon's blood, fire and the action of goats and rabbits caused the extinction of the junipers and the disappearance of practically the entire population of dragon trees.

In 1455, the Italian merchant Luís de Cadamosto wrote about Porto Santo, referring specifically to the technique of extracting resinous dragon's blood from the dragon trees, and describing the manufacture of varnish and ink for dyeing fabrics. According to that Italian navigator, the dragon's blood extractors "struck knife-blows into the foot of the tree and the following year, at a certain time, these cuts bleed resin, which they cook and purify to obtain dragon's blood".

In his manuscript, de Cadamosto also writes about the local agriculture. The crops grown in Porto Santo, he says, included "wheat and barley for their own consumption". He did not refer to the vine, perhaps because in those by-gone times grapes were not yet grown on the island, or the production was as yet insignificant.

At present, the vine is the most important crop on the island, followed by cereals.

The production of cereals depends directly on rainfall and on the time of year in which this falls. When it does not rain in winter, it is not possible to sow barley, wheat or rye. The people of Porto Santo have suffered many crises as a result of food shortages. As recently as the

The buttercup (*Ranunculus cortusifolius*) prefers the humidity of the Madeiran forest

mid-18th century, two famine years occurred in quick succession, times of great suffering as we can see from examination of the island's municipal records:

"The people ... had hardly ceased groaning under its afflictions, drying the tears caused by the food shortage of 1847 when shortly after, in 1850, we were once more cruelly punished by the torment of a new fearful drought the like of which had never been recorded in the annals of this island, depriving the people not only of the cereal harvest, causing the loss of practically all of two sowings, but also of the grape harvest..."

Cereal-growing depends exclusively on rainfall - cereals are a dry-farming crop - whilst grapes and vegetables are irrigated by the tiny amount of water retained by the island's small dams during the sporadic rains of autumn and winter.

Another factor limiting grape production is the wind. Whilst the problem of water is that there is too little, winds are excessive.

Carefully-built stone walls, cane fences or hedges of dried bushes are used to shelter the vines against the destructive action of the wind. With sufficient water and protection against the wind, the vineyards produce excellent table grapes, the delight of visitors to the island during the hot summer months.

To scare off birds, which also find the grapes of Porto Santo a great delicacy, the farmers place scarecrows and noisy distraction devices between the rows of vines. Observing the struggle between man and birds, we might easily believe that each grape is worth its weight in gold.

The fish of the waters around the island have never much attracted the people of Porto Santo, who have always preferred farming to fishing, even though environmental and social conditions were often hard.

With poor agriculture and without other sources of wealth, conditions never allowed the architecture of the island great refinement. Though degraded now, it is still possible to find houses here with roofs made of *salão*, a ferrous, clayey earth found abundantly around Porto Santo. Freely available largely, and with good sealing capacity, this material was used to roof many local houses, particularly those of the poorer members of the population.

Pico Castelo began to be forested in the early 20th century

For five centuries, Porto Santo has been on the road to desertification. The peaks became bare and the soil covering the mountainside was washed into the sea by torrential rain during stormy periods. The wind also helped sweep away the fine topsoil, leaving a barren, rocky surface.

Only a new covering of forest would be capable of halting this degradation of the mountain slopes, allowing infiltration and increasing the volume of water in the springs.

But was it possible to cover a desert with greenery?

The first positive response to this question was given during the opening years of the 20th century by a man named António Schiappa de Azevedo who, despite the enormous difficulties and the general misgivings of the population, began the reforestation of Pico Castelo. Some of the Monterey cypresses *(Cupressus macrocarpa)* which Schiappa de Azevedo planted on that high ground are still standing. For three decades, his work was not continued, but, finally, in 1954, the work of reforesting Porto Santo began in earnest and with gread intensity. The plantings were extended around Pico Castelo and the first trees were established on the hills of Branco, Juliana, Facho and Gandaia.

Over the last twenty years, reforestation work has also been carried out at Zimbralinho, the Morenos area and on Pico de Ana Ferreira. During the 1980s, over 200,000 trees were planted, testifying to the tremendous efforts being expended to combat the desertification of this island, which lies little over 600 kilometres from the Sahara.

The most frequently-planted tree is the Aleppo pine (*Pinus halepinsis*), whilst the dragon tree (*Dracaena draco*), Monterey cypress (*Cupressus macrocarpa*), casuarina (*Casuarina cunninghamiana*) and Canary island palm (*Phoenix canariensis*) are found in smaller numbers. Little by little, the green of this vegetation is hiding the scars left by erosion. This impressive rehabilitation, which began almost nine decades ago with the embellishment of the

MF

Aleppo pines on the western slopes of Pico Ana Ferreira

upper slopes of Pico Castelo, will continue with new interventions, helping this tiny island to regain all its original beauty.

MF

The Levadas
(Irrigation channels)

T he agricultural terraces and irrigation channels are the most valuable items of Madeira's cultural heritage and the living expression of how human intervention was possible without causing significant damage to the functioning of the local ecosystems. Through the construction of small *poios*, (terraces of arable soil), and the irrigation of the drier lands of the south side of the island, past generations created spectacular humanised landscapes worthy of the admiration and respect of the visitor.

The network of irrigation channels is, without doubt, the most impressive of monuments, one which is not more famous only because it does not reach up towards the heavens, but is hidden amongst leafy trees and green farmlands. I do not know if anywhere on the planet there exists such a great density of irrigation channels.

One thousand four hundred kilometres of aqueducts on an island just 737 square kilometres in size is really hard to beat!

In Madeira, the story of the levadas is inseparable from that of man.

The first of these channels were built at the dawn of settlement, and since then more and more have been added in an endless process. As Maria Lamas writes, "For this people, the problem of levadas is life itself. Without water, the land would be barren.

For water, the people of Madeira became giants in the struggle with another giant: the mountain.

For water, they were capable of superhuman efforts, supplying what nature did not.

For water, they defied death and, many times, were vanquished."

Skirting mountain ridges, descending slopes or crossing through hard

basalt rock, the irrigation channels are the indelible mark of the laborious work of generations of Madeirans.

Generations who carved out a life for themselves on an island of stony soil with an orography to dismay the most valiant.

Here, man did not give up his struggle with the environment. The first irrigation channels were built during the times immediately after the first settlement of the island in the 15th century. According to the chronicles of the time, these were open channels of little length made from wooden planks.

As water demand grew to irrigate the sugar cane fields and the vineyards, the network of irrigation channels was extended and better techniques used in their construction. Channels began to be built in solid masonry, replacing the original wooden troughs. Nowadays, new channels are built and old ones repaired using reinforced concrete.

The use of explosives greatly facilitated the opening of tunnels and galleries to collect water. The length of the channels gradually grew, and their width was increased.

The oldest irrigation channels are less than one metre in width and have a depth of between 50 and 60 centimetres. Those built over the last 50 years have a much greater capacity, with depths of between one metre and one metre twenty centimetres and widths of over one metre. In any case, the levadas continue to be narrow channels, thus, preventing loss of too much water through evaporation. Their longitudinal profile is normally designed with enormous precision. The slope is gentle to ensure the slow movement of the water, and what was once a rapid mountain torrent racing to the valley below becomes a slow-flowing current channelled by a narrow watercourse.

Be they new or old, there is always a path running alongside these irrigation channels. These paths, some wide, some narrow, are shaped according to the demands of the local topography.

In some places, these paths are so wide as to resemble avenues, whilst in others they scarcely allow room to walk. In some areas, they are bordered by sheltering heather and bilberry plants, giving walkers greater security. In others, the deep abyss looms sheer below, challenging even brave spirits in search of adventure. The irrigation channels reveal a majestic Madeira which remains hidden from the eye of the hurried tourist or the resident over-dependent on the motor car. Walking along the levadas, it is possible to discover spots of indescribeable beauty, to tread the most idyllic landscapes and to admire the rich flora of Madeira, with plants and flowers which are unique in the world.

Some cross densely wooded areas. Others run at lower altitudes and lead us to contemplate the multicoloured pattern of cultivated lands. For centuries, the irrigation channels were built solely by the force of brave men using the most rudimentary tools. These early builders worked in wicker baskets hanging from ropes tied to tree trunks or rocks above. In their hanging baskets, they cut into the rocks to open up channels through which the precious water could pass.

The work of building new channels and repairing existing ones is now somewhat less laborious. The use of modern machinery reduces labour and speeds up the working rhythm, but death still awaits the slightest distraction, the smallest error. Life is not easy for those who, from morning till night, carry bags of sand or cement along narrow paths beside awesome sheer drops.

What suffering, what labour, so that the water can reach the hydro-electric power stations.

What suffering, what labour, so that the water can reach the city and the fields.

Throughout the year, on the edge of precipices, brave men risk their lives for a trickle of water.

In the last decade of the second millennium, on this tiny island in the northern Atlantic, the search for water continues to be an epic struggle.

An epic struggle which began over five centuries ago, and which is destined to continue for many years to come.

Of the oldest irrigation channels, some have been lost, not even traces remaining.

Others, though old now, continue to fulfil the mission for which they were built.

But there also exist many newer ones, as well as those which have yet to be built.

The first irrigation channels were privately-owned. They were ordered to be built by rich men, owners of springs and farmland. The owners of these first levadas administered the water at their pleasure. When they had more water than they needed, they sold it to tenant farmers and settlers, who were often the victims of speculation.

As far back as the 15th century, however, other privately-owned irrigation channels were built by associations of "heréus".

"Heréus" are farmers who own part of the water from an irrigation channel. They pay for the conservation of the channel and elect from amongst them a committee to administer it.

Finally, individually-owned irrigation channels disappeared completely and there survive only a few associations of "heréus", still maintaining their irrigation channels in good condition.

The construction of irrigation channels with public money began during the first half of the 19th century. The Velha do Rabaçal irrigation channel was one of the first to benefit from public funds. Work on its construction began in 1835 but was not completed until 1860, testifying to the technical and financial difficulties of the enterprise.

Up to this point, state action had been limited, reduced to merely granting rights to explore waterways and to passing laws governing the administration of private irrigation channels.

However, state intervention became much more intense when in 1947 the Madeira Administrative Commission on Hydraulic Resources launched an ambitious plan for the construction of new irrigation channels.

At this time there already existed some 200 levadas forming a total network of around 1,000 kilometres. In spite of the size of this system, studies recommended a significant increase in irrigated areas and the use of the water to produce electrical power.

The island of Madeira has an area of 737 square kilometres. Of this, due to its mountainous nature and the characteristics of its soil, only 300 square kilometres are considered arable. In 1947, the irrigated area was less than 110 square kilometres, clearly insufficient.

Thanks to the expert work of a group of specialists and the spirit of sacrifice of many hundreds of local workmen, by 1967 practically the entire arable area was irrigated and the total length of the island's network of irrigation channels had been increased from 1,000 to 1,400 kilometres.

In just 20 years, almost 400 kilometres of channels were built and 209 square kilometres of land converted from dry to irrigated farming.

Moreover, four hydroelectric power stations were built, producing around 20% of the region's total power consumption.

The work carried out was particularly noteworthy due to the difficulties encountered. Almost 100 kilometres of irrigation channels were opened up at altitudes approaching 1,000 metres, in zones of frequent fogs and heavy rainfall.

Of the total of 100 kilometres of channels built above the hydropower stations, some 20 kilometres are in tunnels.

At lower altitudes, irrigation channels were opened up to carry water for irrigation and drinking water supply after passing through the turbines of the hydropower stations, located at altitudes of around 600 metres.

To further its work of opening up new irrigation channels, the state took over control of many privately-owned waters.

This was not always a peaceful process, some of the former owners reacting at times violently to government moves. The conquest of water generated much drama and more than one tragedy on this island.

Lives were lost in the heroic task of excavating into rocky slopes, opening up paths for the water, building the most splendid of monuments.

RQ

Lives were lost ingloriously in absurd struggles for the possession of a trickle of water to irrigate a tiny patch of ground.

Water has been the source of love and of hate, of co-operation and of war, of joy and of suffering.

Beyond the control of passions and conflict, the water continues to flow, gently and silently, along the irrigation channels built by countless anonymous heroes.

Lavradores market, Funchal

Population

In March 2001, when the fourteenth population census was done, there were in the Autonomous Region of Madeira 242,603 people: 238,202 living on Madeira island; 4,441 on Porto Santo. These figures give the following statistics with regard to population density:

- Madeira: 323 inhabitants/square kilometre
- Porto Santo: 106 inhabitants/square kilometre

Madeira is a very mountainous island with a high population density. However, between 1981-1991 there was a gradual population decline (1981 - 248,468 inhabitants; 1991 - 248,339 inhabitants). From 1991 to 2001 the population decreased by a further 10,000 people. On the island of Porto Santo the population fell by 265 inhabitants.

The distribution of the population in Madeira is very irregular. About 93% (220,338 inhabitants) live on the southern slopes of the island and the remaining 7% (17,864 inhabitants) are confined to the northern areas.

Funchal, the regional capital, has 43% of the population (102,521) and when combined with the adjacent municipalities of Câmara de Lobos and Santa Cruz accounts for 70% of the island's inhabitants. A remarkably high population density.

MF

Funchal

I n our discussion of the population of the island, the figures for Funchal stood out head and shoulders above all others and, therefore, even if no other reasons exist, this would suffice in itself to justify special mention of the capital of Madeira.

It is not my intention here to present an inventory of the most important architectural elements in the city. I prefer to take a quick glance from the point of view of town planning. I am particularly interested in the way, or perhaps I should say art, by which buildings are placed in relation to each other, how the roads are arranged and how they cross one another, how the squares and the small open spaces establish the urban image. In short: the way in which the urban space is organised and lived in.

Funchal was born beside the sea, in the broadest bay there was on Madeira to shelter the first city built by the Portuguese off the Iberian Peninsula.

A port city, the life of Funchal has been linked to the sea since its earliest origins. The relief posed difficulties for laying out the streets of the city. It has always been difficult to use the set-square and the ruler on Madeira.

The street known as Rua Direita or Directa was the basic line along which the original settlement was organised. Despite the name ("Straight Road"), this street is anything but straight. It linked Largo do Pelourinho with Rua da Carreira, for many years the western exit route from the city.

None of the original buildings remain now on Rua da Carreira, yet this street continues to be one of the most interesting in Funchal.

Despite the difficulties imposed by the terrain and the spontaneous way in which the city first came into being and grew, much of the oldest part of the capital obeys a geometric layout.

From the point of view of the early city, Rua de Santa Maria is a very important thoroughfare.

Rua de Santa Maria is almost rectilinear, running parallel to the coast, and has served as the organising element for successive generations of urban growth.

The houses built in the 15th century have disappeared completely. What remains is a harmonious urban centre with buildings dating to the 17th and 18th centuries rehabilitated as dwellings, shops and other services.

A view of Funchal from the east

Various secondary roads cross Rua de Santa Maria perpendicularly.

This simple layout is also found in the urbanised area around Rua da Alfandega, originally known as Rua dos Mercadores.

Why was the oldest nucleus of the city built in this way?

Why did those originally responsible for town planning here opt for winding roads with no apparent order?

The solution employed in Funchal, as in Ponta Delgada and Angra do Heroísmo in the Azores, reveals, perhaps, the early influence of the Renaissance ideas in the building of the Atlantic cities of Portugal.

Due to its rapid growth, stimulated by the sugar trade, Funchal was elevated to the category of city on 21 August 1508 by Royal Charter of Don Manuel. Funchal lived its childhood and adolescence when Renaissance ideas were spreading in southern Europe, ideas which, in terms of architecture, gave rise to Manuelin and Baroque styles.

The Colegio Church is the finest baroque construction. Built by the Jesuits in the 17th century, its high altar is richly engraved and gilded.

One of the most characteristic architectural features in the historic city centre of Funchal are its towers and viewpoints with their views over the sea. These towers are often built a little back from the façade of the buildings.

A delight to the eye, the beauty and harmony of Funchal is particularly impressive when viewed from the sea.

The bay and the three rivers flowing down from the high moun-

MF

Funchal from the sea

tain peaks are essential signs of identity of the capital of the Autonomous Region of Madeira. Funchal grew up here much in the same way as a climbing plant might. With its roots clinging to the edge of the bay, it gradually extended around this vast amphitheatre. The tiny houses hidden amongst the grapevines growing along the ridges separating the streams. The green of the gardens and farmlands dominated the landscape of this garden city.

Towards the end of the 1960s, new hotels began to be built in the west of the city. Many workers came from the country to take part

Santa Catarina park, Funchal _{MF}

in construction work, and the township spread higher up on the hillside. The woods which formerly supplied Funchal with firewood were cut back, many gardens were devoured by the new developments. Even so, the city continues to boast the appearance of a garden city, green areas still occupying a significant proportion of the urban space.

Funchal was born beside a bay of calm waters, but grew with its back to the sea. The housefronts always faced inland, as can be seen by the arrangement of Rua de Santa Maria and Rua da Alfandega.

The city only began to turn its face towards the sea in the 1940s, when Avenida do Mar was built. This development heralded the golden age of public works of the *Estado Novo*.

The results soon began to be seen. Avenida do Mar, the sea front, became the principal meeting-point in the city, particularly on summer afternoons, evenings and nights.

More recently, during the 1980s, the construction of the marina created a new space to socialize in Funchal. Here, cultures meet in perfect harmony. The young and the old, taking the iodine of the sea breeze far from the noise and fumes of cars, find pleasure here. European development funds have had a powerful impact on Madeira's road network. New fast roads connect the capital with the rest of the island, so that it is now easy to reach, by public or private transport, places all over the island which form the starting-point for the most delightful walks to discover rural landscapes filled with ethnographic interest, magnificent forests of indigenous trees, awesome volcanic rocks carved out by the force of water, all this and much more.

Walks

Lagoa do Vento - Risco - 25 Fontes

We need to walk more, to improve our health, to get to know these lands better. Let us begin around Rabaçal, on the western slopes of the only large plateau on Madeira, Paúl da Serra.

Take one of the next couple of weekends or a public holiday. Prepare food and drink, ensure you have suitable footwear, pack a pullover and an anorak in your rucksack.

Remember that you are going to visit spots at an altitude of around 1,000 metres, where rain is much more frequent than in Funchal and where temperatures are, on average, around 6ºC lower than on the southern coast of the island.

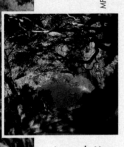

MF

Lagoa do Vento

Get a group of friends together and start out in good time. The ideal is four or five people to a car. That way you save petrol and pollute less. When you reach the flat top of Paúl da Serra, before descending to the hostel at Rabaçal, stop and go up to the fire lookout post on the peak overlooking the regulating reservoir of Calheta hydroelectric power station. On a clear, mistless day, we can enjoy a fine view of the bare plateau, from which waters run north and south down to the sea. The views from here of Lombadas da Calheta, on the south side, and the deep, narrow Ribeira da Janela Valley, winding away to the north, are extraordinarily beautiful.

Starting-point:
Paul da Serra, by the great reservoir.

Arrival points: 1)
Paul da Serra; 2)
Lombo do Salão,
Calheta.

MF

View point at Risco

If during the descent to the house at Rabaçal you cannot find the entrance to the narrow path which runs amongst heather to Lagoa do Vento, ask the guards at the house for precise directions.

Some two kilometres of difficult terrain separate the house from the lake known as

Length:
1) 12 km;
2) 15 km

Lagoa do Vento (Lagoa da Àgua do Vento), so allow 45-60 minutes to complete this stretch.

Words cannot express the marvels of the landscape around this tiny lake, carved into the surrounding cliffs. When the

sun rises over Paúl da Serra plateau and the wind creates a veil from the water emerging from the rocky heights, we can often witness a spectacular rainbow. Seeing is believing. The return route is along the same path to the house. From here, we visit Risco, one kilometre away. The path is flat and just fifteen minutes later we will be standing before an impressive landscape nothing could possibly prepare us for as we cross the harsh, monotonous surface of Paul da Serra. The water descending from the Lagoa do Vento, hid-

Risco

den a hundred metres further up, only becomes calm when it reaches the Poço do Risco, more than a hundred metres below the path. From the small viewpoint, we can contemplate this grandiose natural monument, formed by the persistent action of water on the volcanic rock over hundreds of thousands of years. The damp habitat of the enormous rockside is decorated and filled with mosses, ferns, grasses and bushes adapted to this environment.

Once you have absorbed the scenery at Risco, we can start out for the 25 Fontes. Returning towards the house at Rabaçal, a signpost to the 25 Fontes indicates a path to the right. Take this path downwards until you come to an irrigation channel, walk in the opposite direction to that of the water running along it.

The route is not difficult, though at some points the path beside the channel becomes very narrow and is unprotected, making this walk unsuitable for those who suffer from vertigo. Just over an hour after starting out along the channel, we come to a tiny lake surrounded by dense vegetation, into which a series of fountains from the rocky walls spill their waters. We have reached the 25 Fontes!

It is natural to wish to halt here for a time to listen to the murmuring of the water and the chant of the birds which wing amongst the branches of the laurels and the heather. It is possible to lose all notion of time here, particularly if one is interested in ferns, such is the variety found here.

MF

25 Fontes

But do not wait until the day begins to end before starting out on the return route to Rabaçal, for weather conditions can change very quickly at these altitudes. The sky can be completely blue, but in just minutes the mist descends rapidly along the hillside, invading the valleys, and visibility is reduced to practically zero, causing serious problems to those who do not know the island interior well.

Those walking along this levada cannot fail to ask themselves where this water goes. Well then, here is the answer: the water from the Levada das 25 Fontes (or Levada Nova do Rabaçal) supplies the Calheta hydroelectric power station, after which it flows into two smaller channels watering the hot lowlands of Calheta and Ponta do Sol.

MF **Levada from 25 Fontes**

Finally, those not wishing to return to the original starting-point of this first walk may opt to return by going through the tunnel and thence descend to Calheta.

LAGOA do VENTO
Risco
25 FONTES

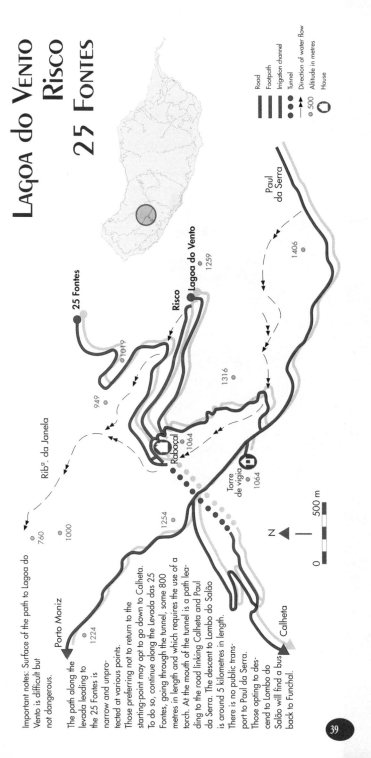

Important notes: Surface of the path to Lagoa do Vento is difficult but not dangerous.

The path along the levada leading to the 25 Fontes is narrow and unprotected at various points.

Those preferring not to return to the starting-point may opt to go down to Calheta. To do so, continue along the Levada das 25 Fontes, going through the tunnel, some 800 metres in length and which requires the use of a torch. At the mouth of the tunnel is a path leading to the road linking Calheta and Paul da Serra. The descent to Lombo do Salão is around 5 kilometres in length. There is no public transport to Paul da Serra. Those opting to descend to Lombo do Salão will find a bus back to Funchal.

Legend:
Road
Footpath
Irrigation channel
Tunnel
Direction of water flow
500 Altitude in metres
House

Rib.ª da Janela

760
1000

Porto Moniz
1224

25 Fontes
1019
949

Risco
Lagoa do Vento
1259

1316

1254

Rabaçal
1064

Torre de vigia
1064

Paul da Serra
1406

N

0   500 m

Calheta

GalHano

T owards the end of 1961, notices were published calling for tender for the construction of the irrigation channel to supply water to the Ribeira da Janela hydroelectric power station.

In September 1965, a firework display celebrated the inauguration of the new hydroelectric power station along what is Madeira's longest watercourse.

Time:
7 hours

Ribeira da Janela Valley and dike islet

The outcome of almost four years of work full of risk and danger, often under bad weather conditions. Only men of the highest courage could make it possible to build this enormous monument with its 16-kilometre length and its

Starting-point: Paul da Serra, beside the Fonte do Bispo forestry post.

Arrival point: Ribeira da Janela hydroelectric power station regulating reservoir, at Lamaceiros, hamlet above Porto Moniz.

Length:
19 km

twelve tunnels. Blood, sweat and tears were shed before the turbines could begin to turn from the force of the flowing water after falling some 400 metres.

How about a walk along this levada?

That is exactly what we shall do, in a walk from Fonte do Bispo, situated on the edge of Paúl da Serra above the slopes of Faja da Ovelha. Passing through Campo Grande do Paúl, on the descent to Porto Moniz, we come to the forestry post at Fonte do Bispo on the left. Opposite the entrance to the house at Fonte do Bispo, on the north side of the road and duly signposted, is

the path which goes down through Fonte do
Galhano and ends at the irrigation channel
which feeds the regulating reservoir for the
Ribeira da Janela hydroelectric power station. Downhill all the way, the path is some
7 kilometres in length, but only steeper and

a little more difficult towards the end. In any case, a walking stick
will be of enormous assistance over this first stage of our walk,
which begins at an altitude of 1250 metres and takes us down to
400 metres above sea level.

Parish of Ribeira da Janela RQ

In the Paul, when the wind is strong, all protection seems insufficient. Braken and the odd heather bush form the epidermis of this
almost skeletal soil. Nothing better to warm ourselves up than a
brisk walking pace.

After a few minutes, conditions become much less unpleasant.
Heather begins to abound, accompanied by bilberry plants. Laurel,
til-trees, lily-of-the-valley trees, Madeira mahogany, all welcome
the visitor who can now take off anorak and pullover. Already close
to the levada, the warm, damp air provides perfect conditions to
allow this dense and beautiful variety of vegetation to prosper.

Two hours or so suffice to reach the cabin used by the irrigation channel maintenance personnel. This point marks the end of the first
stage of our excursion. Now we must have a good lunch, for we
have another twelve thousand metres to walk before we reach the
regulating reservoir of the Ribeira da Janela hydroelectric power
station. You should allow from four to five hours for this second leg
of the journey. If time and stamina allow, the interval between the
two stages can be filled with a visit to the bed of the Janela River,
which is where the irrigation channel collects most of the water it

transports. The source of the irrigation channel is around one kilometre from the path, and to get there we have to cross a tunnel some 200 metres in length.

On arrival by the stream one feels small before such grandeur. The crystalline water babbles gently over the rounded pebbles! Those sides carved almost vertically by the water in times of fury! How many shades of green?

RQ

Descent the Galhano to irrigation channel

From the right-hand side of the river the walker can observe another short irrigation channel-around 3 kilometers in length- which empties its waters into the source of the great canal. From here to the reservoir, with its capacity of fourteen thousand cubic meters which feeds the hydroelectric power station, is a walk of almost 13 kilometers.

Everything ready for the second stage? Everything OK? Let us start out, then, before it gets too late.

Torch in hand, wearing our waterproofs, ready to cross the first of the eight tunnels we shall find along the way. It is only 200 metres in length. Only? Yes, only. What are 200 metres compared to the almost 1,200 metres of the second tunnel, which we shall shortly encounter?

This is a tunnel worthy of the name. Those wishing to cross it should prepare themselves mentally to walk for twenty minutes through the very heart of the rock, and for a good bath towards the end, where water gushes from a crevasse in a basalt dike.

After the darkness of the tunnel, the joy of the light reflecting on the waters of the Ribeira das Lajes Negras do Galhano, a tributary of the great Janela River.

The three tunnels which follow are all short, the third just 30 metres in length, the fourth almost 80, the fifth around 50.

The sixth of these tunnels is somewhat longer, about 200 metres. The seventh is shorter again but, being curved, we shall only be able to catch a small glimpse of the light at the opposite end fom the half-way-point.

Between these two tunnels stands a small house beside the aqueduct, rarely used by the watchmen, who know it as the Casa do Mestrezinho. The house marks a point just under five kilometres

A tunnel of the Galhano irrigation channel

RQ

from the end of the levada, and stands on a ridge preceding a beautiful wooded area with Canary willows and lily-of-the-valley trees. The seventh tunnel ends beside Morcegos or the Aguagens creek, where a great landslide once occurred, destroying one section of the canal. The necessary repair was extremely difficult, but it is now completely safe to walk along.

Shortly after this creek, we come to the mouth of the eighth and last tunnel, less than 200 metres in length. For a few hundred metres more, ferns of various species and forms continue to cover the slopes and to carpet the bottom of the tiny valleys. Leaping from the til-tree to Madeira mahogany and from these to the laurels and wax myrtles, the climbing plant which produces the *maracujá* banana accompanies us almost to our destination.

Meanwhile, the appearance of the terraces (*poios*) near the irrigation channel indicates the proximity of Lamaceiros in Porto Moniz.

On the other side of the valley, the houses of the tiny village of Ribeira da Janela huddle around the simple but pretty church. A new road winds up the hillside towards Fanal.

Down below, the mouth of the great river and the rock which permanently watches over it. What a picture!

GALHANO

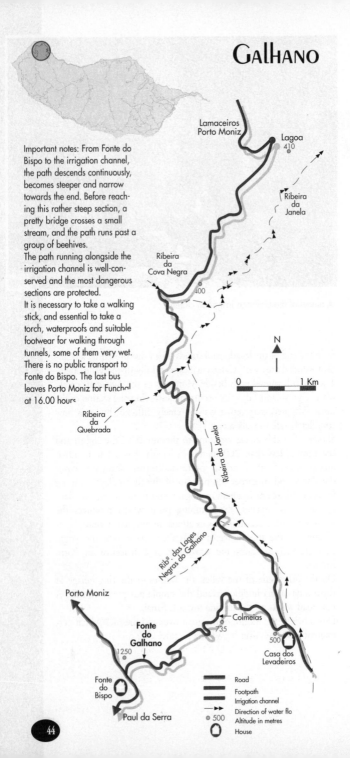

Important notes: From Fonte do Bispo to the irrigation channel, the path descends continuously, becomes steeper and narrow towards the end. Before reaching this rather steep section, a pretty bridge crosses a small stream, and the path runs past a group of beehives.

The path running alongside the irrigation channel is well-conserved and the most dangerous sections are protected.

It is necessary to take a walking stick, and essential to take a torch, waterproofs and suitable footwear for walking through tunnels, some of them very wet. There is no public transport to Fonte do Bispo. The last bus leaves Porto Moniz for Funchal at 16.00 hours.

Lamaceiros
Porto Moniz

Lagoa
410

Ribeira
da
Janela

Ribeira
da
Cova Negra
400

N

0   1 Km

Ribeira
da
Quebrada

Ribeira da Janela

Ribª. das Lages
Negras do Galhano

Porto Moniz

Colmeias

Fonte
do
Galhano
735

500

Casa dos
Levadeiros

1250

Fonte
do
Bispo

Paul da Serra

Road
Footpath
Irrigation channel
Direction of water flo
500 Altitude in metres
House

44

FROM RIBEIRO FRIO
TO PORTELA

T his walk can be made in complete safety by anyone who enjoys walking. The route covers a total of ten kilometres, eight along the flat path beside the Levada da Serra do Faial from Ribeiro Frio to the house marking the point where

Time:
Without hurry-
ing, 4 hours

Serra do Faial irrigation channel   ≥

the waters divide, and another two km. from this building, dated 1906, to the Portela viewpoint.

Mist and rain are frequent at these altitudes, and the temperature is, on average, 5º lower than in Funchal. Wear suitable shoes or boots for walking in wet terrain, and don't forget your waterproofs.

Unhurriedly, enjoying the grandeur of the landscape and the delicate shapes of its life forms, the walk along this stretch of the Levada da Serra do Faial also allows us to appreciate just how difficult it must have been to open up these channels to

Starting-point:
Ribeiro Frio
forestry post

Arrival point:
Miradouro da
Portela

Length:
Approximately
10 kilometres

45

Ribeiro Frio forestry post

carry water from the northern springs to the dry lands of the southern coast.

This irrigation channel originates in the Faial mountains, winding for 54 kilometres around slopes and valleys to reach Choupana, in the eastern heights of Funchal. The first attempts to build this aqueduct date to 1830, but it was not until 1871 that the work really got underway. The irrigation channel was completed in 1905.

In September 1905, water finally began to flow from the source of the levada to the farmlands of Caniço, São Gonçalo and Santa Maria Maior. The result of over 30 years of work carried out at enormous risk, suffering, tears, of basalt rock stained with the blood of Madeira.

The impressive cutting into the rocks at Cabeço Furado and the many stone walls which support this aqueduct clinging along the edge of the precipice are clear testimonies to the epic nature of this task. This text is a simple homage to those anonymous Madeirans who lost their lives in this noble, difficult mission.

Before starting out, walk around the Ribeiro Frio Forest Park which is adjacent to the levada. As well as the trout farm, you will have the opportunity of observing many rare species of the Madeira flora. Thanks to the unstinting work of the Forestry Service, the original flora of this phytoclimatic site is gradually being recovered.

As we walk along the aqueduct, we will see, amongst the multifarious green tones of the woods, delicate flowers bursting forth from the tiny plants whose habitat is this environment of high humidity and little light.

Look at them, photograph them, practise your artistic skills on them, but do not pick the tiny flowers and plants which adorn the embankments of the irrigation channel. They are very sensitive, and they would not even reach Funchal in good condition. Apart from this, the local ecosystem is very fragile, and the next visitors would not be able to enjoy this enormous natural wealth.

Pride of Madeira
(Echium candicans)

The tiny wild orchid with its delicate pink and white flowers, geraniums with their bright pink-purple flowers, or isoplexis with their bunches of orange-tinted corollas, pride of Madeira with its great panicles of purple flowers, buttercups with spectacular yellow flowers, marguerites with their white flowers, Madeira mountain stock and shrubby sow thistle, all these are species which are found here in their splendour in spring and early summer, flourishing beneath the canopy of leafy trees which covers the slopes of Ribeiro Frio and the headlands of the Tem-te-não-caias river.

Laurel, wax mytle, lily-of-the-valley tree and heather tree are the most frequently found trees here. There are also til-trees and hollies, whilst Madeira mahogany and aderno grow here and there. These are all evergreen trees which flourish in this damp climate, their trunks decorated by an enormous variety of algae, lichens, mosses and ferns.

During this voyage within the interior of purifying nature, we may see firecrests, known here as *bisbis*, the smallest of the birds which populate Madeira, hopping from branch to branch in search of larvae and insects, softly singing *bis, bis, bis...*

We can also see the blackbird here, looking for berries and small insects, brightening the landscape with its strong melodic song. Also frequently-seen in this forest are the chaffinch and the wagtail, providing cheerful concerts as they search for food. More uncommon is the large laurel pigeon.

With a little luck, we may spot the buzzard, a bird of prey which visits the forest to hunt birds, rabbits and mice and to make his great nest at the top of the laurel trees.

On a clear, mistless day, it is possible, from certain sections of the irrigation channel, to observe the landscape beyond the forest. We are surprised by the fields of Faial, São Roque do Faial and Porto da Cruz, villages scattered amongst the flats and plateaux of the mountain peaks. The enormous rocky mass of Penha de Águia, looking out over the Atlantic, protects the Bay of Faial to the east, whilst to the west the Ponta dos Clérigos does what it can to shelter the area from the harsh northeasterly winds. Exhausted from their journeying, the waters of Riberia da Metade and Ribeira Seca merge near the sea, together disappearing into the great ocean.

Studying plants and animals in isolation or systematically analysing the entire environment, listening to the silence and breathing pure air, ecologists or simple nature lovers will find ample cause for pleasure and reflection along this route.

Important notes: Most of the route runs along the Levada da Serra do Faial irrigation channel and is protected by railings and natural hedges.

The descent to Portela is not too steep, and offers no danger. The ground is in good condition.

Although a signpost in Ribeiro Frio indicates that it is eight kilometres to Portela, the truth is that the distance between the two places is just over 10 kilometres. It is 8 kilometres from Ribeiro Frio to where the waters of the irrigation channel divide. From there to Portela is another 2 kilometres.

The route to Portela is downhill all the way. Around 200 metres below the aqueduct is the Lamaceiros forestry post, and a little further on we have a choice of two routes. Portela or Santo da Serra or, more correctly, Lombo das Faias. Taking the way towards Portela, we can even choose between the path to this viewpoint and the descent to Referta in Porto da Cruz.

Those wishing to go to Santo da Serra should continue along the irrigation channel for another two kilometres until they come to a second division of the waters. From here, descend along a beaten track to the road joining Portela and Santo da Serra. The Church of Santo António da Serra soon comes into view from here, and the rest of the route is along this road. It is just over 3 kilometres from the irrigation channel to the church.

It is around 13 kilometres from Ribeiro Frio to Santo da Serra, some four or five hours on foot.

There are buses to Ribeiro Frio, and from Portela and Santo da Serra to Funchal.

From Ribeiro Frio to Portela

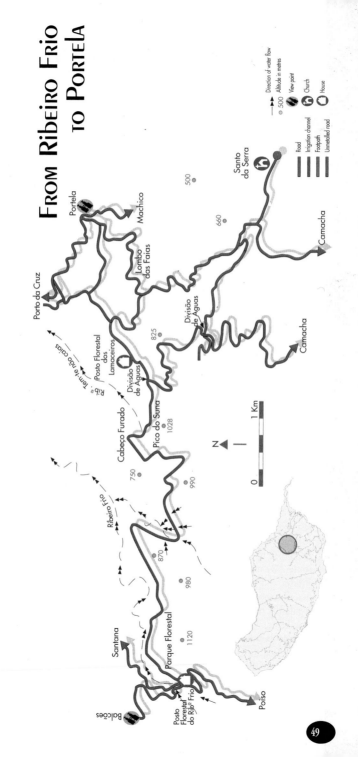

Key

road
irrigation channel
footpath
unmetalled road

Direction of water flow
500 Altitude in metres
View point
Church
House

0   1 Km

N

Portela
Machico
Porto da Cruz
Lombo das Faias
500
660
Santo da Serra
Camacha
Camacha
Divisão de Aguas
825
Posto Florestal dos Lamaceiros
Ri.º
Divisão de Aguas
Cabeço Furado
Torrente não caios
Pico do Suna
1028
750
Ribeiro Frio
990
870
980
Santana
Parque Florestal
1120
Balcões
Posto Florestal do Rib.º Frio
Poiso

49

Fajã da Nogueira

Fajã da Nogueira is one of the most beautiful inland regions of Madeira, and all lovers or students of nature should visit it at least once.

But how can we get there?

Here are two suggestions. The final choice is up to the reader.

A bus leaves Funchal or, more correctly, Almirante Reis, for Boaventura at seven o'clock in the morning. Take this bus to Ribeiro Frio, where you will arrive shortly after eight. Once there, lose no time in making for the Balcoes, where on a clear day, you can see a good stretch of the central mountain range of the island, and the lovely valley of the Metade River. Also, the Penha de Águia, beside the great Atlantic, completes the breathtaking geological panorama from this viewpoint.

Taking the Levada da Serra do Faial - dry here - we come to the Fajã da Nogueira hydroelectric power station. However, some 500 metres after the Balcoes, we leave the aqueduct path to descend by a narrow path which is not signposted.

Amongst til-trees, wax myrtle, *"pau branco"*, heath trees, lily-of-the-valley trees and many oak trees, we finally come, after walking for an hour and a few minutes, to a small house beside the path, half a kilometre or so from the power station.

Once we reach the hydroelectric power station, we will be at an altitude of 620 metres above sea level, some 280 metres below the Balcoes viewpoint. We can rest awhile here and eat some of the provisions in our rucksack in the shade of a cherry or a beech tree.

At the start of this text, I mentioned two possible routes. We are going to take the second of these now, shorter and less demanding than the first, before we describe the ascent to the hydroelectric power station regulating reservoir.

Just before Cruzinhas do Faial is a bridge over the Metade. Beside the bridge is a sign indicating the way to the Fajã da Nogueira hydroelectric power station. Drive along the beaten track which runs parallel to the river towards its source. No doubt during the ascent you will want to make several stops to appreciate the scenery.

Time:
Longer walk: 8
or 9 hours
Shorter walk: 4
or 5 hours

Starting-point:
Ribeiro Frio
forestry post

Arrival points:
Cruzinhas

Length: Longer
walk (Ribeiro
Frio - The
Balcoes - Fajã da
Nogueira hydro-
electric power
station - regulat-
ing reservoir -
Cruzinhas):
14 km

- Shorter walk
(hydroelectric
power station -
regulating reser-
voir - hydroelec-
tric power
station):
8 km

You can get to the power station by car or on foot, but from this point on you should walk, for only in this way will you be able to appreciate the extraordinary riches of Madeira's geological architecture and the different species which make up the endemic forest.

The Fajã da Nogueira area is the repository of a veritable botanical treasure-trove, and for this reason is part of the Madeira

Fajã da Nogueira

Natural Park. It is a pity that some visitors do not respect the environment, leaving behind them the pollutant traces of their presence. It is a pity, too, that there are goats and pigs inside the Integral Reserve area, as these threaten to finally cause the extinction of many rare plant species. The damage caused by these animals to the ecosystem is clearly visible.

Amongst the many plants which grow in these mountains, the til-tree stands out due both to its size and sculptural shapes. Some trees of this species are thought to go back to before the first human settlement of Madeira. Right by the path, just before it forks, stand two of these gentle giants of the Madeira forest, survivors of the devastation caused by fires started by criminal hands.

On reaching the point where the path forks, we take the left-hand route. Further on, we come to the bed of the Fajã da Nogueira River, on crossing which we ascend to a beautiful sweet

RQ

Til-tree *(Ocotea foetens)*

chestnut wood with two tiny houses inhabited by personnel in charge of the maintenance of the irrigation channels. Now we need merely to continue straight ahead for a little over half a kilometre to find the regulating reservoir, situated at an altitude of 1000 metres above sea level. The climb can be completed in around two hour's steady walking.

From the viewpoint, situated beside a tiny reservoir carved into the rock, we can enjoy magnificent views of the soaring peaks of Areeiro to Pico das Torres, getting a bird's-eye view of the deep meanders of the Ribeira do Juncal. If it is misty, do not despair, the weather can clear up in just a few minutes.

We now descend to the sweet chestnut wood, rising again to the left to find the irrigation channel which carries water from the Caldeirão do Inferno.

From now on, continue along the path which runs beside the levada, heading towards its source. An hour and a half later, approximately, you will come to a beaten track leading down back to the hydroelectric power station.

Continuing along the aqueduct, you would come to the Caldeirão do Inferno after two hours walk crossing through several tunnels, one of them 2,400 metres in length.

During the descent, we can observe some of the most beautiful Madeira mahogany trees forming part of the flora of Madeira. Here, the Laurisilva, though diminished, takes on an immense variety of green hues, forming surprising natural sculptures and bringing forth delicate flowers. Plunging 50, 100, 200 metres, various waterfalls further embellish this great natural spectacle.

Meanwhile, we notice that, having descended for some 15 or 20 minutes, we find ourselves once more at the fork in the path, beside the two giant til-trees tortured by fire. From here there is a half-hour descent to the hydroelectric power station.

Hydroelectric power station

RQ

Those without a car should note that from the hydroelectric power station it is another 4 kilometres walk to the main road, about 90 minutes walking time, and remember that the last bus to Funchal leaves Cruzinhas at 18.00. During this part of the walk, you will be able to appreciate the large-scale crumbling of the sloping mountain peaks over thousands of years, eroded by the violent energy of flowing water. The river runs wide through the softer rocks, then forms a narrow gorge where the lava beds and basalt dikes present stronger resistance to its erosive action. In the depths of the valley, enormous blocks of rock testify to the landslides caused by the persistent action of the water as it opens up a path down to the sea.

Fajã da Nogueira

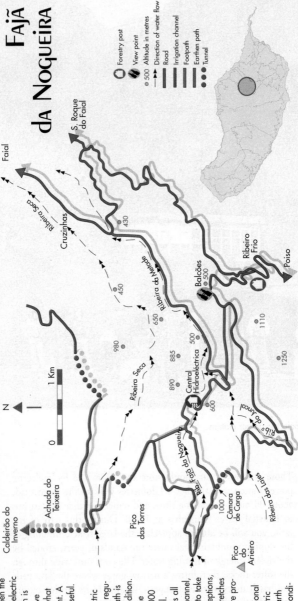

Legend:
- Forestry post
- View point
- 500 Altitude in metres
- Direction of water flow
- Road
- Irrigation channel
- Footpath
- Earthen path
- Tunnel

Labels on map: Faial, S. Roque do Faial, Ribeira Seca, Cruzinhas, 430, Ribeira da Metade, 450, 650, Ribeiro Frio, Poiso, Balcões, 500, 1110, 980, 885, 890, Central Hidroeléctrica, 500, 1250, Ribeira Seca, Achada do Teixeira, Caldeirão do Inverno, N, Pico das Torres, Rib.ª Fajã da Nogueira, 600, Rib.ª do Cidrão, Pico do Arieiro, Câmara de Carga, 1000, Ribeira das Loiras, 0 1 Km

Important notes: Between the Balcões and the hydroelectric power station, the path is narrow. Landslides have made the route somewhat dangerous at one point. A walking stick is very useful.

Between the hydroelectric power station and the regulating reservoir, the path is wide and in good condition. The only difficulty is the ascent from 600 to 1000 metres above sea level. There are small tunnels all along the irrigation channel, and it is a good idea to take a torch. With few exceptions, all the most difficult stretches along the aqueduct are protected.

The way from the regional road to the hydroelectric power station is an earth road, but is in good condi-

Caldeirão Verde

Caldeirão Verde, what beauty! The water, embellished in all the colours of the rainbow, flows down the slopes into the lake it itself constructed at the bottom of that semi-cylindrical formation. But some have never been here, out of fear of the path or some other reason, and harbour a burning desire to visit this spot, as remote as it is absolutely wonderful. I shall now attempt to guide visitors by providing some indications, which I feel are important, for readers who have never been to Caldeirão Verde. For those who have already visited the site, I shall suggest an alternative route. And, since we are going to Caldeirão Verde, we shall also take the opportunity of making a short detour to Caldeirão do Inferno.

But let us begin at the beginning, that is to say, at Queimadas.

Get things ready early in the morning: put food, good boots for walking in wet conditions, waterproofs and a torch into your rucksack and get on the road.

It is six kilometres from the Park Queimadas to Caldeirão Verde, an hour and a half walking briskly and without allowing time to admire the scenery. But hurrying along without stopping in this way does not give us the chance to observe the many plants and geological formations we

Caldeirão Verde

FM

Time:
A) 5 to 6 hours
B) 7 to 8 hours
C) 8 to 9 hours

Starting-point:
Parque das
Queimadas

Arrival points:
Queimadas or
Cruzinhas

Length:
A) Queimadas -
Caldeirão Verde
- Queimadas:
12 kilometres
B) Queimadas -
Caldeirão do
Inferno -
Queimadas:
16 kilometres
C) Queimadas -
Caldeirão do
Inferno - Fajã da
Nogueira -
Cruzinhas:
19 kilometres

MF

House at Queimadas

AF

Caldeirão Verde

find on the way, nor to enjoy the marvellous scenery of Santana and São Jorge.

On leaving Queimadas, admire the cylindrical forms of the Japanese cypress *(Cryptomeria japonica* var. *elegans)* which stand just below the irrigation channel, the reddish, leafy Europoean beech and the Madeira cedar with its hanging branches, we see, far below, a tiny plateau dotted with houses and barns standing amidst cultivated fields. This flat, isolated land amongst the rocky peaks and a river valley is Achada do Marques. For many years it formed part of the parish of São Jorge, but now a new parish called Ilha, and which enjoys the status of a Protected Landscape within the Madeira Natural Park.

Stopping here to observe a waterfall, there to admire the flight of the laurel pigeon, stopping once more to photograph a fine example of til-tree, an interesting *pau branco* or a group of holly trees, time passes without us even realising.

Enventually, we come to the first tunnel, short and with a small bend. Further on, just at the entrance to the second tunnel, almost 200 metres in length, is the signposted path to Vale da Lapa. We take this second tunnel, however, towards Caldeirão Verde: the path leads to the Vale da Lapa forestry post, from which it descends towards Achada do Marques or Ilha. We carry straight on, for our destination is Caldeirão Verde.

Shortly after we emerge from this second tunnel, we come to a third, not very long and with even a window-like opening in the middle, but low and with a generally damp floor, and therefore requiring special care as we cross it.

The fourth and last tunnel is a little further on, and is very small. There is less than a kilometre between this tunnel and Caldeirão Verde. Take care! Caldeirão Verde cannot be seen from the irrigation channel, and as the signpost sometimes disappears, some pass by without ever finding this beautiful spot. Caldeirão Verde lies to the left of the aqueduct, and

The Laurisilva, designated a World Heritage Site in December 1999 by UNESCO

to reach it we walk some 50 meters along an ascending way by the bank of the river which carries excess water from the natural lake.

Once we have paused sufficiently to admire the scenery at Caldeirão Verde, those with enough time and not afraid to continue along the unprotected path beside the levada can visit Caldeirão do Inferno.

To get there, it is necessary at a certain point to descend to the bottom of a depression where there was once a little waterfall. This is now dry, as its waters have been diverted into the irrigation channel which has its source at the top of Caldeirão Verde and which, in turn, feeds the Fajã da Nogueira hydroelectric power station.

Passing through this cavity, carved into the rock, we come to the old aqueduct, now dry. Continuing straight on, we find a steep, narrow path leading down to the bed of the Ribeira São Jorge and, through a long tunnel, to Fajã do Penedo in Boaventura.

AF

**Caldeirão
do Inferno**

But, for now, our objective is Caldeirão do Inferno.

Carry on straight ahead to a the many steps which we have to ascend to reach a flat area beside which is the entrance to a great tunnel leading towards Fajã da Nogueira and which forms the meeting-point of two aqueducts, one of which has its source above Caldeirão Verde and, taking water from there, diminishes the water flow and hence the beauty of the waterfall in summer. The other, on the right as we go up, carries water collected in the Caldeirão do Inferno area. Taking this second levada, we come to Caldeirão do Inferno. It is just one thousand metres long, some of it through small tunnels.

It is called "Caldeirão", but is nothing like Caldeirão Verde, for this is a gorge, or canyon, carved out by the waters along a line of less resistant rocks. And why "Inferno"? Was this paradise of green, filtered light and clear waters once inhabited by the devil?

Well, it is a shame, but we have to leave the Inferno and return to the city. Those not wishing to take the same way back can opt to cross the long tunnel, 2,400 metres of it. Almost an hour of walking underground brings us to the Ribeira Seca do Faial valley. A few more tunnels lead to the descent to the Fajã da Nogueira hydroelectric power station. It is approximately a three-hour walk from the end of the great subterranean pathway to the hydroelectric power station, and an hour or more from here to the regional road, and remember the last bus to Fuchal leaves Cruzinhas at 18.00 hours.

These, then, are my suggestions. The choice is up to the reader.

CALdEiRÃO VERdE

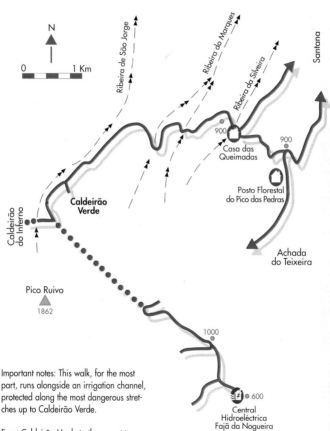

N

0   1 Km

Ribeira de São Jorge

Ribeira do Marques

Ribeira da Silveira

Santana

900

Casa das Queimadas

900

Posto Florestal do Pico das Pedras

Caldeirão Verde

Caldeirão do Inferno

Achada do Teixeira

Pico Ruivo
1862

1000

Important notes: This walk, for the most part, runs alongside an irrigation channel, protected along the most dangerous stretches up to Caldeirão Verde.

From Caldeirão Verde to the ascent to Caldeirão do Inferno, the levada is dry and has no protecting railing.
The mountainside between the two aqueducts is difficult and the terrain slippery, and it is important to take great care. A walking stick is always very useful.
The Caldeirão do Inferno aqueduct is in good condition and walking along is not dangerous.
There are several tunnels along the route, making waterproofs and torch essential.

600
Central Hidroeléctrica Fajã da Nogueira

	Road
	Footpath
	Irrigation channel
●●●	Tunnel
→►►	Direction of water flow
● 500	Altitude in metres

Pico Das Pedras - Queimadas - Vale Da Lapa - Ilha

The Pico das Pedras nursery in Santana parish lies at an altitude of 900 metres above sea level. Many indigenous species are cultivated here with the aim of repopulating those mountains of Madeira which are at present bare due to fire and pasturing. Apart from visiting this nursery, we also recommend a walk around the picnic park, where beautiful plants and bushes grow. Various indigenous bird species are also kept in captivity here, such as the buzzard, the largest of the birds of prey of Madeira, and the laurel pigeon.

The first section of this walk runs along the beaten track, long, without precipices, to Queimadas, some three kilometres away. Here there is another lovely forest park, with large thatched houses.

We already described the walk from Queimadas along the Serra de São Jorge aqueduct as part of the Caldeirão Verde route.

The second stage is along this aqueduct, which transports water from Caldeirão Verde. The first tunnel we pass through is small and does not require the use of a torch. We now continue along the irrigation channel until we see the second tunnel. Beside the mouth of this tunnel, on the right, lies the path to the Vale da Lapa forestry post.

This is an area of indigenous forest mixed with many sycamores, which tend to be invasive.

The third stage of our walk begins here. Starting out along the path, after just a few metres we are confronted by a choice of route: to carry straight on or to climb up to the peak where the forestry post lies. Though the first option is the shortest path to Ilha and Achada de Marques, the second possibility is, without a doubt, the most interesting.

Climbing up for a few minutes, the path begins to offer spectacular views. Words cannot express all that we can see from this point. Pico Ruivo and Pico das Torres soaring up. Houses, now dotted everywhere,

Time:
4 to 5 hours

Starting-point:
Pico das Pedras, Santana

Arrival points:
Ilha municipal road, close to the entrance to Achada do Marques.

Length:
12 kilometres

now forming orderly rows, in Santana and São Jorge. The agricultural lands of lighter greens and gentler slopes, contrasting with the dark green of the Laurisilva which covers the mountainsides. The São Jorge River flowing between Achada de Gramacho to the east and the lands of São Jorge, slightly more undulating, to the west.

On a clear day, the ideal spot for a picnic and to recover our strength is, without doubt, at the natural viewpoint beside the forestry post.

Until now we have been ascending almost constantly along the irrigation channel, with just a slight descent towards the end, the fourth stage of the route is downhill all the way. On our downward route, a stick will help to prevent us from slipping.

A little further on, the path runs into a beaten track leading to Ilha, whose tiny church can be seen below. During the final stage, close now to the centre of this small parish, you join the tar macadam road.

MF

High up between two river valleys - Ribeira de São Jorge and Ribeira dos Arcos, or do Marques - seen from the distance Ilha looks just like an island, hence its name (Ilha = island in Portuguese). Apart from its church, of little interest, the centre of Ilha has a school, administrative centre, grocery shops with bars and a cluster of houses.

MF

The parish of Ilha

The surrounding farmlands grow maize, sweet potatoes and vines, stretching from the hillside down into the two valleys. There are more women than men working the fields, and the men are usually of an advanced age. The young lads prefer city jobs, or emigrate seasonally to the British Channel Islands. Working on farms or in hotels, they earn the English Pounds they need to build a house and improve the purchasing power of their families.

But this walk would not be complete without a visit to one of the most characteristic spots on the entire island, Achada do Marques. It is easy to get to Achada do Marques. Just take the only road down to the fork. The right-hand path leads to a tiny plateau hidden behind the rocks. Emerging from the tunnel, we come head-on to the lovely little village. Great lemon trees grow around the houses of Achada do Marques, which has a population of around 50 people. Almost all the *palheiros,* or small, thatched cowsheds have lost their thatching and now sport zinc roofs, painted in an attempt to imitate the colour of straw and not damage the harmony of the landscape.

It is half an hour there and back, plus the time to chat to the friendly residents and to buy some of the excellent lemons.

Pico das Pedras
Queimadas
Vale da Lapa
Ilha

Important notes: The first stage of the walk, between
Pico das Pedras and Parque das Queimadas, is easy.

From Queimadas, the most dangerous points along
the path to Vale da Lapa are protected.

The descent from the forestry post is along a path
which is normally rather slippery, and a stick should
be taken.
Waterproof clothing and good boots are also recommended.

▬▬▬ Road
▬▬▬ Footpath
▬▬▬ Irrigation channel
▬▬▬ Earthen path
--▶▶ Direction of water flow
◉ 500 Altitude in metres

⌂ House

FolHadal

Folhadal is a place with many lily-of-the-valley trees - *folhados* or *folhadeiros*, as they are known to the local people.

But what are lily-of-the-valley trees? Urbanites with less contact with the language of the country will ask. *Folhados* (lily-of-the-valley trees) are indigenous trees of Madeira found in the forest known as Laurisilva and which are covered by bunches of white, aromatic flowers between July and September. It is thanks to this intense flowering that during the summer and early

Time:
A) 5 hours
B) 5 hours

Starting-point:
Encumeada
Viewpoint

Arrival points:
Feiteiras, São
Vicente;
Estanquinhos
forestry post,
Paul da Serra

RQ

**Lily-of-the valley tree
(*Clethra arborea*)**

autumn the forests of Madeira are dotted with clear white patches amongst the multiple tones of green.

As well as being one of the most common trees in the forests of Madeira, the decorative qualities of the lily-of-the-valley tree means that it is grown extensively in the gardens of Monte, Camacha and Santo da Serra. These trees also line many roads, and it is a pity it is not planted more frequently for its decorative qualities along roads and paths between 500 and 1200 metres altitude. Nevertheless, the aesthetic qualities of the lily-of-the-valley tree is what least interests the countryfolk, who hold the tree in esteem above all as a source of feed for cattle when grass is scarce, and the new branches of this tree are frequently chopped off for this purpose.

Length: A)
Encumeada -
Folhadal - Ginjas
- Feiteiras:
13 kilometres
B) Encumeada -
Folhadal -
Caramujo -
Estanquinhos:
10 kilometres

But the lily-of-the-valley tree is not only sacrificed for forage. Light, strong walking sticks can be made from the straight new stems of these trees. There is no tree better in our mountains for the purpose.

If these trees are so common nowadays on Madeira, it is because of their great facility to regenerate from the stumps and from seed.

But, what am I writing about?

Well, when I sat down at the computer it was with the intention of describing a walk from Encumeada to Feiteiras in São Vicente, passing through Folhadal and Ginjas. I do not know whether due to the influence of the green characters running across the screen, but something got me talking about a species of tree. Forgive me, but I am incorrigible. I am not worth psychoanalysing.

Let us get on with our walk then, starting at the Encumeada view-point from where we can see Ribeira Brava to the south and São Vicente on the other side of the island.

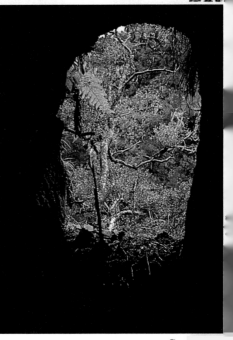

RQ

Knapsack on back, we start out walking west along the Levada do Norte, which carries water to the Serra de Água hydroelectric power station.

The first stretch of the irrigation channel crosses land beside the Ribeira Brava, where we can still see the mark of fires which damaged the forest. Beside the path we see *pau branco*, til-tree, Madeira cedar and European beech, embellishing the route. The views of the different tributaries of the Ribeira Brava and the crests of the mountains of the Serra de Água help make this first stage particularly pleasant.

About a kilometre from Encumeada, the irrigation channel divides into two. It is at this point that the Levada do Norte receives water from the Levada das Rabaças, which has its beginings at the source of the Ribeira da Ponta do Sol on the south side of Paul da Serra.

RQ

House of the levada watchmen

Those wishing to visit Lombo do Mouro or Rabaças should carry on straight ahead, bearing in mind that in order to admire the beautiful Rabaças waterfall and the Ribeira da Ponta do Sol Valley they will have first to go through a tunnel over two kilometres in length.

But the objective of this walk is to reach the village of Feiteiras in São Vicente, and we therefore have to walk along the Levada do Norte. In other words, at the meeting-point of the two irrigation channels the correct option is to take the one which reaches this point through a 300 metre long tunnel.

At the other end of this tunnel, the irrigation channel is surrounded by great trees of various species, til-trees, laurels, *pau branco*, wax myrtle, a few Madeira mahogany trees and many lily-of-the-valley trees (*folhados*). It is not surprising that this place is called Folhadal!

In summer the flowers of the lily-of-the-valley trees are the stars in that great green theatre. In spring, floral beauty is provided by pride of Madeira, geraniums, buttercups, white-flowered marguerites and Madeira mountain stock, whilst a little later the scene is dominated by wild orchids.

After Folhadal, the irrigation channel now skirts a valley, now runs along the hillside. The forest continues to be thick and green, and we come across many waterfalls.

One of the six tunnels along this route

RQ

To reach the house used by the irrigation channel watchmen, close to the track between Ginjas and the Estanquinhos forestry post in Paul da Serra, we have to pass through another five tunnels, three longer than the first and two short ones.

In all, it is around seven kilometres from Encumeada to Ginjas, with over two kilometres of tunnel. The discomfort of the underground sections of the walk is amply compensated for, however, by the beauty of the views over the São Vicente Valley.

Along the track, whose construction destroyed the old path and disfigures the zone around Caramujo, we can ascend to Paul da Serra or descend to São Vicente.

It is just over three kilometres from the levada watchmen's house to Estanquinhos, enough, however, to see how the trees have been cut back and the heather has expanded, whilst close to the top of the plateau we can observe the domination of bracken ferns.

From that watchmen's hut to the regional road at Feiteiras is a journey of around six kilometres. Little by little, before we reach the cultivated lands of Ginjas, the forest of varied species gives way to pine and eucalyptus woods and the landscape on either side of the path becomes monotonous.

Folhadal

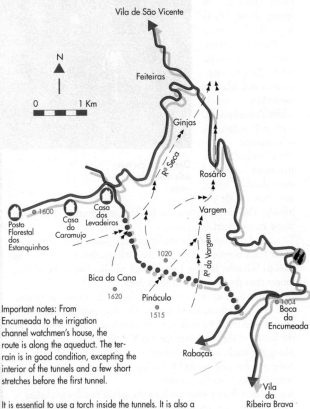

Vila de São Vicente

Feiteiras

Ginjas

Rosário

Rª Seca

Vargem

Casa dos Levadeiros

⊙ 1600

Casa do Caramujo

Posto Florestal dos Estanquinhos

Rª da Vargem

1020 ⊙

Bica da Cana

1620 ⊙

Pináculo

1515

1004 ⊙ Boca da Encumeada

Rabaças

Vila da Ribeira Brava

Important notes: From Encumeada to the irrigation channel watchmen's house, the route is along the aqueduct. The terrain is in good condition, excepting the interior of the tunnels and a few short stretches before the first tunnel.

It is essential to use a torch inside the tunnels. It is also a good idea to take waterproofs and suitable headgear, as it is easy to hurt one's head on the rocks projecting from the roof of the tunnels.

The path up to Estanquinhos or down to Ginjas is of beaten earth and is completely safe.

Each of the alternate routes take around ninety minutes to complete. Those going down to Feiteiras can catch a bus back to the starting-point. Those ascending to Estanquinhos should arrange transport, as there is no bus back from Paul da Serra.

An early morning bus leaves Funchal for São Vicente, passing through Encumeada.

🎯 View point
━━ Road
━━ Footpath
━━ Irrigation channel
━━ Earthen path
▸▸ Direction of water flow
⊙ 500 Altitude in metres
●●● Tunnel

Fajã da Ama

T he wheat is turning yellow, just here and there are a few scattered stalks and ears of green. July is here and, weather permitting, the threshing machine will pour forth grain to make white flour, the essential ingredient in the local home-made bread. The potatoes have been picked from the ground and, combined with salted tunafish, make a fine meal in these times of

Time:
Route A) 4 hours
Route B) 5 to 6 hours

Starting-points:
Ginjas or Ribeira da Vargem

Arrival points:
Ginjas or Ribeira da Vargem

The São Vicente Valley seen from Fajã da Ama

MF

Length:

Route A)
Ginjas -Ribeira do Inferno - Ginjas: 10 kilometres
Route B)
Ribeira da Vargem - Caminho das Ginjas - Ribeira do Inferno - Ribeira da Vargem: 16 kilometres

saints' feast-days. The beans have already been sown now, and the sweet potatoes are being planted in the soil.

This is what farming is like in Vargem, in Ginjas, in Lanço, in Cova da Fonte and in many other places in the upland areas of São Vicente. Here, unlike in the coastal zones, the vine is scarce and mixed farming dominates, with successive crops on the same terraces (*poios*), using just rainwater until spring and taking water from the Passada

MF

The Fajã do Rodrigues or Fajã da Ama irrigation channel

and Fajã do Rodrigues irrigation channels in summer. Fajã do Rodrigues, or Fajã da Ama are the two names by which the same aqueduct is known. Its source is in the Ribeira do Inferno, which separates the lands of Seixal from those of São Vicente, and winds its way along ridges and small valleys to Vargem, to above the Church of Nossa Senhora do Rosário. It flows little above Cova da Fonte and just below Curral dos Burros, crossing the pretty Fajã da Ama which gives it its name.

There is little agriculture in Fajã da Ama: eucalyptus, pines, wax myrtle, heather, brambles and the occasional laurel inhabit these lands, crossed by beaten tracks used by land rovers. It was this network of access roads that allowed timber to be felled more easily, as well as enabling the appearance of small meadows of apple trees on the cleared land.

Fire has visited this area more than once, and the results are clear to the eye: the pine forests are clearly regressing, whilst the eucalyptus population, whose seed are actually stirred into life by fire, is gaining ground. Here, as in many parts of the mountainous regions of the island, eucalyptus is spreading, blissfully unaware of the law passed by parliament restricting its expansion. A lack of harmony between the laws of nature and the laws of the Regional Assembly?

In February 1989, when I was heading with a group of friends to carry out a field study in the Ribeira do Inferno, we came across a young girl of about thirteen years and her older brother close to the irrigation channel. They were from Passo and had gone up to Fajã do Rodrigues to cut some wax myrtle for stakes. The girl told us she was still in her third year at school and did not know if she would pass, but meanwhile showed us that she knew a lot about work in the fields. But what good is such knowledge for passing school exams? I never saw them again. I don't know whether the girl passed her exams or whether she left school once she got to school-leaving age, as her brother had done. I don't know whether the walk they went on with us up to the source of the irrigation channel left them more sensitive to nature. I only know that those children, and many more like them, will continue to cut wax myrtle for stakes with the same exper-

Great care needs to be taken at certain points

tise and endure the same lack of success at school as their parents and grandparents as long as education continues to be incapable of understanding and teaching the laws of nature.

It was the first time the two young people had been to the source of the irrigation channel, as was the case, moreover, of most of the people in our group. It was a sunny day, making the specta-cle of the waterfall cascading down the rocks above the aqueduct into the pools at the bottom even more beautiful.

As we approach the first tunnel, the views of the São Vicente Valley are truly lovely. Down below is Lanço, whilst further east is Ginjas and, a little further down, Passo and Poiso. On the right-hand side of the river soars Pico da Senhora de Fátima with the belltower of a church never built in the lands of Lameiros.

As we got closer to Ribeira do Inferno, the vegetation is ever rich-er and more varied. Til-tree and Madeira mahogany become more frequent along the way, dominating the forest with their great height. Pretty holly trees, laurels, lily-of-the-valley trees, *sanguinho* and enormous exemplars of *pau branco* lined the irrigation channel, particularly after the long tunnel.

It was not difficult for the young people to see that these great trees still remain in these places because of their inaccessibility, making it impossible to fell them and carry off their valuable timber. This fact led us naturally to a discussion of the importance of conserving the forest and gave us the chance to tell them that, though it is no sin to cut some wax myrtle to make stakes, they should also be aware of the damage done to nature by random cutting. We advised them to ask the forest keepers whenever they should need more stakes. Whether or not our advice did good I do not know for, as I said, I never saw them again.

Wallflowers (*Erysimum bicolor*)

MF

The forest around the aqueduct is much more than trees. Ferns are abundant here in all their beauty, from small species with kidney-shaped leaves - which, with selaginella, liverworks and mosses, cover the humid rocky walls - to the great chain ferns which dominate and embellish vast areas.

Buttercups, geraniums, marguerites, orchids. What a marvel!

Chaffinches, firecrests and blackbirds. Splendid soloists!

Waterfalls, rivers, streams: in this polluted world it is still possible to find clean waters. Please, let them be.

At last, the Ribeira do Inferno valley. It is the work of the Creator. And there the Great Architect of the Universe excelled Himself! To return, retrace your journey back to your car.

Fajã da Ama

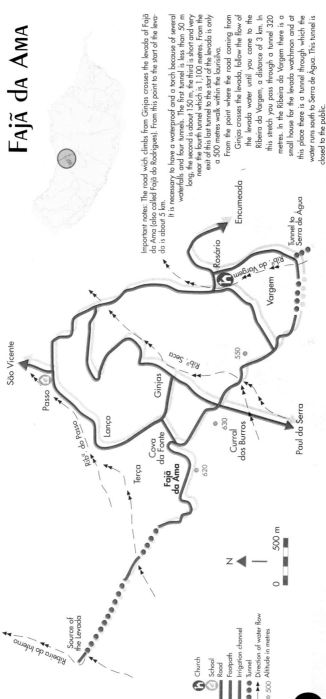

Important notes: The road wich climbs from Ginjas crosses the levada of Fajã da Ama (also called Fajã do Rodrigues). From this point to the start of the levada is about 5 km.

It is necessary to have a waterproof and a torch because of several waterfalls and four tunnels. The first tunnel is less than 50 m long, the second is about 150 m, the third is short and very near the fourth tunnel which is 1,100 metres. From the exit of this last tunnel to the start of the levada is only a 500 metres walk within the laurisilva.

From the point where the road coming from Ginjas crosses the levada, follow the flow of the levada water until you come to the Ribeira da Vargem, a distance of 3 km. In this stretch you pass through a tunnel 320 metres. In the Ribeira da Vargem there is a small house for the levada watchman and at this place there is a tunnel through which the water runs south to Serra de Água. This tunnel is closed to the public.

The dangerous parts of this walk are protected by fences.

Legend:
- Church
- School
- Footpath
- Irrigation channel
- Tunnel
- Direction of water flow
- 500 Altitude in metres

N

0 500 m

73

FROM CURRAL TO BOAVENTURA

A quarter to six. The city still slept when the bus to the Curral das Freiras left Avenida do Mar. In darkness, we passed through Santo António, Estrela and Eira do Serrado. In darkness we reached Achada do Curral das Freiras and stopped outside its church.

Time:
8 to 9 hours

MF
Basalt dikes

It was Saturday and few locals were waiting to take the bus to Funchal. In the bars, which have the pretentious name of *pastelarias*, there was coffee which, though not of the finest quality, was more than welcome.

Some early-risers were breakfasting on a glass of wine or something stronger. They downed their fire water without the hint of a grimace, and some even broke into tuneless song amidst the alcoholic fumes.

In just a few minutes, dawn had banished dark night from this village in the centre of the island, showing us clearly the Boca dos Namorados, Pico Serradinho, Pico Grande, Pico das Torrinhas, Pico Cidrao...

On the grey mountain slopes, brownish sweet chestnut woods stood out, their trees still bare.

In the sky, the first rays of sunshine filtered through stratocumulus clouds. A sign of good weather.

Seven o'clock. Time to start out on our walk. In the branches of the laurel trees, blackbirds offered passers-by a morning concert.

It is three kilometres from the church to Fajã dos Cardos. Since 1994, it has been possible to drive there along the new road which at some points follows the course of the old path.

Starting-point:
Casas Próximas,
Curral das
Freiras

Arrival point:
Regional road, at
the meeting-point
with the road to
Falcas and
Lombo do Urzal.

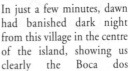
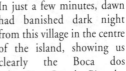
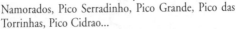

Length:
approximately
16 kilometres

For centuries, this path was the only link between the upper Curral and the centre of the parish. It was along this path that building materials, goods and the sick were transported. The hammocks used to carry those in need of medical attention have been kept for posterity.

It is 1,100 metres from the church to the bridge over the Cidrão, with a tunnel in between. The bridge provides fine views of the conflu-

A view of the Curral das Freiras from Eira do Serrado. Near this viewpoint there is a good hotel

ence of this river and the Ribeira do Curral. This latter river, receiving water from various tributaries upstream, then becomes known as the Ribeira dos Socorridos.

Immediately on crossing this first bridge, the road runs parallel to the stream, between fields of crops, sweet chestnut woods, willows and a few vineyards. The houses are arranged in line, with a slight tendency to group in the Fajã Escura, Colmeal and Fajã dos Cardos.

Some 700 metres beyond the bridge, there is a dam on the Ribeira do Curral from which water is taken through a tunnel to feed the Socorridos hydroelectric power station.

Farther on, in Colmeal, a bridge leads to Fajã Escura and the path to Pico Grande.

It is another 1,400 metres from Colmeal to the tiny square at the end of the road where a bridge marks the beginning of the footpath to the tiny village of Pico Furão. Passing these humble dwellings the path continues towards Pico Ruivo.

But neither of these is the correct path we need to take for Boaventura. Around 1 kilometre after the bridge at Comeal, four hundred metres before the Pico Furão bridge, in Fajã dos Cardos, is a third bridge. This is the one we need to cross. It is here that the path begins which, winding for three kilometres, rises up to Boca das Torrinhas, at an altitude of 1450 metres.

The narrow path, which begins at an altitude of 650 metres, passes shortly afterwards through Cabeço da Fontinha and then through Beira do Poiso. Higher up is the Cabeço do Lombo

MF

Fajã dos Cardos

Grande. At first, we walk through fields where potatoes, sweet potatoes, beans, peas and taro grow.

Little by little, the path becomes steeper, and we leave the cultivated lands behind. Winding ever upwards, the path leads us through eucalyptus, pines and Madeira mahogany as we gradually ascend to an altitude of 800 metres.

The difficulty of the climb is compensated for by our constant pauses at each bend in the path to enjoy a succession of magnificent views of Curral das Freiras, its hamlets scattered over the platforms, plateaux and ridges formed over millions of years by the flow of torrential waters which collect lower down in Ribeira dos Socorridos.

Close now to Boca das Torrinhas, heather begins to dominate amongst the covering of this shallow soil. In this tiny gorge between Pico das Torrinhas to the west and Pico da Laje to the east, we find the Curral and Boaventura paths, which cross the trail between Pico Ruivo and Encumeada.

To catch the bus which goes through Fajã do Penedo at 16.00, we have to leave Torrinhas at around 11 o'clock.

From here on, it is downhill all the way along the narrow path which is at times more like a stream. It is just over 6 kilometres to Lombo do Urzal.

Crossing Boca das Torrinhas, we note a change in the vegetation. We are now on the north side of Madeira, more exposed to the north winds, more frequently visited by mist, more humid, more rainy. The vegetation is not only denser than on the Curral side, but is also richer in species. Here, the heather shares its space with laurels, til-trees, *pau branco*, lily-of-the-valley trees, aderno and bilberry. The floor is adorned with a multitude of geraniums, buttercups, white-flowered marguerites and ferns. After mid-April, flowers abound, and the forest floor becomes a festival of colour. Those who visit this forest never forget the spectacle of forms and colours laid on here by Mother Nature. Apart from the extraordinary beauty of the plants, there are also basalt dikes emerging from the mantle of green. The result is an astounding symbiosis of the mineral world with the vegetable kingdom.

Little by little, we come closer to the houses and the cultivated lands of Achada da Madeira and Lombo do Urzal, the most remote hamlets in the *freguesia,* or parish of Boaventura.

MF

Lombo do Urzal

It is almost four kilometres from Lombo do Urzal to the regional road beside Fajã do Penedo. Along the way, we pass through Falca de Cima and Falca de Baixo, two populated areas where in March it is possible to see the gathering, boiling and peeling of the osiers.

In short: almost 16 kilometres of unforgetable beauty, but only for the strong walker as, after a steep climb from Curral das Freiras to the mountains forming the dorsal spine of Madeira, there follows a long, difficult descent which is wearing and tiring on the muscles and joints of the legs.

If you are not fit enough, or lazy, content yourself with reading this description of the walk.

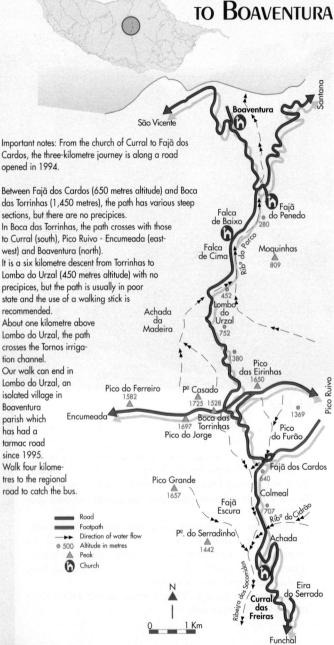

Important notes: From the church of Curral to Fajã dos Cardos, the three-kilometre journey is along a road opened in 1994.

Between Fajã dos Cardos (650 metres altitude) and Boca das Torrinhas (1,450 metres), the path has various steep sections, but there are no precipices.
In Boca das Torrinhas, the path crosses with those to Curral (south), Pico Ruivo - Encumeada (east-west) and Boaventura (north).
It is a six kilometre descent from Torrinhas to Lombo do Urzal (450 metres altitude) with no precipices, but the path is usually in poor state and the use of a walking stick is recommended.
About one kilometre above Lombo do Urzal, the path crosses the Tornos irrigation channel.
Our walk can end in Lombo do Urzal, an isolated village in Boaventura parish which has had a tarmac road since 1995.
Walk four kilometres to the regional road to catch the bus.

São Vicente
Boaventura
Santana
Falca de Baixo
Fajã do Penedo
280
Falca de Cima
Moquinhas
809
Ribª do Porco
452
Lombo do Urzal
752
Achada da Madeira
1380
Pico das Eirinhas
1650
Pico Ruivo
Pico do Ferreiro
1582
Pº Casado
1725 1528
1369
Encumeada
Boca das Torrinhas
1697
Pico do Jorge
Pico do Furão
Fajã dos Cardos
640
Pico Grande
1657
Fajã Escura
Colmeal
707
Ribª do Cidrão
Pº. do Serradinho
1442
Achada
Ribeira dos Socorridos
Eira do Serrado
Curral das Freiras
Funchal

Road
Footpath
Direction of water flow
500 Altitude in metres
Peak
Church

N

0   1 Km

Curral de Baixo

Not all the population of Curral das Freiras lives in the houses clustered around the church: most of the people of this village live along the narrow banks of the great Socorridos river and its tributaries both upstream and downstream from the centre of the parish. We described the places upstream as part of the walk between the Curral and Boaventura, but now we are going to take a look at the area below the church.

Down at the bottom, some 200 metres below the level at which the parish centre stands, we find the tiny hamlets of Lombo Chão, Seara Velha, Balseiras, Terra Chã and Capela, with a total population of around one thousand souls. The walk from Corticeiras near Estreito

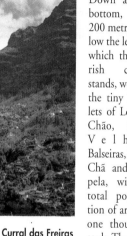

MF

Curral das Freiras

de Câmara de Lobos and Casas Próximas in Curral das Freiras offers us the possibility of appreciating the profound contrast between a landscape which is splendid to the eye of the visitor and ruinous for the local inhabitant. The wealth of nature and human poverty are near neighbours here!

Two kilometres, more or less, separate the primary school at Corticeiras from the viewpoint at Boca dos Namorados. Then, above the school, beside the farm whose door bears the sign "Mios Muchachos", the path forks, one stone track rising, the other, of beaten earth, going straight

Time: 4 hours

Starting-point:
Corticeiras,
Estreito de
Câmara de
Lobos

Arrival point:
Casas Próximas,
Curral das
Freiras

Length:
7 kilometres

The descent from Boca
dos Namorados

ahead. Both lead to Boca dos Namorados, but the first is somewhat shorter and steeper. Whichever you choose, the landscape
up to that viewpoint is unspectacular.

At the start of the climb up, the vegetation is dominated by cherry trees, particularly lovely when in early spring, before their
leaves begin to shoot forth, they are covered by white flowers, or
when in summer, now fully arrayed in green, they are adorned
by tiny red fruit.

Farther ahead, farmlands give way to a wood of little biological
or scenic interest. This is the dictatorship of the eucalyptus, with
a few acacias attempting to prove that there is democracy...

At the end of the ascent, we come to Boca dos Namorados. A
small clearing, the meeting-point of several paths, where we see
for the first time the enormous, beautiful depression of Curral
das Freiras. In the foreground lie Lombo Chão and Seara Velha,
the schoolhouse rising above the surrounding buildings. More
distant, on a small, raised platform, is Casas Próximas, its principal landmark the church.

The descent to the Curral begins here, at Boca dos Namorados.
At first, the path is still bordered by eucalyptus, but we soon
enter the realms of the sweet chestnut. How beautiful is the light
as it filters through the soft green foliage!

Beyond the sweet chestnut woods, the rocky walls are covered by
rich and varied flora: houseleek, penny wort, shrubby sow thistle, Madeiran germander, sorrel, and groundsel, St John's wort,

melliferous spurge, prickly cardoons, various grasses, and many ferns. Identifying one, admiring the beauty of another, noting the type of leaf or the size of yet another, we lose all notion of time and barely notice the ascent to Pico do Cedro.

RQ

Here it is obligatory to halt awhile. Only those of little sensitivity will fail to sit down to enjoy the views of the Ribeira dos Socorridos valley, dotted with the fields and houses of Curral de Baixo. We begin to descend once more from Pico do Cedro. The thin soils of the mountainsides are covered by wax myrtles, laurels, Canary holly (*Ilex canariensis*) and heather.

Before we come to Lombo Chão, we encounter a river where the people from the area wash their clothes. This is known as Corgo do Murtal. Corgo comes from *córrego*, meaning creek or gully, whilst Murtal refers to the myrtles which abound on the riverbank. Here we can also find the exotic prickly pear and the indigenous globularia.

Shortly afterwards, we spot the first houses of Lombo Chão. The appearance of these dwellings does not hide the poverty of their inhabitants. The cultivated terraces descend the mountainside to an almost impossible depth.

From Lombo Chão, we ascend a short way to Seara Velha, where the only school in Curral de Baixo is found. Straight ahead is the gentle descent to the bridge over the Socorridos river, known locally as the Ribeira do Curral. Along the way, we pass through the place known as Balseiras.

Why Balseiras? This is the name of an ancient grape-growing method, by which the vines grew up the trunks of trees. Possibly imported from the Minho region in the north of Portugal during the early times of the colonisation of Madeira, this was a frequently-used method all along the northern coast of the island and in Curral before the destruction of the vineyards by phylloxera during the second half of the 19th century.

We can take either the road or the footpath to get from the river to the church. The old path is both shorter and more pleasant.

Curral de Baixo

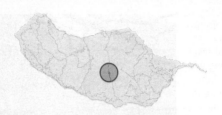

Important notes: This is a walk without precipices. There are two alternative routes between the school at Corticeiras and Boca dos Namorados. The old path is a little shorter, but steeper at first. Both are accessible to cars.

Between Boca dos Namorados (altitude 1060 metres) and Corgo do Murtal (430 metres) the path descends all the way, except for a short climb before Pico do Cedro (908 metres). The path needs repair here and there but is not dangerous at any point. It is 2.5 kilometres from Corgo do Murtal to the bridge over the Socorridos River - known there as Ribeira do Curral - the path continually rising and falling. It is another 2.5 kilometres from the bridge to the church, uphill along the road. The old path is the shorter route 1 km., but this is in any case the most demanding part of the walk. Those wishing to avoid this ascent can catch the bus at Balseiras or Seara Velha.

Funchal

Casas Próximas

Curral das Freiras

Terra Chã

Capela

630

Balseiras

430

Ribeira dos Socorridos

Seara Velha

Lombo Chão

450

Ribeira do Murtal

Pico do Cedro
908

N

0   500 m

Boca dos Namorados
1060

1000
950
900
850

Jardim da Serra

750

Estreito

Road
Footpath
Unmetalled road
Direction of water flow
500 Altitude in metres
Church
School

82

Levada of Curral and Castelejo

Now it is a ghost village, but it once had a population of 30 people who, little by little, tired of their isolation. The last inhabitants moved away around 20 years ago.

It is called Fajã do Poio or, simply, Fajã, and it belongs to the Santo António parish in the district of Funchal. So near and yet so far!

There are some ten houses, partially covered by brambles, on a tiny sun-drenched plateau on the

Time:
4 or 5 hours

MF

Starting-point:
Santa Quitéria,
in Santo António

Arrival point:
Casas Próximas,
Curral das
Freiras

Length:
10 kilometres

right-hand bank of the Lapa, a tributary of the great Ribeira dos Socorridos. Houseleek spontaneously decorates the roofs, the thresholds of the doors and the windows. The domestic water tanks, the sinks for washing and the little fireplaces remain. In the gardens are avocados, custard apples and loquat trees, fighting for sheer survival against the invading brambles and white eupatorium.

At weekends, a few of the former inhabitants continue religiously to visit the village, tending a few plots planted with potatoes and banana trees. To me, this is a moving labour of love, particularly in view of the sacrifice entailed in transporting the products back to their homes.

RQ

But, how do we get to Fajã?

The Levada do Curral and Castelejo, which collects water from the Curral das Freiras to irrigate the lands of Santo António and São Martinho, is the only access route to this isolated spot. This route, however, also allows us to visit the abandoned Fajã and to take a walk up to Curral das Freiras.

There are various ways up to the levada. I suggest you start walking at Santa Quitéria, immediately after the last bus stop.

A few minutes after starting out along the aqueduct, we encounter a tiny bridge over the Arvoredo river. The houses lining the irrigation channel before we come to the river belong to the village of Preces, whilst those on the right-hand side belong to Viana. The beautiful views over the river Socorridos, Pico da Cruz and the ridges rising up from the Câmara de Lobos to Estreito form a pleasant counterpoint to the lack of architectural or aesthetic interest of most of these buildings.

MF

Little by little, houses become more rare, and cultivated soil gives way to bare lands. Here, woad, a tiny plant used for making dye, pushes forth its yellow flower amongst hay and brambles. Around the rocks, Canary laurels begin to appear, but eucalyptus is the most common tree here until we reach Ribeira da Lapa, on the right bank of which we find the abandoned hamlet of Fajã.

Tunnel near Fajã do Poio

There are two routes to choose from to get to Fajã: either to continue along the aqueduct or to descend by a path to the left of it and climb up on the other side.

I strongly urge you to take the latter route because, although it is longer, it is much less dangerous. Those choosing the first route should take enormous care. The ledge running beside the aqueduct is narrow, there are many leaking cracks, the ground is muddy and the protection in poor condition. A torch should also be carried to avoid problems crossing the tunnel.

By one route or the other, with or without-adventure we reach Fajã. How about lunch on a high spot, in the shade of a tree which does not refuse to do this service in spite of its long years of abandonment? A few hundred metres after leaving Fajã, we begin to glimpse, on the right-hand side of the Socorridos river, Fajã das Galinhas, a rather isolated village pertaining to Estreito de Câmara de Lobos. It is called "Fajã", but this is not a sedimentary platform at the bottom of the valley. The few dozen dwellings, some recently built, stand on the more gentle mountain slopes. The terraces stretch up towards the peak and below the inhabited area almost to the very floor of the valley, which takes on its most spectacular forms in this area.

In their mad, torrential flow down to the sea, these waters encounter rocks of very different hardnesses. Over millions of years, the longitudinal and transversal profiles of the river evolved in accordance with this titanic struggle. Narrow meanders, with tiny *fajãs* - plaforms in the convex stretches and steep rocky banks in the concave sections form a succession of shapes of strange beauty. The gigantic wells carved into the ochre tuffs, the basalt dikes and mantles, are just some of the actors on this natural stage of outstanding drama and beauty.

Canary and Azorean laurels, holly, wax myrtle, Madeira mahogany, heather, soft broom and globularia convert some of these areas into a transitonial ecosystem in which indigenous species typical of the first phytoclimatic area and those of Laurisilva live side-by-side.

In Lombo da Partilha, which separates the lands of the Curral and Santo António, the water cascades from the rocky heights, detained only by the valley floor, hundreds of metres below the

MF

irrigation channel. A small tunnel allows safe passage from one side to the other of this splendid waterfall.

A little before passing through this scenic spot, similar to Risco in Rabaçal, we begin to glimpse, on the other side of the river, the houses of Curral do Baixo. At first, Lombo Chão is hidden behind a rocky mass, so that Seara Velha - easily-identified by its school - appears to be the most distant site.

As we approach the Curral, sweet chestnut woods become more common, reddish in hue from winter to mid-spring, dressing in pale green to celebrate the summer solstice and offering a fine banquet for the festivities in honour of All Saints' Day. Meanwhile, the aqueduct reaches the road between Casas Próximas and Capela. Murteiras is the name of this place. This is practically where our walk ends, a walk of rare beauty and many great abysses.

Levada of Curral and Castelejo

Important notes: This walk is almost as dangerous as it is beautiful. From just before Fajã do Poio to Curral das Freiras, the aqueduct ledge is narrow, in some places in bad condition and railings are practically non-existent. We therefore recommend the greatest care when making this excursion to ensure that a moment of pleasure does not turn into hours of nightmare.

The most dangerous stretch is the part just before Fajã, and walkers are therefore recommended not to carry on along the irrigation channel but to take the path along the bottom of the Ribeira da Lapa.

Between Fajã do Poio and Lombo da Partilha, the aqueduct changes level twice. Take the alternate path near these points where the level changes. Walkers should take special care if they choose to start out from the Curral for Santo António, as the first turn-off is not signposted and the natural tendency is to go straight along the aqueduct path. If you reach a point where it is impossible to continue walking along the levada, turn back and look for a way down on the right. The ground may be slippery, and great care is needed. The access to Santa Quitéria is easy. There are buses from 6 a.m., departing from Avenida do Mar, by Alfândega. The return trip from the Curral can also be made by bus.

Road
Footpath
Irrigation channel
Direction of water flow
• 500 Altitude in metres
Church   View point

THE SNOW ROUTE

Fernand Bradel, in one of the most important works of modern historiography, "O Mediterrâneo e o Mundo Mediterrânico", writes that, "in the 16th century, snow water was so widely found in Turkey that it was not even a privilege of the rich. In Constantinople and, for instance, in Tripoli too, travellers often note the abundance of sellers of snow water, of ice and of water ice, all obtained for little money.

In other parts it was, on the contrary, a luxury item. For example, in Egypt where relays of horses were used to transport it from Syria to Cairo; in Lisbon, which sent out afar for snow... in Malta where, to believe their own words, gentlemen died for the lack of snow supplies from Naples, their illness requiring this sovereign remedy. Snow appears, however, to have been generally available all over Italy and Spain. In Italy, this explains the precocity of its peoples in the art of making ice creams and water ice, and in Rome its sale was so lucrative that it became the object of a monopoly. In Spain, snow is conserved in wells until summer".

On Madeira, as in many Mediterranean regions, wells were also built to store snow or hail which fell on the high points of the central mountains during the winter. According to the "Elucidário Madeirense", at the turn of the century there still existed, in the proximity of Pico do Areeiro, and the São Roque mountains above Funchal, "a number of snow wells, some in ruins, others in a good state of conservation". Nowadays, just one of these still exists near the Poiso-Pico do Areeiro road. It is in a good state of repair, and is an interesting part of our architectural heritage, showing the Mediterranean influence on our culture.

The frozen water collected, whose scarcity made it a precious item, was used by water ice makers, hotels and hospitals.

Packed into leather bags and then wrapped in straw, the ice was carried in wicker baskets by robust men, rapidly completing the descent from the mountains down to Funchal. Along three narrow paths, they came to Funchal through Carreiras near Camacha, Alegria at São Roque, or Laranjal in Santo António.

Time:
3 hours

Starting-point:
Poço da Neve,
near Pico do
Areeiro

Arrival point:
Laranjal, Santo
António

Length:
8 kilometres

In Camacha there are still those who remember "O Lobo", one of the last carriers of ice to Reid's Hotel.

More slowly, and without the weight of ice on our backs and with time to admire the scenery, we are going to complete the route between Poço da Neve and Laranjal.

Levada da Negra

MF

When we reach Poço da Neve, if there is no mist, we shall get a glimpse of part of Funchal through the opening of the Santa Luzia Valley. A few hundred metres to the west, on the right-hand bank of the Santa Luzia river, a small aqueduct begins. The mountainsides are bare and ravines are frequent.

Crossing from one side to the other is relatively simple, following a path built many years ago when a series of weirs were built along the river's course to break the force of the torrential water during strong storms. Without covering vegetation, the path was converted into a stream and the little soil which remains is continually being washed away into the river.

Reaching the Levada da Negra, we walk along the path which runs parallel to it, following the flow of the water. A few minutes

Poço da Neve

later, the water begins its descent towards Terreiro Fecho. On this plateau of reddish soil, at the base of Pico Escalvado, there are a series of circular constructions made from slabs of basalt dislodged by the effect of rain and snow over thousands of years from the rocks high above. These structures are used during the sheep-shearing ritual which takes place here every 10 June.

It is difficult to find words to describe this landscape, which combines the green tones of the meagre pastureland with the ashy colours of the basalt crests and brings together a few sweet chestnut trees and the reds of the oxidised rocks.

Just below Terreiro Fecho, close to a small iron aqueduct crossing a river, is an unmarked path leading to Alegria in São Roque. This path is in poor condition, with many tree-trunks lying along it.

The pretty pine forests which covered the basins of the Santo António and Santa Luzia rivers have been almost completely destroyed by summer fires. Thousands of trees, consumed by fire and wind, were denied the honour of dying on their feet. Lombo da Alegria is in such condition that even the agile ice-carriers would not be able to pass through.

MF

To soothe the spirit, dismayed by this Dantesque scene, we enjoy spectacular views of the Bay of Funchal and its urban amphitheatre. Images delighting all those who venture along the Levada da Negra. The path running parallel to this irrigation channel has been maintained in a good state of repair and it is possible to reach Lombo dos Aguiares, Laranjal and Barreira in Santo António along it.

To reach Laranjal, we cross through terrain with many eucalyptus and some pine trees until we come to the point where the waters divide. Here, we take the path leading downwards.

The first dwellings here, below the eucalyptus woods, form part of Curral Velho in Santo António parish. The houses for the most part line the steep stony road leading down towards Laranjal. Despite the architectural poverty and the unsuitable location of many of these houses, it is refreshing to notice the care with which the lovely flowering plants in the little gardens are tended. There is no rose without a thorn!

THE SNOW ROUTE

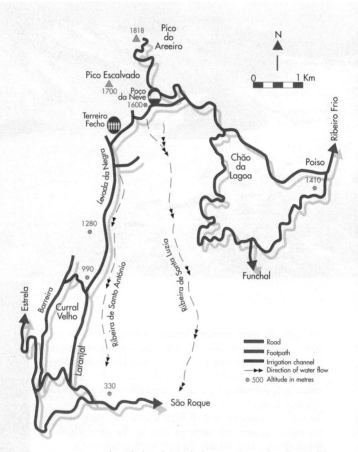

Important notes: The path along the Levada da Negra is in good condition and there are no abysses. Nevertheless, great care should be taken on very misty days.

It is not advisable to take this route during snow or hail, as the irrigation channel can no longer be seen and therefore cannot serve us as a line of reference.
There is no public transport to Pico do Areeiro, though there are buses to Poiso. It is about 3.5 kilometres from Poiso to Poço da Neve, around one hour on foot.
There are buses from Laranjal to the centre of Funchal throughout the day.

Poço da Neve -
Levada do Barreiro -
Casa do Barreiro

he prime point of interest on this route is, without doubt, the snow well, *poço da neve* located in the heights of the Funchal Ecological Park, at an altitude of 1600 metres. Ordered to be built in 1813 by an Italian who produced icecream, this unique example of Madeira's heritage has been the property of the Municipal Council of Funchal since 1936.

Time:
2 to 3 hours

MF

Levada do Barreiro

Starting-point:
Poço da Neve
(1,600 metres
above sea level)

Arrival point:
Casa do Barreiro
(970 metres)

Length:
6 kilometres

This storage place, dug into the ground to keep temperatures low and prevent the ice from melting, is cylindrical in shape and has a hemispherical covering made from basalt slabs. With a height of eight metres and a diameter of 7.5 metres, it holds up to 265 cubic metres of ice. In spite of its dark colour, its shape is reminiscent of an Eskimo igloo.

The ice could be stored in this well for several months without melting. Though we call it a snow well, in fact more hail was stored in it, as hailstorms are more frequent in the mountains of Madeira than snowfalls. This may possibly be the well mentioned by two foreign visitors to the island during the 19th century. Alfred Lyall, in his book "Rambles in Madeira and in Portugal in the Early Part of 1826", refers to a snow well "located very near to the highest point of the mountains visible from Funchal".

In 1851, John Adams Dix, in his book "A Winter in Madeira" speaks of the excellent water ice made by Baxixa, a trader in Rua da Carreira, from ice brought from a well in the mountains.

It is approximately 300 metres from Poço da Neve to Pico dos Melros. On this tiny elevation and in the valley separating it from the plateau where the weather station is located, are found two of the most interesting nuclei of high altitude vegetation on the entire island.

Tree heath (*Erica arborea*) and Madeira billberry (*Vaccinium padifolium*) are the predominant species here, though other heaths (*Erica scoparia ssp. platycodon*) also form part of the vegetation.

Madeira bilberries are picked in September and October. Rich in vitamin A, they also make excellent jam.

Heather does not produce edible fruit, but not for this is it any the less important to the quality of life of the people of Funchal. Its tiny leaves retain large amounts of water from mist, making a decisive contribution to restocking the springs of Tornos.

MF

In this vegetable formation, we can observe laurels (*Laurus azorica*) which, due to the cold and wind, grow less and have smaller leaves than in the Laurisilva, holly (*Ilex perado*) and Madeira rowan (*Sorbus maderensis*).

The rowan, known here as *sorveira* or *tramazeira,* is a small deciduous tree of the Rosaceae family, endemic to Madeira. There are scarcely a hundred individuals of this species on the island, however, distributed around this nucleus on the Pico dos Melros and around the

nucleus covering the slope to the northeast of the Meteorological Station. With such a rare species, we need to take

the greatest care of it and take all necessary steps to increase its population.

It cannot be said that there are many birds around Pico dos Melros, but we may easily spot the firecrest (*Regulus ignicapillus maderensis*) and the chaffinch (*Fringilla coelebs maderensis*) hopping from the heather to the bill-berry. At its origin, the Levada do Barreiro channel is rather narrow. After running through large heather bushes, it then joins another canal, whose source is in a river where, shel-tered from the wind, grow willows (*Salix canariensis*), lily-of-the-valley trees (*Clethra arborea*) and laurels (*Laurus azorica*). It is well worth mak-ing a short detour to the source of this second aqueduct.

The levada continues through a pine forest planted during the 1930s, now in decline due to various forest fires and strong winds. The Funchal Ecological Park management plan provides for the removal of dead pines and those in an unhealthy condition and the planting in their place of indigenous species with the aim of increasing the variety of vegetation on

Bushy vegetation, Pico dos Melros

Pico dos Melros.

Three years after the removal of the sheep and goats which grazed freely around here, the signs of self-regeneration of the vegetative covering are clearly visible. Heather grows vigorously everywhere, and human action is now limited to planting other indigenous species in order to ensure the biodiversity characteristic of moun-tain bushy formations.

Still in the pine forest, the irrigation channel clearly descends to flow into the waters of a stream forming a tributary of the Santa Luzia river. This is the section of the walk where we need to take most care. Now, the descent becomes steeper and we must walk along the riverbed, passing over the stones which escaped from a quarry operational until a few years ago higher up the mountain. After this short odyssey, we finally reach the main channel of the Levada do Barreiro, close to the point where this crosses with two paths: that leading to Chão da Lagoa, passing through the old quarry and which has now been reclaimed; and that leading to the Tornos water treatment station, which requires repair at certain points to ensure a safe passage along it.

Our objective is Casa do Barreiro and we must therefore continue walking along the path which runs parallel to the aqueduct.

No one knows for sure when the Levada do Barreiro was built, but it is certainly one of the oldest irrigation channels on the island. It really is a magnificent work. It continues to flow between the volcanic tuffs into which it was carved, receiving from time to time the water offered to it by narrow little channels fed by tiny springs.

The source of the Levada do Barreiro is hidden amidst a dense thicket of heather; it's a remarkable water route for the study of nature, but further on throws open wide windows over the Ribeira de Santa Luzia, with delightful waterfalls during the rainy season and pretty basalt dikes throughout the year. On the other side, we can view perfectly three irrigation channels running through the practically bare rock. From here, we can easily see the steps to Tornos and the tiny houses, where the water from various sources converges. Seagulls fly up the valley in search of freshwater and any odd titbit, whilst buzzards (*Buteo buteo harterti*) and kestrels (*Falco tinnunculus canariensis*) make reconnaissance flights in search of their favourite prey.

As we walk along, we enjoy a delightful series of views of Funchal from different perspectives. Which is the most beautiful?

At the end, the irrigation channel is surrounded, principally by exotic trees: holm oak (*Quercus ilex*) sweet chestnut (*Castanea sativa*) and maritime pine *(Pinus pinaster)* from southern Europe, and from Australia eucalyptus *(Eucalytus globulus)* and various acacias (*Acacia dealbata, Acacia elata, Acacia mearnsii, Acacia melanoxylon*).

As we approach Casa do Barreiro, our final destination on this walk, we see til-trees, laurels, Madeira mahogany, Canary laurel, lily-of-the-valley trees, wax myrtle, *pau branco*, recently planted in an area where eucalyptus, acacia and pine have been cut down, beginning the regeneration of the original forest which, at this altitude, close to 1,000 metres above sea level, is different from the vegetation we observed at Pico dos Melros.

Poço da Neve
Levada do Barreiro
Casa do Barreiro

Important notes: This entire hike is contained within the borders of the Funchal Ecological Park, in an area where work is being undertaken to regenerate the original indigenous plant covering.

The path is marked and the most dangerous spots are protected by railings.

A stick should be taken for walking, and suitable footwear for slippery terrain. Don't forget your waterproofs, particularly in winter. The route ends at Casa do Barreiro, one of the various Park centres for receiving groups of young people taking part in environmental education projects.

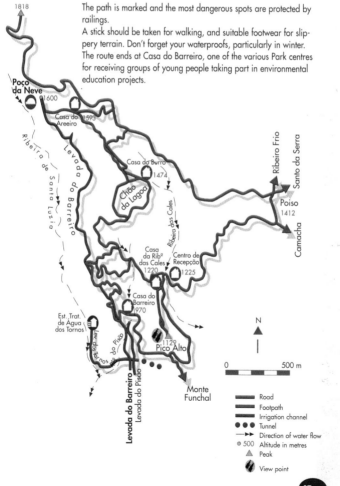

Pico do Areeiro
1818

Poço da Neve
1600

Casa do Areeiro
1593

Ribeira de Santa Luzia

Levada do Barreiro

Casa do Burro
1474

Chão da Lagoa

Ribeiro Frio
Santo da Serra

Poiso
1412

Ribeira das Cales

Camacha

Casa da Rib.ª das Cales
1220

Centro de Recepção
1225

Casa do Barreiro
970

Est. Trat. de Água dos Tornos

Levada dos Tornos

Levada do Piso

Pico Alto
1129

Levada do Barreiro
Levada do Piso

Monte Funchal

N

0   500 m

	Road
	Footpath
	Irrigation channel
●●●	Tunnel
►►	Direction of water flow
◉ 500	Altitude in metres
▲	Peak
◍	View point

FROM AREEIRO TO PICO RUIVO

Time:
- 3 hours for Route A without the ascent of Pico das Torres. Five hours with the ascent of Pico das Torres.
- Close to a hours for Route B: 6 hours with the ascent of Pico das Torres.
- Around 7 hours to Santana: 9 hours with the ascent of Pico das Torres.

S ome boast of having done the Pico do Areeiro-Pico Ruivo trek in two hours. Some even place their record at just sixty minutes. I, quite honestly, cannot walk the length of this path in less than three hours. And I am no mean walker! When not pursued by mist, not even four hours are enough to appreciate the enormous diversity of forms and colours provided here by Mother Nature.

Tiny orange lichen, moss and ferns springing from the cracks in the basalt, the green rosettes of the house-leek, silvery-green grasses hanging from the rock walls, the golden yellow of genista, the fluorescent branches of white -flowered marguerites, the twisted, rugged old forms of the heath tree - all thrive in a hostile environment! At this altitude such surival is quite remarkable as the summers are hot and dry while in winter hail and snow occur and throughout the year the daily temperature variation is enormous.

And the geomorphology? What wealth!

The sills and the basalt dikes supporting volcanic waste and tuff less resistant to the draining waters and the battering of the wind. The red of the iron oxides in the volcanic ashes, contrasting with the black solidified basalt lava...

Monotony? Repetitive forms?

Not a bit of it! Each point along the path gives the walker a different, but always succulent bit of the landscape.

Around a quarter of an hour from Pico do Areeiro -having spotted in the distance, to the left of the path, the thatched cowsheds of Pico Furão in Curral das Freiras - the Ninho da Manta buzzard's nest viewpoint appears.

From this high lookout, where that noble bird of prey, the buzzard, once nested, we can see, in Fajã da Nogueira, the network of creeks and streams which flow into the Ribeira da Metade and, more distant still, Achadas do Pau Bastião and Cedro Gordon in the area of São Roque do Faial.

The walk along the basalt dike separating the courses of the Fajã da Nogueira and Cidrão rivers is absolutely marvellous. The first is a tributary of the Ribeira da Metade - or Ametade, as they say in Faial - running

Starting-point: Pico do Areeiro

Arrival point: Pico Ruivo; Achada do Teixeira; Santana

Length: A - 10 kilometres, including the ascent and descent of Pico das Torres; 6 kilometres going through the tunnels of Pico das Torres.
B - From Pico do Areeiro to Achada do Teixeira (Homem em Pé) it is just over 8 kilometres: 12 kilometres including the ascent to Pico das Torres.
C - From Pico do Areeiro to Santana, around 16 kilometres including the ascent to Pico das Torres

northwards, whilst the second flows into the Socorridos river, whose mouth is near Câmara de Lobos.

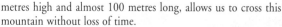

Later, Pico da Gato appears, 1,780 metres high and sporting a mushroom shaped rock on the summit and slopes steep enough to deter the finest mountaineer. A tunnel, two metres high and almost 100 metres long, allows us to cross this mountain without loss of time.

Fantastic! Just before the tunnel entrance, we see before us one of the rivers which converge at Curral das Freiras and some of the hamlets of this parish, dominated by the dark rock of Pico Cidrão.

Over there to the west, behind Pico Grande, the sun shines down over the plains of Paul da Serra. Emerging from the tunnel, we come face to face with the source of the Fajã da Nogueira river. Further upstream are the plateaux and ridges of São Roque do Faial.

Pico do Areeiro

MF

The second tunnel, some 200 metres in length, is the longest of the five along this route, passing through Pico das Torres. The other three are small, and also cross through that great monument of silvery-red rock.

On entering Pico das Torres tunnel, we left behind us another tributary of the Curral river, and on leaving at the other end we meet the Seca do Faial river. Inattentive observers might easily become confused, not knowing whether they are facing north or south.

On emerging from the last tunnel, we join the Pico das Torres path. Before describing the final stage of our excursion, up to Pico Ruivo, I should like to tell you a little about this path, which is a longer, harder alternative route through Pico das Torres.

In a small flat area between Pico do Gato and Pico das Torres, before the second tunnel, the path divides into two. Passing through the iron gate, we begin the climb up. In a few places, broom lies between the path and the precipice, and where it does not, there is a railing.

The ground is covered by slabs of basalt rock ripped from the encircling mountains by the force of the ice which formed in the rock fissures over thousands of years. Where there is no basalt, the path is excavated into volcanic tuffs and waste.

MF

Pico das Torres

The vegetation throughout the ascent is poor, dominated by broom bushes and the bracken *(Pteridium aquilinum)*, a cosmopolitan species not to the liking of sheep and goats. Ironwort *(Sideritis candicans* var. *candicans)*, known here as *selvageira* or *erva branca,* is the only endemic species with widespread presence amongst these bare rocks.

All along the path, we come across several caves excavated into the volcanic tuff, where livestock takes shelter during bad weather and which also served as a refuge for the men engaged in building this difficult track.

The most demanding stage of this journey is the final stretch of the ascent. We must climb up hundreds of steps carved into the reddish rock before we come to a basalt dike which marks the beginning of the descent.

If the ascent is a veritable trial of strength for the heart, the descent is a true test for our leg joints and muscles. The stone slabs seem to rush by under our feet.

This side of Torres is a monument of dikes, sills and periglacial formations. Sculptural heather bushes, hundreds of years old, grow proudly on a bare rock stage, crumbling here and there.

The two paths come together once more at the mouth of the last tunnel. Both lead through Pico das Torres, the path I have just described beng the older and longer of the two.

Just before the meeting-point of the two tracks, the old Torres path passes by a trail leading down into Fajã da Nogueira. With great care and, above all, a good knowledge of the terrain, it is possible to make this descent, passing through an Integral Reserve which contains, amongst many other tree species, a rare group of yew. But this is one of those paths which should only be taken with scientific objectives and in the company of an expert guide.

Continuing our walk to Pico Ruivo, over half an hour from the last tunnel along Torres, we come across a beautiful patch of

Hundred-year-old heath trees between Pico
das Torres and Pico Ruivo

enormous old heather trees. The last part of the path before we
reach the hostel, is up hill all the way.

This is the hardest part of the hike, excepting the ascent of
Torres. But why cover this stage in a hurry if we are not trying
to break any records? Stop, sit down in the shade of one of these
magnificent trees, contemplate the peaks of Torres, let your
mind soar over the Ribeira Seca Valley, enjoy the silence, for at
any moment the birds will start their concert.

Now, let us walk once more, reaching the mountain hostel, which
fits harmoniously into the scenery, unlike the hotel at Pico do
Areeiro. Leave your rucksack in the house and, lighter now, walk
up to the top of the highest mountain in Madeira.

Crossing through that patch of heather which has resisted hundreds of winters and countless windy storms, you will be able to
see, if there is no mist, the lands of Curral das Freiras, the majestic Ribeira Grande de São Jorge valley and the plateaux of
Santana. If surrounded by a sea of cloud, do not despair. Let your
spirit sail gently over the waves of the stratocumulus. Now,
retrace your way back to the hostel and return to Pico do Areeiro
follow the good path down to Achado do Teixeira.

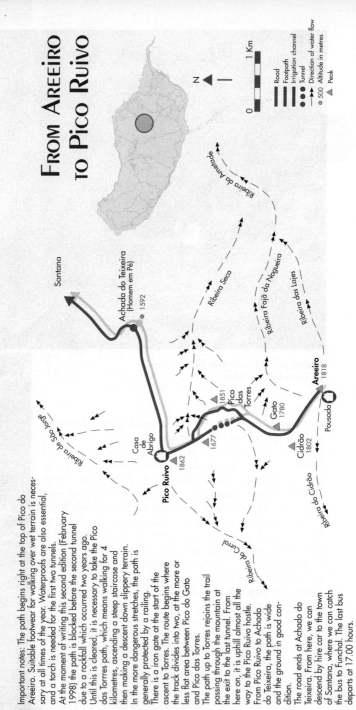

FROM AREEIRO TO PICO RUIVO

Santana

Achada do Teixeira
(Homem em Pé)
▲ 1592

Ribeira da Ameixade

Ribeira Seca

Ribeira Fajã da Nogueira

Ribeira das Lajes

Casa de Abrigo

Pico Ruivo
▲ 1862

▲ 1851

Pico das Torres

1677

Gato ▲ 1780

Areeiro
▲ 1818

Pousada

Cidrão ▲ 1802

Ribeira do Cidrão

Ribeira de Curral

Ribeira de São Jorge

0	1 Km

N

━━━ Road
━━━ Footpath
∙∙∙∙ Irrigation channel
▪▪▪ Tunnel
→ Direction of water flow
● 500 Altitude in metres
▲ Peak

Important notes: The path begins right at the top of Pico do Areeiro. Suitable footwear for walking over wet terrain is necessary at all times of the year. Waterproofs are also essential, and a torch is needed for the first two tunnels.

At the moment of writing this second edition (February 1998) the path is blocked before the second tunnel due to a rockfall which occurred two years ago. Until this is cleared, it is necessary to take the Pico das Torres path, which means walking for 4 kilometres, ascending a steep staircase and then making a descent down slippery terrain. In the more dangerous stretches, the path is generally protected by a railing.

There is a iron gate at the start of the ascent to Torres. The route begins where the track divides into two, at the more or less flat area between Pico do Gato and Pico das Torres.

The path up to Torres rejoins the trail passing through the mountain at the exit to the last tunnel. From here on, it is uphill almost all the way to the Pico Ruivo hostle.

From Pico Ruivo to Achado do Teixeira, the path is wide and the ground in good condition.

The road ends at Achado do Teixeira. From here, we can descend by hire car to the town of Santana, where we can catch the bus to Funchal. The last bus departs at 17.00 hours.

102

From Pico Ruivo
to Encumeada

I was still just a schoolboy when I and a group of friends decided to climb from Santana to Pico Ruivo for the first time. The aims of that summer expedition were to see the Homem em Pé and the sunrise from the highest peak on Madeira.

As we got closer to Achada do Teixeira, and one of my companions pointed out the Homem em Pé to me, I was amazed. In the end, the stone giant (Homem em Pé means "Standing Man") which I had imagined as a child, when listening to stories about Pico Ruivo, did not exist, and the Homem em Pé was just a pretty-looking, tame, basalt eminence which stoically resisted the erosive forces of the waters as they drained away.

The fantastic emergence of the sun from the sea of red clouds at five in the morning surpassed, however, my greatest expectations and fully justified the hard climb.

Now, times have changed, and an excursion to Pico Ruivo is a much easier mission. You can get to Achada do Teixeira by car, and from there to the top the path is in such a good state of repair that ladies have been known to walk up it wearing high-heeled shoes. There are small shelters along the path and, more or less halfway up, the water which filters into the rocks with the passing of mistclouds or the occasional hailstorm, surges out once more from a crevasse between two prisms of basalt to refresh tired walkers.

Slowly, take it easy, enjoy the views of the São Jorge River basins to the west, the Seca do Faial River to the east, and in an hour's time we shall be at the Pico Ruivo hostle. You may be interested to learn that this shelter was built in 1939, and was recently extended and living conditions in it improved. Before this house existed, those who came up the mountain to cut heather to make fences, or to collect fire-

Time:
8 hours

Starting-point:
Achada do
Teixeira (Homem
em Pé)

Arrival point:
Encumeada

Length:
18 kilometres

"Homem em Pé"

wood, and hikers caught by nightfall or thick fog could take shelter a little further down in the Lapa da Cadela cave, which lies close to the Encumeada path.

If climbing Pico Ruivo is no longer an adventure, then, at least from the Santana side, the truth is that the spectacular views over the landscape on clear days makes a visit to the peak more than worthwhile. And if the unpredictable mists obscure the highest parts, do not despair, for the weather will surely be kinder next time.

Apart from the magic of the light and the colours when the sun rises, or slips away over the horizon, it is always a pleasure to observe the deep, V-shaped narrow valley of the São Jorge river, separating the Achada do Gramacho from the lands of the parish of the same name, or Pico do Arco de São Jorge, with its television transmission tower, bringing Brussels closer to Ribeira Funda. From here we can also see the end of the São Lourenço Peninsula and the arch formed by the Desertas Islands, the bare flats of Paul da Serra and the shapes of Porto Santo.

More than this we cannot see, for Pico das Torres is somewhat large, and hides a slice of the landscape from the walker.

It is on Pico Ruivo that the walk I propose really begins. The first part was just to whet your appetite, or for those who were abandoned by the spirit of adventure in their adolescence. It is some 16 kilometres in length, with more descents than ascents, following a path running along the island's mountainous backbone.

Just after commencing the descent, before reaching the Lapa da Cadela cave, we can see, down there in the distance, the houses of Curral da Cima, Fajã dos Cardos and Colmeal, beside the river and on a platform on the right-hand side lies Fajã Escura. Only after some distance will we see the plateau with the centre of Curral das Freiras, its houses huddling around the church. From Pico Jorge, we can even see the Socorridos river mouth and the church of São Martinho.

Meanwhile, we hardly notice the kilometres passing by, as our attention is divided between the

Sunrise at Pico Ruivo

AR

grandiose forms of the volcanic skeleton of the island and the minuscule elements of its vegetable epidermis.

It is quite possible that the mist may appear, gradually covering the great depression of the Curral and only leaving the surrounding mountains visible. In just a few minutes, the Grande, Cedro, Cidrão and Torres peaks are transformed into tiny islands of black and red rock amidst a sea of whitish stratocumulus.

But when the great landscape disappears from view, not all is lost, for the sides of the path are rich in shapes, forms and colour.

Skirting around Pico da Lapa da Cadela, passing through Torrinhas, winding below Pico Jorge or crossing the peaks of Encumeada and Meio, the path becomes hidden between ancient heather bushes, broom with its golden flowers, and bilberry. Laurels, Madeira mahogany, lily-of-the-valley trees, the odd beefwood, holly and even the rare barberry, are the denizens of these extensive, beautiful spontaneous forests.

Hundreds of mountain orchids, patches of marguerite with their white flowers, and pride of Madeira with its lilac blooms, decorate the rocky walls, whilst the path is carpeted with thyme, marjoam, mint, all impregnate the air with their scent.

June and July are the months when the great festival of these flowers takes place along the narrow path winding through the sources of the Socorridos and Brava rivers and which from Cumeada Alta penetrates into the Ribeira Brava and São Vicente valleys.

But those who walk this path at any other time of year will not consider their time wasted, for the more journeys one makes along this path, the more plants and capricious geological forms one discovers.

From Pico Ruivo to Encumeada

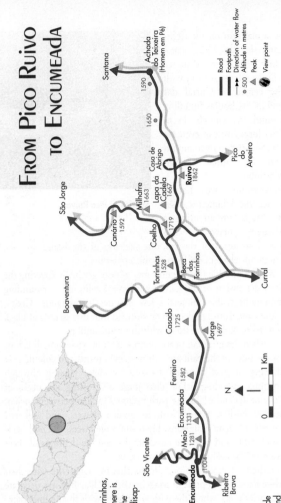

Legend:
- Road
- Footpath
- → Direction of water flow
- ● 500 Altitude in metres
- ▲ Peak
- 🔄 View point

Map labels:
- Achada do Teixeira (Homem em Pé)
- Santana
- 1590
- 1650
- Casa de Abrigo
- Milhafre 1663
- Lapa da Cadela 1667
- Ruivo 1862
- Pico do Areeiro
- São Jorge
- Canário 1592
- Coelho
- 1719
- Torrinhas 1528
- Boca das Torrinhas
- Curral
- Boaventura
- Casado 1725
- Jorge 1697
- Ferreiro 1582
- Encumeada 1331
- Meio 1281
- 1004
- São Vicente
- Encumeada
- Ribeira Brava

N — 0 — 1 Km

Important notes: From Achada do Teixeira to Pico Ruivo - less than three kilometres - the path is excellent, and even allowing time to enjoy the scenery the walk takes less than an hour.

It is approximately 16 kilometres from Pico Ruivo to Encumeada, with more descents than ascents, as the beginning of the path is at an altitude of nearly 1850 metres and the end at 1004.

Right at the start, we come to a gravely area where care is needed to cross the slippery terrain. Later, the path improves again, though along some stretches we may find loose stones. The path linking the Curral das Freiras and Boa Ventura crosses our way at Boca da Torrinhas, however, about a kilometre before we get to this point there is another track on the left hand side which also leads to the Curral - this is not sign- posted. Indeed, sinposting also disappears at times in Bocas das Torrinhas.

The most difficult stretch of this walk is the steep ascent from Boca das Torrinhas to the summit of Pico Jorge, after which the path runs downhill all the way.

There are no sheer drops along this path, and in some places the broom which grows alongside is so dense as to make it difficult to continue.

Waterproofs should be taken, along with warm clothes and suitable boots.

It is advisable to carry water as there is just one small spring, almost dry in summer, at Pico Ferreira, which is almost dry in summer.

The offices of the Regional Secretariat for Tourism provide information about bus times from Funchal to Santana and from Encumeada to Funchal.

Pico Grande

I t is big. It is enormous when seen from Curral das Freiras or Serra da Agua. It soars up to a height of 1,657 metres above sea level, loftily tending over the separation of the waters which run gaily down into the Brava and Socorridos river valleys.

But how can we get to Pico Grande? What path must we take to visit this grandiose natural museum adorned with many giant sculptures, carved by the wind and the water in the red tuffs and volcanic waste?

The easiest way up is by the old path from Estreito de Câmara de Lobos to Encumeada, much-used in the past by the people of São Vicente and other parishes in the north of the island to come to the city before the advent of the motor-car. There are still some old folk who recall the adventure of a journey to Funchal on a day of terrible heat or showers or through shadowy mist. There are also those who remember with nostalgia the groups of - pilgrims; who sang lustily as they crossed these mountains at the time of the feast of Senhor Bom Jesus in Ponta Delgada.

There are a variety of possible walks along this path, which links the north and the south of Madeira.

For the hardiest hikers, I recommend the route from Corticeiras through Chão da Relva to Encumeada. For those who prefer to take their car to "Casa Florestal", near Pico da Malhada the walk to Pico Grande with return to the starting-point is an excellent option.

There are frequent buses to Corticeiras throughout the day, but it is a good idea to start out early to reach the "Casa Florestal" during the cool morning hours. From the bus stop to the lovely Quinta do Jardim da Serra, with its fine old house surrounded by lovely woods of indigenous and exotic trees, the path is more downhill than up.

Things get a little more complicated from this point to the "Casa Florestal". The path is uphill all the way, though the road is good and even suitable for cars.

Time:
A: 4 to 5 hours
B: 6 to 7 hours

Starting-point:
Corticeiras or the
Boca da Corrida
Forestry Lodge
("Casa Florestal")

Arrival points:
Boca da Corrida
Forestry Lodge or
Encumeada

Length:
A: Forestry
Lodge - Pico
Grande -
Forestry Lodge:
10 kilometres
B: Corticeiras -
Chão da Relva -
Encumeada:
16 kilometres

This first part of the walk is some four kilometres in length and takes around one and a half hours to complete on foot. At first, the path is lined by houses whose poor architectural quality is in stark contrast with the pretty little fields of crops. Here, cherry trees surround the plots of cabbages, potatoes and taro.

Wallnut and sweet chestnut are frequently found in this rural landscape and at one point the path runs through a lovely wood of sweet chestnut which in autumn, in an atmosphere of gently flitering sunlight, offers the traveller its fruits, once freed from the confines of its hedge-hog like shell.

Even without their fine foliage these sweet chestnut trees become a pleasant reference point, marking practically the end of our steep climb.

MF

Those who make the ascent to the house of the forest keepers can never even suspect the presence here of a viewpoint commanding views of the entire parish of Curral das Freiras and the opposite side of Eira do Serrado.

The depression of the Curral, seen from just east of the "Casa Florestal" viewpoint, looks much larger than when observed from Eira do Serrado. From this vantage point the observer can see the dwellings of that parish scattered on the ridges and plateaux carved out by the water from the mountain torrents which converge in the Ribeira dos Socorridos Valley.

After a few moments for rest and contemplation, if the clouds permit, we continue along our way once more. It is four kilometres to this point, and it is another four kilometres to Chão da Relva, encountering no steep ascents or descents along the way. At first, if the day is clear of cloud, we can enjoy different views of the Curral

Pico Grande

and, in the distance, the mouth of the Socorridos and the lands of São Martinho.

Farther along the path, we go across a basalt ridge separating the basins of the Socorridos and Brava rivers. Here, our visual horizon is even broader. the Curral continues to fill our eyes with beauty, and Encumeada appears on the other side, with the Vinháticos Pousada and even a few houses at Serra de Agua.

Eventually we find a narrow path leading off to our right. Those heading for Encumeada should make a brief detour along this route to Chão da Relva. From that tiny platform, carpeted with grasses, adorned with sweet chestnut trees and embellished with fine views, paths start out which lead to the summit of Pico do Grande and to Fajã Escura in Curral das Freiras.

It is around one kilometre along the path from Chão da Relva to the top of Pico do Grande. The steps here are very high, and there is no protection on either side.

The forms sculpted by the wind and draining water have created a fascinating geological park here. Rounded shapes carved from the red tuffs: columns and colonnades; blocks somehow maintaining an uncertain balance; cavities built by the wind.

Close to the top are the low walls of drystone enclosures, evidence of the sheep and cattle once kept here, and which finished off the vegetation around about.

Beyond these enclosures is a short-cut linking up with the Pico Ruivo-Encumeada path.

It takes another twenty minutes from the top of Pico do Grande to Chão da Relva. From here, we can descend to Fajã Escura in the Curral or continue towards Encumeada.

MF

**Path from Boca da
Corrida to Pico Grande**

It is around eight kilometres from Chão da Relva to Encumeada,
with more downhill than uphill sections, the path passing through
stony ground more often than through wooded areas. The path
crosses rivers and streams converging in Serra de Água, the source
of the Brava.

Some 3.5 kilometres from Encumeada, the path runs through
lands which are still cultivated and where we find a number of *palheiros* - small, thatched cowsheds. This is Curral Jangão, the
remotest hamlet of the Serra de Agua parish and through which
runs the Ribeira do Poço, a tributary of the great Ribeira Brava.

The path ends at the regional road, some 500 metres below Boca
da Encumeada. Nothing better to round off this day's hiking than
by going up to the viewpoint, which commands views of São
Vicente to the north and Ribeira Brava town on the other side of
the island.

Waterproofs and warm clothes are recommended for this walk,
particularly in winter.

Pico Grande

N

0   1 Km

Boca da Encumeada
● 1004

Ferreiro
▲ 1582

Curral Jangão

Central Hidroeléctrica
da Serra de Agua

Ribeira do Poço

Pico Grande
1657 ▲

Faiã Escura
(Curral das Freiras)

Pousada
dos
Vinháticos

Chão
da Relva

Ribeira Brava

Serradinho
▲ 1442

Ribeira do Pico

Cavalo
▲ 1357

Malhada
▲ 1203

Casa
Florestal

Quinta
do Jardim
da Serra

Corticeiras
(Autocarro)

Important notes: The path to Chão da Relva is in a good state of repair and is not at all dangerous.

There is a short stretch just after Chão da Relva on the way to the summit of Pico Grande which is narrow, steep and unprotected.
There are a number of sections in poor condition between Chão da Relva and Encumeada, and a walking stick is useful here.
Waterproofs and warm clothes are also recommended for this walk.

Road
Footpath
▶▶ Direction of water flow
● 500 Altitude in metres
▲ Peak
View point

From Serra de Água to Curral das Freiras

ombo Moleiro lies at the inland end of the road which runs past the church at Serra de Água, a parish which grew gradually, extending along the bottom of the Ribeira Brava valley. At this point the new 3,000 m road tunnel to São Vicente starts.

The waters of the Achada and Poço rivers meet at Lombo Moleiro. A bridge over the river here leads to Caminho Matias, a path ascending to Curral Jangão. The Caminho Matias path passes over the Levada do Norte or, better, over the main tunnel. Care is needed to find the path leading to the tunnel mouth, beside the Poço River.

Time:
A: 5 to 6 hours
B: 3 to 4 hours

Starting-point: The regional road beside the entrance to the church of Serra de Água

Arrival points: A - Church of Curral das Freiras
B - Encumeada viewpoint

The ascent from Lombo Moleiro to Curral Jangão is somewhat tiring. The path is some two kilometres in length, beginning at an altitude of 440 metres and terminating just below the 900 metres mark.

At first, the track runs through mixed-crop farming lands, with beans, cabbage and potatoes growing side-by-side. Next we begin to see many Canary holly trees (*Ilex canariensis*), as well as the odd laurel, Madeira mahogany and even one or two specimens of *pau branco*.

MF

Terraces at Serra de Agua

Length:
A - 14 kilometres
B - 8 kilometres

Once in the heart of the forest, the path divides into two: the gentler of these leads off to the left towards the Levada do Norte irrigation channel, the Serra de Água hydroelectric power station and the Vinháticos Pausado; the other, steeper, continues straight ahead to Curral Jangão.

There are still some houses and small, thatched cowsheds standing in Curral Jangão which testify to the by-gone period when intensive crop-farming and cattle-breeding were important activities here.

At Curral Jangão, the path ascending from Lombo Moleiro joins the old track between Estreito de Câmara de Lobos and Encumeada. From here, it is possible either to head towards Chão da Relva or to make for Encumeada.

From Curral Jangão to Chão da Relva (Pico Grande), the path rises a little more, up to nearly 1300 metres above sea level. It is just over 4 kilometres along the path which until the turn of the XX century was the main communications route between Funchal and São Vicente.

In somewhat degraded condition in parts, this path runs through a bush formation where the scars can be clearly seen of forest fires which have on repeated occasions ,disfigured this beautiful landscape.

From Chão da Relva, we can continue towards the Boca da Corrida forestry lodge ("Casa Florestal") or down to Fajã Escura in Curral das Freiras. It is just over three kilometres along the sloping path, the ground somewhat slippery. It takes around one hour to reach the bridge of the Socorridos river.

Curral Jangão

One of the most beautiful elements of the scenery here is a great rock on whose peak perches the rounded, isolated shape of a sweet chestnut tree. It is as if this tree had been planted here on purpose to embellish the rocky eminence which has withstood the erosive forces of the elements for thousands of years.

We frequently find sweet chestnut trees on our descent, along with eucalyptus woods which are expanding to the detriment of the pine

MF

The Ribeira do Poço valley

forests, decimated by successive forest fires. Also common here are foxgloves, their pretty purplish flowers beautifying the floor, where ferns also grow. In Fajã Escura there is a dwelling carved into the rock. Could this be a shelter built by the early settlers of these isolated areas in the inland regions of Madeira?

The poor architectural quality of some more recent houses here is alleviated a little by the beautiful gardens with their varieties of flowers. In May, the potato fields are in flower. This is time to plant the cuttings of sweet potatoes, bought in the lands bordering the sea as the cold winters in the Curral do not allow this plant to survive here from one year to the next. The way sweet potatoes is propagated in these parts is interesting. Cuttings, 20 to 30 centimetres in length, are inserted into the soil, previously turned and fertilised with the aid of a heather pitchfork. It is fascinating to the see the speed and dexterity with which the women carry out this task. Next, the soil is watered, a process which is repeated throughout the summer whenever the ground becomes dry, until the roots acquire sufficient starch and sugar to be picked.

On the marshy lands on the banks of rivers and streams, willow trees grow abundantly, supplying the cottage wicker industry. Until 1995, when the road was finally opened, willow was carried down on shoulders to the centre of the Curral, from where it was dispatched to Camacha. Also carried down where baskets made in the little cottages of the area for export to Europe and North America.

FROM SERRA DE ÁGUA TO CURRAL DAS FREIRAS

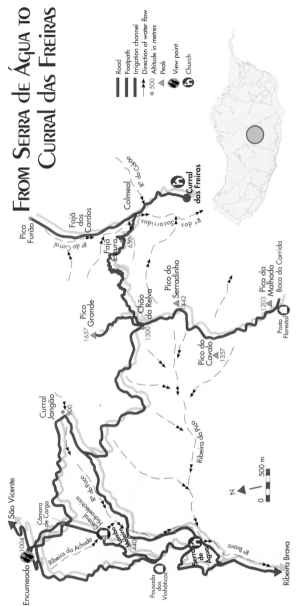

Important notes: The walk begins in Lombo Moleiro, near the new road tunnel which links Serra de Água to São Vicente. It is two kilometres from Lombo Moleiro to Curral Jangão, ascending 400 metres in altitude.

Parts of the old path between Encumeada and Boca da Corrida, partly used for the two suggested routes, are in poor condition, and a walking stick is useful. A stick is also needed for the descent from Chão da Relva to Fajã Escura.

For those opting to continue to Encumeada, it is a further three kilometres from Curral Jangão.

Map legend:
- Road
- Footpath
- Irrigation channel
- Direction of water flow
- 500 Altitude in metres
- Peak
- View point
- Church

Map labels:
- São Vicente
- Encumeada 1004
- Câmara de Carga
- Curral Jangão
- 900
- Central Hidroeléctrica
- Ribeira da Achada
- Rª do Poço
- Pousada dos Vinháticos
- Lombo Moleiro 440
- Serra de Água
- Rª Brava
- Ribeira Brava
- Ribeira do Poço
- Pico do Cavalo 1357
- Posto Florestal
- Boca da Corrida 1203 Pico da Malhada
- Pico do Serradinho 442
- Chão da Relva 1300
- Pico Grande 1657
- Fajã Escura
- 650
- Rª dos Socorridos
- Colmeal
- Rª do Cardo
- Fajã dos Cardos
- Rª do Curral
- Pico Furão
- Curral das Freiras

0   500 m

115

From the Serra de Água power station to Eira do Mourão

O ne never tires of walking the innumerable irrigation channels which are cut into the slopes of Madeira. Each time, one discovers a new view of a landscape one had never before fully appreciated. Everywhere one goes, one finds new plants whose detail and beauty strikes the imagination.

Some go into the mountains to "burn up" kilometres, to break records, to be able to boast that they can do such-and-such a route in spectacular time. But there are also those who go into the mountains in search of peace, of harmony, to discover the infinite complexity of nature.

Time:
5 to 6 hours

Starting-point:
Pousada dos
Vinháticos

Arrival point: 1 -
Boa Morte,
where the aqueduct crosses the
road
2 - Fajã da
Ribeira, on the
left-hand bank of
the Ribeira Brava
River, a little to
the north of the
town of Ribeira
Brava.

MF

Serra de Agua hydro-electric power station

Length:
1 - 15 kilometres
2 - 13.5 kilometre

But there are levadas and levadas. Some are accessible to anyone who likes walking. Others are only to be recommended to those who are reasonably used to hard hiking, to looking down into the depths without protective railings, to narrow, waterlogged tunnels.

The levada which begins at the Serra de Água hydroelectric power station forms part of this latter group, particularly the section from its origin up to Eira do Mourão in the parish of Ribeira Brava. From there to Estreito de Câmara de Lobos, where it ends, the channel passes through less mountainous terrain, much less dangerous.

But those who seek powerful emotions are strongly recommended to try the walk from the hydroelectric power station to Eira do Mourão.

At first, everything seems easy, even until the first tunnel, which appears less than one kilometre from the power station. We can also get through this without problems, it being just 50 metres in length and with a concrete floor. We do not even require a torch. The second tunnel is separated from the first by a stream which carries very little water in summer. It is more or less double the length of the first and is dry with a cement floor. Nevertheless, it is advisable to use a torch to get through. Up to this point, the vegetation is a mixture of indigenous and exotic plants. Lovely sweet chestnut trees stand beside laurels and holly trees. Sarsaparilla (*Smilax*), with strong, heart-shaped leaves, is often found winding around the trees trunks.

Emerging from the second tunnel, we are welcomed by a delegation of fine, varied ferns. Here also are chestnut, walnut and willow, offering a lovely spectacle of filtered light. In this spot, even the brambles are pleasant, giving sweet berries in August.

Some five hundred metres after this second tunnel, a trickle of water falls into the levada, refreshing both walkers and the plants below, who are also God's children. This section is easy in summer, but becomes more complicated in autumn. Then, the water rushes down, sweeping everything along with it. All it needs is a good shower.

Prevention being better than cure, the irrigation channel is covered over for a length of around 50 metres so that problems are not caused by occasional falls of stones and sand. Here, the irrigation channel passes through a zone of volcanic ash and waste with little plant covering. Nevertheless, a few hundred metres farther on, we come to a lovely river with interesting forms carved out by the water in the volcanic ash and waste which continue to dominate the scenery.

At this point we can observe the water flow gauge of the Ribeira do Poço where the levada passes on a bridge. Just after the bridge we come to the largest tunnel, which has a low roof and is very damp. It is 1,100 metres in length and takes 15 minutes to walk through at a reasonable pace. It is advisable to wear protection for the head due to the danger of striking against the low roof of the tunnel, which goes through Pico da Pocinha, a peak with an altitude of 879 metres above sea level, ending beside Pico do Meio

Vintém, a lower summit (622 metres).

Before crossing the Ribeira do Pico Valley, the aqueduct passes along the side of Pico do Búzio (798 metres), going through a small tunnel with a dry floor and a roof a little higher than the previous one.

The Ribeira do Pico Valley is particularly lovely. Here, the water gurgles its way under the shadow cast by sweets chestnuts and willows. The mountainsides are densely covered with a variety of forest. Side by side we find deciduous trees from the Atlantic areas of Europe and indigenous evergreens. In the Ribeira do Pico, we find the mouth of a 3,000-metre-long tunnel which ends near Terra Chão in Curral das Freiras. This tunnel was built in the 1990s to feed the the Socorridos hydroelectric power stations and the drinking water treatment station at Covão, Câmara de Lobos and Santa Quitéria in Funchal.

When this tunnel was built, the Levada do Norte had already irrigated the lands of Ribeira Brava and Câmara de Lobos for 50 years. Since when it rains the croplands are not irrigated, in winter the surplus water is now channelled to this new tunnel. This water supply is added to that collected from the Curral and channelled through yet another tunnel to the lagoon in Covão.

The tunnel to the Curral is not open to the public, and our route therefore continues along the Levada do Norte.

Soon after crossing the bed of the Ribeira do Pico, the aqueduct begins to run parallel to the left-hand bank, and in some places is carved into the rock. Below the canal, the rock falls sheer down into the valley bottom, and small stones occasionally crash down from the rocks above, so that extreme caution is recommended to pass along this section.

At those points where the path running alongside the irrigation channel broadens, one cannot help but stop to admire the landscape. Above is the imposing Pico Grande, separating the basins of the Brava and Socorridos rivers. Below, the waters of the Ribeira do Pico murmuring as they wend their way through the

Levada do Norte between Espigão and Eira do Mourão

forest. On the other side, Pousada dos Vinháticos and the edge of Paul da Serra.

From time to time, a laurel pigeon flits through the laurels at an unbelievable speed. On noticing human presence, the much-hunted bird beats its wings with such force that it causes a sharp noise similar to that of a gunshot. Those not familiar with the habits of this pretty native bird can even be frightened by this sudden outburst, and may not recover quickly enough to see the bird as it wings away.

Stopping here and there, we finally reach the fifth tunnel, some 200 metres in length. This tunnel is waterlogged from end to end, and we can only pass by walking through the mud. In fact, going through this tunnel is no easy matter, but our efforts will shortly be rewarded by the amazing views we shall enjoy over the Serra de Água.

The sixth and seventh tunnels are short and easy to traverse.

Beside the mouth of the last, in a wall of decaying basalt rocks facing south, live some plants of the endemic *Musschia aurea* species, which flowers in August.

The eighth tunnel is about 50 metres long, has a bend in the middle and is waterlogged. Just at the exit mouth is a waterfall over the aqueduct. Here we need to take great care, for the ground is slippery and there is a drop of over 100 metres.

There follows a section of canal built into the rock and completely unprotected, crossing the rocky crest which gave its name - "Espigão" - to a small village in the Ribeira Brava hills.

From the Espigão tunnel to Eira do Mourão, there is just one more tunnel very small, and the path alongside the aqueduct is also unprotected. It is around 10 kilometres from the Serra de Água hydroelectric power station to Eira do Mourão, with 3,325 metres of tunnel and some five kilometres beside sheer drops. A walk recommended for those who enjoy powerful emotions. But, be careful, very careful, for the tiniest error could be fatal.

Is a hamlet Eira do Mourão, whose population lived in great isolation for many years. In 1952, when the water began to flow

MF

Levada do Norte

along the Levada do Norte, the surrounding landscape began to become greener in summer, and agriculture became possible throughout the year.

On reaching Eira do Mourão, we have two choices: to continue along the irrigation channel towards Boa Morte, or to descend by the very steep path to Fajã da Ribeira.

It is 3.5 kilometres more along the aqueduct to Boa Morte. To Fajã da Ribeira, on the left-hand bank of the Ribeira Brava river, almost two kilometres, downhill all the way, a good supplement to the ten kilometres we have already put under our belts along the aqueduct.

From the Serra de Água power station to Eira do Mourão

Central Hid. Serra de Água
600

Ribª do Poço

Pousada dos Vinháticos

Lombo Moleiro
440

Serra de Água
310

650

Ribª do Pico

Curral das Freiras

N

0   500 m

Ribª Brava

600
Espigão

140

Ribª do Espigão

600

Meia Légua

Eira do Mourão

São Paulo

Ribª Funda

Ribeira Funda

90

Fajã 250

Boa Morte

Vila da Ribeira Brava

Important notes: It is just over one kilometre along the road from Pousada dos Vinháticos to the Serra de Água hydroelectric power station.

From the hydroelectric power station, the route is along the Levada do Norte. It is around 10 kilometres to Eira do Mourão, including 3,325 metres of tunnel and many sections along sheer drops with no protection. From Eira do Mourão to Boa Morte is another 3.5 kilometres along the aqueduct.

There is a two-kilometre descent from Eira do Mourão to Fajã da Ribeira, down steps quite hard on the legs. A walking stick should be taken, and waterproofs and torch are absolutely essential.

Road
Footpath
Irrigation channel
Direction of water flow
500   Altitude in metres
Tunnel
Church

Caldeira,
Câmara de
Lobos

Levada do Norte (From Cabo Girão to Boa Morte)

Time: :
A - 3 hours.
B: 4 hours

Starting-point:
Where the
regional road
crosses the
Levada do Norte,
between
Garachico and
Cabo Girão.

Arrival points: A
- Crossing of the
aqueduct with the
municipal road at
Boa Morte,
B: Town of
Ribeira Brava

T his walk begins close to Ribeira da Caldeira, where the aqueduct crosses the regional road, below Cabo Girão. Some 750 metres farther on is a tunnel with a length of around 300 metres.

After passing through the tunnel, another 500 metres and the aqueduct crosses the road once more, now in the parish of Quinta Grande.

Over this first stretch of our walk, we can feast our eyes on the marvellous views over the vast area extending from Câmara de Lobos to Funchal. The Convent of Caldeira, inhabited by the nuns of the St Clare Order, stands out amidst the urbanized basin to the east of Cabo Girão.

The water transported by the Levada do Norte is the chief element responsible for the many hues of green which adorn the immense chessboard of terraces which extends

Length: :
A - 10 kilometres.
B: 13 kilometres

MF

MF

before us down to the coast. Until 50 years ago, the fields of Quinta Grande and Campanário, now extensively cultivated throughout the year, could only be sown after rain. What is now green in summer, five decades ago was brown and yellow. Human action here has made Nature provide nourishment without harming her.

Although there exist abandoned fields, even today there are those who build new walls to grow their crops in little parcels of allogenous soil. In winter, the fields are covered by the yellow flowers of sorrel and marigolds, and the staircases of spontaneous gardens are astoundingly beautiful.

From the irrigation channel, we can also see the distribution of the houses in this rural environment. These dwellings are scattered amongst the plots of land, conveying an image of individualism. We can also appreciate how the old paths and the more recently-built roads help to generate a certain order in the arrangement of housing here.

MF

From the regional road in Quinta Grande to Boa Morte, we have to walk 8.5 kilometres, a distance which can be covered quite easily in about two and a half hours, allowing time to observe the landscape and to study the many wild plants which populate the hillsides around the Levada do Norte.

Some of the bends in the aqueduct form veritable viewpoints from where we can enjoy magnificent views over the farmlands of Campanário in the foreground and of the coast up to Ponta do Sol.

Those wishing to continue the walk should now descend to the town of Ribeira Brava, taking the old path, which is easily found, down to the bus stop for Boa Morte.

The descent is steep but rewarding, as it offers an excellent opportunity to admire the gardens filled with lovely flowers. Some of these are a veritable hymn to beauty and love of plants. An hour, downhill all the way, but with many flowers to photograph or to film.

Levada do Norte (From Cabo Girão to Boa Morte)

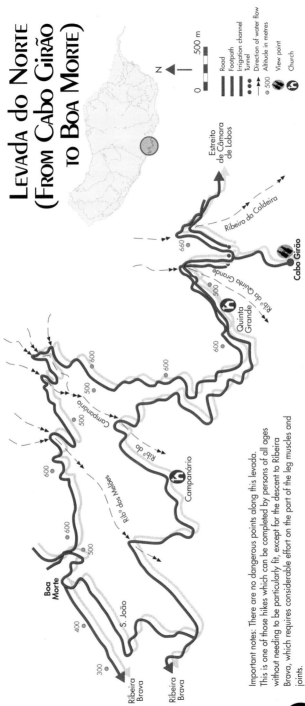

Road
Footpath
Irrigation channel
Tunnel
→ Direction of water flow
• 500 Altitude in metres
View point
Church

0 ___ 500 m

N ←

Estreito de Câmara de Lobos

Ribeiro da Coldeira

660

Cabo Girão

500 Rib.º de Quinta Grande

Quinta Grande

600

600

Campanário

500 Rib.º de

600

500

Rib.º dos Melões

600

Boa Morte

S. João

600

600

500

Ribeira Brava

Ribeira Brava

400

300

Important notes: There are no dangerous points along this levada. This is one of those hikes which can be completed by persons of all ages without needing to be particularly fit, except for the descent to Ribeira Brava, which requires considerable effort on the part of the leg muscles and joints.

Beyond Calvário

I t was a rainy morning, and when we reached the Church of Estreito de Câmara de Lobos, few in our group believed that the hike planned for that Saturday would turn out to be feasible.

Since the rain did not look like stopping, we decided to pay a visit to the old but well-conserved baroque-style church. Here, we gazed at the paintings on the ceiling and the interesting paintings covering the side walls, stopping also to admire the gilt carving of the altarpiece. We were particularly impressed by the fine furniture which decorated the sacristies, as well as the sturdy carved stone font. And as there were amongst our number those well-versed in the lives of the saints, we were given details of the stories of those represented in this church, with especial attention to the life of Francis of Assisi, patron saint of ecologists, our favourite saint.

It was almost 10 o'clock, and the rain continued to fall with an intensity such that we were practically all convinced that the walk would not be possible. Not even the priest, with whom we had fallen into conversation, believed that the weather might improve.

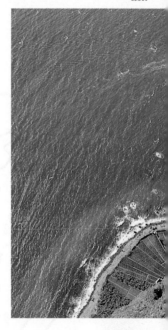

I don't know whether by the grace of Saint Francis or a mere thermodynamic caprice of the atmosphere, but the weather finally cleared, however, and we began to ascend the Calvário path towards the Levada do Norte.

We had just reached the second of the fourteen Stations of the Cross when the rain blew up again. As there was no church there to give us shelter, we made for the bar. But the rain did not last long, and the sun was soon smiling once more through the threatening clouds.

We started out along our path once more, stopping before the seventh cross, not due to more rain or to fatigue, but to strike up a conversation with the last shoemaker in the Estreito de Câmara de Lobos parish. On his workbench were his awls, dyes, nails, threads and his pieces of leather. To one side were the old wooden lasts for all sizes of feet. Nor were benches for customers awaiting repairs lacking here. On the wall, taking pride of place, a pair of horns and a horseshoe to ward off evil spirits.

MF

Cabo Girão

Cobbler Tolentino plies his trade in the traditional way, a space for working and chatting, the old centre of popular culture. And so that his art does not become extinguished in the parish, he teaches his two children the finer points of the trade once they have finished their schoolwork.

Meanwhile, the weather had improved greatly, and we easily reached the tiny Chapel of Calvário, last station of the *Via Sacra*. Festivities are held here for the Vera Cruz, and there is a procession to Senhor dos Passos at Lent.

Ascending a few dozen metres more, we finally reached the Levada do Norte, which winds through hills and valleys from the Serra de Água hydroelectric power station. The aim of our hike that day was to reach Cabo Girão.

Two and a half hours are sufficient to reach the end of that section of the aqueduct which crosses through vineyards and cherry orchards. This is a lovely place to walk, particularly when the cherry trees are in flower or loaded down with fruit, but is no less interesting in autumn, when the scenery is dominated by the copper colours of vine leaves. The immense staircase of terraces, descend-

MF

Fajã at the base of Cabo Girão

MF

**The coast line
to the east of Cabo Girão**

ing down into the bottom of the valleys, is another beautiful incentive for those who decide to walk in these lands around Estreito de Camara de Lobos.

The first houses which appear near the irrigation channel after Calvário belong to Quinta de Santo António. A little farther on, we come to Foro de Baixo. Beyond this tiny nucleus of houses, the rocks over the aqueduct make the path more difficult to follow, and it is advisable to make a detour along the path descending to the left.

Between Foro and Garachico, on the banks of a stream flanked by cherry trees, there is an enormous Canary laurel with dark, shiny green leaves. Nogueira is the last village the aqueduct passes through before crossing the regional road. Down below the road, the irrigation channel brings water to the lands around Ribeira de Alforra or Fonte Garcia.

To reach the Cabo Girão viewpoint, 580 metres above sea level, we continued our walk along the Levada do Norte. We only walk on tarmac when there is no other choice! After a few minutes, we stood before a tunnel which passes under Cruz da Caldeira. We did not enter it, but walked along the little canal, crossing a path and finally taking the track leading to a spot close to the viewpoint.

At last, seated on stone benches under the rounded canopy of an old stone pine, we drank in the vast landscape which extended before us as far as Ponta do Garajau. The terraces or *poios* on the edge of the abyss are a veritable hymn to the Madeiran farmer.

Since our destination was Câmara de Lobos, necessarily going past the Convent of Caldeira, we took to our way once more. There are various paths down from here, but we chose the track which begins at the entrance to Cabo Girão.

Enjoying a constant sequence of spectacular views over the landscape, we followed the old stone path - in good condition - as it twisted and turned towards Caldeira, thus known because during the early times of settlement on the island, those uncultivated lands belonged to João Caldeira, the Elder.

In the idyllic peace of that vale of carefully-tended green fields, the convent, home to a small community of nuns, stands out.

There they live, within the convent walls, in contemplation, removed from the outside world, taking as their model the life of Saint Clare during the Middle Ages.

Just below the convent, we found a path descending to the small town, passing the parish church of Carmo, a new building, unattractive from the

outside, but whose interior reveals great aesthetic value and whose atmosphere is propitious to meditation.

The afternoon was reaching its end, and our walk too. And few of us that morning had believed in the success of this undertaking, which had its start at Calvário.

Important notes: The ascent to Calvário is not steep, and there are even buses from Corticeiras to the start of the Levada do Norte.

There are practically no precipices along the levada, and only just after Foro do Baixo is there a rocky outcrop which makes it difficult to get through. Here, it is advisable to make a short detour along the path to the left.
Crossing the regional road, there is a tunnel which runs under Cruz da Caldeira. Those wishing to continue to the Quinta Grande side should take this tunnel. For Cabo Girão, continue straight along the smaller levada.
Two paths cross the canal: the first goes to the regional road beside the entrance to the Cabo Girão viewpoint; the second ends close to the viewpoint. The latter has been partially lost due to the opening up of a new path.
Take either of these paths to descend down into the town of Câmara de Lobos, though those wishing to visit the Convent of Caldeira should take the first, which is in good condition.
From the convent to the town, take either the road or the path leading past the Church of Carmo.

Beyond Calvário

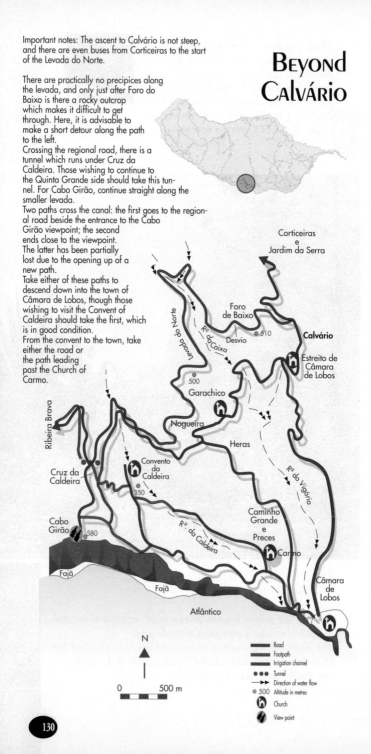

Corticeiras e Jardim da Serra

Foro de Baixo

Desvio • 510

Calvário

Levada do Norte

Rº da Caixa

Estreito de Câmara de Lobos

• 500

Garachico

Nogueira

Heras

Rº do Vigário

Ribeira Brava

Convento da Caldeira

Cruz da Caldeira

• 350

Cabo Girão • 580

Fajã

Fajã

Rº da Caldeira

Caminho Grande e Preces

Carmo

Câmara de Lobos

Atlântico

N

0   500 m

Road
Footpath
Irrigation channel
Tunnel
Direction of water flow
500   Altitude in metres
Church
View point

Lugar da Serra and Espigão

T his is where we find one of the last inhabited thatched dwellings. The straw roof sits on a rectangle of thick stone walls which never saw a drop of whitewash. The two tiny bedrooms are occupied by an elderly couple and their two daughters and one son. Beside it is the small kitchen, hidden from the path by a box-wood fence and a lovely plum tree.

Contrasting with the poverty of the house is the rich garden, the living expression of a great love for plants and flowers. Here we find orchids, azaleas, gypsophylla, cyclamen, a variety of ferns, fuchsia... Clinging to trellises, many good luck plants *(Tillandsia tenuifolia)* prosper. It could not have been planned better!

These poor but noble people live at the top of Fontaínhas, in the parish of Quinta Grande. Getting there today is easy. The path to this sunny ridge starts out just before Cabo Girão and rises parallel to Ribeira do Escrivão. Before coming to Fontaínhas, it passes through Aviceiro.

Time:
8 hours

The road to Espigão MF

In these places, there are many new houses, whenever possible built along the new road. Excepting certain honourable exceptions, the architecture is poor but, in truth, these houses are much better for those who live in them than were the old dwellings.

Between Aviceiro and Fontaínhas, the road is lined by a young pine forest, which gives way to croplands as we approach the inhabited area.

Beside the path, charlock and wild radish plants with their yellow flowers, periwinkle with their lovely blue flowers, fumitory, white allium and

Starting-point: Cabo Girão

Arrival point: Ribeira Brava town

Length:
15 kilometres

MF

tiny daisies form a spontaneous flower garden. In the waters of the Ribeira do Escrivão and its tributaries, we can see arum lilies with beautiful white flowers emerging from the green cape of their large leaves.

Just a little above Fontaínhas, the path forks: the path leading straight ahead takes us to Jardim da Serra, in Estreito de Camara de Lobos; that to the west goes to Terreiros, a village in the Serra do Campanário which was, until recently, very difficult to get to.

Whilst the path has been uphill all the way to this point, from this crossroads onwards we walk along the flat, with just the occasional incursion into tiny valleys. Along the way, at each turn we enjoy superb views over the surrounding countryside.

At one bend, we see Cabo Girão and the staircase of terraces leading down to the Convent of Caldeira. At another, we are surprised by the vast vineyards surrounding the township of Estreito de Camara de Lobos and, beyond, Funchal, stretching out under the sun. The peaks of Torre, Romeiras, Barcelos and Cruz appear to our eye as the most recent marks of the volcanic forces which created the island of Madeira.

But, as nothing is ever perfect, the silence of the mountains is broken by music from pirate cassettes blaring out from vans selling fish, hens, shoes and who knows what else. A good distance along the path, walking almost constantly through eucalyptus, we come to Terreiros. This is one of the most hiddenaway places in Campanário, with the houses grouped on a tiny mountain ridge. The car now reaches this village, as does electricity and television, but the rules of hygiene are conspicuous by their absence. Though plenty of water is available, visitors passing through cannot fail to note and be disgusted by the dirtiness of the place. Later on, we come to Lugar da Serra, which also belongs to Campanário. Here, as in many other parts, the entire family works the land, and even the children sometimes miss school to dig, to collect grass for the cow, to water the crops or to chop wood. If you did not already know, then let me tell you that wood continues to be the main energy source used in the kitchens around here. Gas is used only for the more simple culinary operations.

The striking colours of parsley and the golden petals of gorse and broom cover the fences here, encircling the tiny plots of land where cabbage, sweet potatoes, potatoes, beans, lupins and corn are grown. Meanwhile, we come across the road from São Jão and on to Fontes and the Trompica forest lodge. Below the crossroads is the Chapel of São Paulo, where the road to Espigão begins. This is a village in Ribeira Brava parish with some 60 houses, occupying a triangular peak between the main valley of the Brava River and one of its tributaries.

The houses stand more or less in the middle of the great terraced stairway of *poios*, which even today continue to be built with the greatest love and the hardest efforts. Two modest shops and a school are the only public buildings

RQ

here. The old path, formerly the only way out of Espigão, is well conserved, and can be taken down to Meia Légua, midway between Ribeira Brava and the Church of Serra de Água.

Some say there are 600 steps, others solemnly affirm that there are many more than that, yet others swear that there are not so many. I only know that there are many, but I never stopped to count them, for I am completely absorbed by the beauty of the valleys on either side of the path as I go down it, and by the wealth of vegetation which coves the mountainsides. The only thing I can say for certain is that it always takes me between an hour and an hour and a half to get to Meia Légua and another sixty minutes to get to Ribeira Brava.

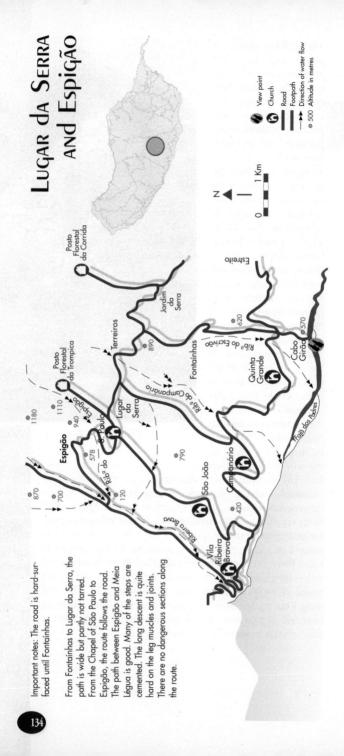

Lugar da Serra and Espigão

Important notes: The road is hard-surfaced until Fontainhas.

From Fontainhas to Lugar da Serra, the path is wide but partly not tarred. From the Chapel of São Paulo to Espigão, the route follows the road. The path between Espigão and Meia Légua is good. Many of the steps are cemented. The long descent is quite hard on the leg muscles and joints. There are no dangerous sections along the route.

Legend
- View point
- Church
- Road
- Footpath
- Direction of water flow
- ⊙ 500 Altitude in metres

N

0   1 Km

Posto Florestal da Corrida

Estreito

Jardim da Serra

Terreiros

⊙ 620

⊙ 890

Fontainhas

Ribª do Escrivão

⊙ 570

Cabo Girão

Quinta Grande

Ribª de Campanário

Posto Florestal da Trompica

⊙ 1110

⊙ 1180

⊙ 940

Espigão

São Paulo

Lugar da Serra

Espigão

⊙ 578

Ribª do Espigão

⊙ 870

⊙ 700

⊙ 120

⊙ 790

São João

Campanário

⊙ 420

Ribeira Brava

Vila Ribeira Brava

Fajã dos Padres

BARBUSANO

Time: between
4 and 5 hours
for those who
do not like
charging
through the
fields.

Barbusano, Canary laurel is a tree forming part of the Lauraceae family which can grow as high as twenty metres. When the lands of Tabua were first populated, there must have been many enormous exemples of this species on the mountain slopes. I say "must have been" because there now remain just a few trees near the mountain rocks to perpetuate the memory of their ancestors, who once had the honour of lending their name to a township. This honour did not, however, prevent the axe and the saw from slicing these trees up into thousands of stakes to support European or American varieties of grape vines.

At the turn of the XX century, Barbusano had a population of some four dozen inhabitants. This number probably increased up to the 1950s, but the exodus which then began was total.

In that tiny group of houses, which time has undertaken to destroy, there are now no inhabitants. Some went to Venezuela, others to France to earn the money they

The Ribeira da Tabua Valley

MF

could not obtain on the sunny slopes of Barbusano.

The few who did not emigrate moved to Candelária, "where at least there is a car for when someone is ill or wants to go shopping".

At Candelária, in Tabua parish, there is a small, unusual church devoted to Our Lady of the Candles. It is some 750 metres along the municipal path from the regional road to this chapel.

From the chapel to Levada Nova da Tabua, it is another 600 metres along a path following the crest of the ridge between the basins of Ribeira da Caixa to the west, and Ribeira da Tabua to the east. The houses form a neat line, interspersed with mixed agricultural land - in one terrace, sweet potatoes, in another, sugarcane, in yet another, bananas. There are terraces planted with cabbage, beans and potatoes, not to mention corn

Starting-point:
Chapel of Nossa
Senhora das
Candeias,
Candelária, in
the parish of
Tabua.

Arrival point:
Ribeira Brava

Length:
9 kilometres

MF

for home-made bread and oats for the cattle.

By the roadside is the bar, well-stocked with a wide range of local and imported drinks.

At first, the ascent is steep, but a little further past the shop the path becomes flatter and the views from here are extraordinary. Down below flow the gentle waters of the Tabua. Seeing it thus, it is hard to imagine that its waters once carved out the entire valley from the edge of Paul da Serra. On the gentler slopes and where the rock is not so hard are the terraces, many of them still painstakingly tended.

Further upstream, the valley broadens out somewhat to form a concave area on the eastern slopes where the first settlers made their home, creating the village of Ribeira.

Between Candelária and Ribeira is a slope populated by a few houses and small thatched cowshed. It is Barbusano! We need to take the Levada Nova to get there. On either side of this irrigation channel, which runs along at an altitude of 400 metres, are many terraces, some cultivated, others abandoned. In the latter and in the rocks not suited to agriculture are laurels, myrtles, globularia, houseleeks, fish stunning spurge, wax myrtle, brambles, sumac and prickly pear. The yellow flowers of the marigold, sorrel and dyer's woad embellish the ground. Acacia, eucalyptus and pine border certain stretches of the *levada* and, from time to time, a young Canary laurel or a pretty holly tree stands. Rarer, but also present, is the decorative Madeira shrubby bittersweet.

It is just over three kilometres along the aqueduct from Candelária to Ribeira da Tabua. Tabua is a small centre of population, with a few scattered houses in the valley, over four kilometres distant from the parish centre.

The only public buildings here are the shop and the primary school. In the tiny school playground, the children play wildly in the short time they have free between class and collecting grass to feed the cows. The shop terrace is the meeting-place for the old men of the village and the one or two younger fellows who have not yet emigrated.

In spite of everything, the village is much less isolated now than in the past. The motor-car has arrived, and electricity allows news of all the latest developments to reach Tabua via the radio and television.

Around two kilometres after crossing Ribeira da Tabua, the aqueduct winds through Corujeira. Here, the *corujas* - owls - from which the village takes its name pass the day hiding in the rocks

or in the branches of trees, waiting for nightfall, when they come out to hunt for food. These birds of prey are most useful in keeping the rat population down, thus saving the crops from these busy rodents.

Corujeira is also a high place in the mountains which commands fine views. From here, we can admire all the beauty of the Ribeira da Tabua Valley. The cultivated terraces on the two slopes, the poplars adorning the river banks, the gently-flowing watercourse. Near the river mouth is Praia with the Church of Nossa Senhora da Conceiçao, built in the late-17th century after the original building was destroyed by flooding.

It was also the fury of the river waters which destroyed, in 1742, the original Chapel of the Madre de Deus. Later, a new chapel was built a good way from the river, on a basalt platform in Corujeira, close to where the regional road now runs. Passing through the upper part of Corujeira, the irrigation channel distributes its precious liquid amongst the cultivated fields of Bica de Pau and Apresentaçao.

Bica de Pau belongs to Tabua, whilst Apresentaçao belongs to Ribeira Brava. The limit between the two parishes is marked by the old path which runs along the summit of Lombo da Apresentaçao. Here, we begin our descent, passing through carefully-cultivated fields until we reach the town of Ribeira Brava.

BARBUSANO

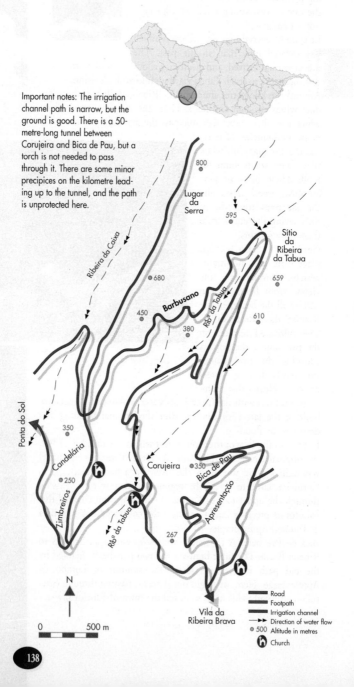

Important notes: The irrigation channel path is narrow, but the ground is good. There is a 50-metre-long tunnel between Corujeira and Bica de Pau, but a torch is not needed to pass through it. There are some minor precipices on the kilometre leading up to the tunnel, and the path is unprotected here.

800

Lugar da Serra

595

Sítio da Ribeira da Tabua

Ribeira da Caixa

680

659

Barbusano

450

Rib.º da Tabua

610

380

Ponta do Sol

350

Candelaria

Corujeira

350

Bica de Pau

250

Zimbreiros

Rib.º de Tabuo

Apresentação

267

N

0   500 m

Vila da Ribeira Brava

Road
Footpath
Irrigation channel
Direction of water flow
500 Altitude in metres
Church

Lombada da Ponta do Sol

etween the River Caixa, whose mouth is in Lugar de Baixo, and the Ponta do Sol river, whose waters flow into the sea in the bay near the town, is a ridge, or *lombada*, extending from the sea to the mountains which, in the early period of the settlement of Madeira, belonged to two sons of João Gonçalves Zarco. Through sale or lease, these extensive lands passed in 1498 into the possession of the Flemish noble man, João Esmeraldo, who, according to the chronicles of the time, was a friend of Christopher Columbus.

The old manor house of the Esmeraldos

In the early 16th century, some eighty Moorish, mulatto, black and Canary Island slaves worked on the Lombada da Ponta estate. Sugarcane was the dominant crop in those days and was grown extensively on those fertile, sun-drenched lands. With the money from this enormous sugar production, João Esmeraldo ordered the construction of the largest and most sumptuous noble house in the Madeiran countryside and, near the same place, a chapel devoted to the Holy Spirit.

Almost five centuries later, with the estate dismantled, the noble house and chapel still stand amidst the fields, which continue to produce good crops. Of the sugar factory which once stood here, only the stones still remain, some of them used to build the support walls for the terraces, where grapes, bananas and vegetables are produced. Just a few terraces still grow sugarcane, which once dominated these lands, providing the raw materials for the production of rum and molasses at the Calheta factory.

The great house, with its rose-coloured walls, was recently rehabilitated and is now an annex of the Ponta da Sol secondary school. The chapel, with its

Time:
3 to 4 hour

Starting-point:
Solar dos Esmeraldos,
Lombada da Ponta do Sol

Arrival point:
Solar dos Esmeraldos,
Lombada da Ponta do Sol

Length:
8 kilometres

rich baroque carvings, is still in good condition and is a fine example of Madeiran religious architecture. According to Father Fernando Augusto da Silva, "the original church was rebuilt, the present structure dates from the first half of the 18th century, and the chapel is the largest, most elegant and most finely-adorned in the entire diocese. Worthy of admiration and appreciation is the lining of glazed tiles which covers the wainscott of the chapel walls, representing in symbolic figures the gifts and fruits of the Holy Spirit."

The path to Lombada starts out at the regional road in a place with the curious name of Formiga ("Ant"). In the space between the old manor house and the chapel, adorned with lovely trees, is where

MF

**Chapel of
Lombada**

the road for cars ends, but not for those who enjoy walking. This is a hike which is really worth undertaking, besides the two interesting items of local building heritage which in themselves justify the journey to Lombada, nature also offers the visitor its finest wares for contemplation.

From the front of the chapel, which stands on the eastern slopes of the Ponta do Sol River valley, we can see a tiny sliver of water down below, winding snake-like between craggy hillsides embellished by enormous, artistically-cultivated terraces.

Just beside the church runs the Levada do Moinho and, 80 metres above this, the Levada Nova. Both of these aqueducts are fed from the waters of the Ponta do Sol River and have their source a little upstream. The Levada Nova carries more water than the Levada do Moinho, and has a wider, better-conserved shoulder.

In some places the brambles and in others the lack of protection constitute the main problems for those wishing to walk the length of the Levada do Moinho. Nevertheless, the walk to the origin of the aqueducts is more interesting if the outward journey is made along the newer of the two and the return journey along the older one.

An ascent of 80 metres over a distance of a little more than half a kilometre separate Esmeraldos from the Levada Nova. A road, beginning before the chapel and continuing along the ridge allows relatively easy access to the aqueduct which irrigates vast areas in

the Ponta do Sol and Ribeira Brava districts.
The Levada Nova runs at an altitude of
around 400 metres through cultivated lands
and, as it gets farther from the populated
zones, spontaneous and sub-spontaneous

plants dominate. Brambles and white eupatorium have inundated
some places, but there is also space for Canary laurel, *pau branco*,
myrtle, globularia and willow trees.

This last species -the willow- also known as *seixeiros,* or *seixos,* is
particularly common where there is abundant water. Its roots work
their way through cracks in the rocks and even penetrate the aqueduct walls in search of water. On reaching the interior of the irrigation channel, the root grows
to an enormous size, taking a
form reminiscent of the tail of
a large fox. In this way, the
tree collects more easily the
mineral salts dissolved in the
water. At the start of summer,
the aqueducts are cleared and
these roots removed.

Around one kilometre before
the source, or *cabo* (as the people of Lombada call it), of the
irrigation channel, there is a
tunnel some 200 metres long.
On either side of the rocky
outcrop through which the
tunnel was bored are depressions similar to those in Risco,
near Rabaçal. Traces of
ancient volcanic craters? I do
not believe so. I think these
are erosive forms created
through the force of torrential
water against rock of varying
hardness. In both cases, strata

Levada Nova

MF

of tuffs of less resistance are clearly visible, and these serve as the
bed for falls of cracked basalt rocks. Even today, we can see falls of
blocks of tuffs and pyroclastic materials, leaving the basalt rock
with no supporting base.

In any case, we can see many beautiful shapes in relief here, out-
standingly that on the side of the aqueduct spring with its large,
splendid waterfall.

Whilst the scenery we see around the path running alongside the
Levada Nova is splendid, none the less interesting is the spot where
it collects its waters. Willows, weeping willows, poplars and pride

Lombada
da Ponta do Sol

MF

of Madeira give life and beauty to the end of the Ponta do Sol river valley. Small lakes, ideal for a swim in summer, add further to the attractions of this natural beauty spot.

We can return to Esmeraldos manor house along the same canal or, as an alternate route, along the Levada do Moinho. To reach the source of the Levada do Moinho, we must go down a narrow path some 500 metres from the source of the Levada Nova.

Without tunnels, but with a great many brambles along the border, the walk along the Levada do Moinho is somewhat more dangerous. The vegetation which surrounds it differs little from that which we have observed along the first aqueduct, but we can see a small group of ironwood trees which have survived the teeth of grazing livestock.

At first sight, the ironwood may easily be confused with the Canary laurel, but closer observation soon makes doubt impossible. The ironwood is a small tree endemic to Madeira, the Canaries and the Cape Verde Islands, now rather rare. Its scientific name is *Sideroxylon marmulano*, it belongs to the Sapotacea family and has a milky sap.

If you reach the end of the route without having discovered the ironwood trees, then at least admire the old mill («moinho»), once used for grinding corn, which gives its name to this aqueduct.

Lombada
da Ponta do Sol

Important notes: The shoulder of the Levada Nova is in good condition, but is not protected, so great care is necessary when traversing the steeper parts. A torch is also required for crossing the tunnel, and waterproofs will save us from a wetting from the waterfall at the tunnel mouth.

The path running beside the Levada do Moinho is narrower and in worse condition. Moreover, the brambles hamper progress in certain sections, and there is no protection.

The two aqueducts are linked by a narrow 500 metres long path. A sharp lookout is required to find this path, as it is not signposted and is often hidden by the long grass.

▬▬▬	Road
▭▭▭	Footpath
▬▬▬	Irrigation channel
●●●	Tunnel
➤➤	Direction of water flow
◉ 500	Altitude in metres
🅗	Chapel

The Ridges and Slopes of Calheta

C alheta is a land of *lombos* - slopes, ridges - of all shapes and sizes. There is Lombo do Doutor, named after a certain Dr Pedro Berenguer de Lemilhana, a Valencian who came to these shores around 1480 and came into possession of these lands. Then there is Lombo Brasil which, according to the experts in the origins of place names, was baptised in

Time:
4 or 5 hours

Starting-point:
Calheta
Hydropower
Station

Arrival point:
Church of
Prazeres.

MF

View of Calheta from the Madalena do Mar viewpoint

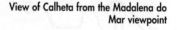

Length:
14 kilometres

honour of some relatives of Dr Berenguer who had helped João Fernandes Vieira in the heroic task of freeing Pernambuco (Brazil) from the naughty Dutch who, taking advantage of the weakness of the Portuguese lads during the Spanish occupation, laid their imperialistic hands on the lands Vera Cruz. And there is Lombo do Atouguia which, it seems, belonged entirely to Luís de Atouguia. And there is Lombo do

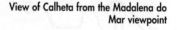

144

MF

Salão, which has nothing to do with people of blue blood, only with the reddish soil of the spot, which produces excellent sweet potatoes and fine potatoes, the delight of one and all, with no distinction of class. And there is Lombo da Estrela, where we find the health centre and the secondary school. And there is even Lombo das Laranjeiras.

In Estreito da Calheta, we find Lombo dos Castanheiros, Lombo dos Lameiros, Lombo dos Serrões, Lombo da Igreja, Lombo Furão...

But there are many more slopes and ridges, large and small, distributed throughout Calheta district. And nothing better to get to know them than one of our walks along a levada, this time the one which has its origin at the Calheta hydropower station.

«The power station building is 600 metres above sea level, at the upper limit of the irrigated lands. After the turbines, the water is channelled along two aqueducts, one of which, some 40 kilometres in length, irrigates the land right to the west end of the island, the other, 14 kilometres long, providing irrigation to the east as far as the Ponta do Sol River» («O Aproveitament da Água na Ilha da Madeira», CAAHM, 1969).

These two aqueducts were completed in 1953 and are responsible for irrigating some 4,000 hectares of land whose production was severely limited for five centuries by the low rainfall in the region, particularly in the hot months.

Our walk takes us along just 14 kilometres of the canal which begins at the power station, on the left-hand banks of the Calheta river, winding through vales and along ridges in the parishes of Calheta, Estreito da Calheta, Prazeres and Ponta do Pargo. The route I describe here ends at Prazeres. From there to the end of the aqueduct in Cabo (Ponta do Pargo parish), it is over 26 kilometres without great novelties as regards flora or the general scenery.

One kilometre, more or less, after the power station, the canal crosses a stone road which runs over the Lombo do Brasil towards Paul da Serra. From here, we can see Lombo do Doutor and, more to the east, Lombo do Atouguia. Despite the differences, there are also striking similarities in the distribution of the houses lining the paths at the highest points of the river valley.

Some 500 metres farther on, the irrigation channel crosses another path, this one leading uphill along Lombo do Salão to the edge of Paul da Serra, near Rabaçal.

On Lombo do Salão, we find the surge tank which, through a penstock, feeds the winter hydropower station at Calheta. This construction, as well as helping to reduce energy dependency, also allows better water management outside the irrigation period, that is, between the first rains of autumn until April or May of the following year, when irrigation begins once more. The water leaving the power station, which lies at an altitude of 600 metres above sea level, no longer flows into the river during the months when it is not required to irrigate the crops, but is reused for electricity production by the power facility installed at the mouth of the Calheta River.

The vegetation of the land around the aqueduct is dominated by acacia, eucalyptus, pines and broom. In more humid, shady areas we find willows struggling for space against the eucalyptus. Also to be found are fine groups of sweet chestnut trees, whilst the occasional oak also appears to add its graceful air to the scenery. The deep, narrow valleys are populated with interesting nuclei of indigenous flora, with the laurel an ever-present feature, as well

as Madeira mahogany with its large oblong lanceolate leaves, pale green when young, red when they fall to carpet the ground. There are also patches of bracken here which, nevertheless, cannot hide the scars left by forest fires in previous summers.

MF

Meanwhile, almost without realising, we pass from Calheta to Estreito da Calheta. In this parish, in the spot known as Atalhinho, we find a point where the great aqueduct divides into two: one section descends, directing its waters to Estreito, whilst the main canal continues towards Prazeres. The space around the tank which divides the waters is a charming mixture of vegetable and flower garden in which we find flourishing side-by-side roses, dahlias, artichokes, ferns, African lilies, beans and lettuce.

It is around five kilometres from Atalhinho to Prazeres along the levada following the sides of the ridges and valleys. One hour's walking after the tank which divides the waters of the levada into two, and we see a tiny plateau with fields of crops bordered by trees surrounding a group of houses built round the Church of Nossa Senhora das Neves. Farther off, the reddish chestnut tones of the football pitch contrasts with the dark green of a small wood. This is the parish of Prazeres and the end of our walk.

The Ridges and Slopes of Calheta

Map legend:
- Road
- Irrigation channel
- Direction of water flow
- ● 500 Altitude in metres
- Church

Scale: 0 — 500 m

N

Map labels: Ponta do Pargo, Prazeres, Lombo Furão, Divisória do Atalhinho, 736, Paul da Serra, Ribª da Achada, Central Hidroeléctrica, Florenças, Lombo do Atouguia, Ribª do Doutor, Lombo do Calheta, Lombinho, Lombo do Brasil, Ribª do lombo das Laranjeiras, Lombo do Salão, Lombo das Laranjeiras, Lombo de Estrela, Lombo dos Castanheiros, Ribª da Achada, Lombo dos Lameiros, Ribª do Farrobo, Ribª dos Serrões, Lombo dos Serrões, Lombo da Igreja, Estreito da Calheta, Centro de Saúde da Calheta, Loreto

Important notes: The path to the hydropower station begins on the regional road between Loreto and Estrela da Calheta. It is two kilometres from the road to the power station along a stone paved road suitable for cars of any kind.

The aqueduct shoulder is in good condition and there are no precipices, and this is a walk perfectly suitable for anyone who enjoys walking.

It is almost ten kilometres from the power station to where the aqueduct divides at Atalhinho, and from here to Prazeres we must add almost five kilometres more. From Prazeres to the end of the channel in Cabo (Ponta do Pargo parish) is over 26 kilometres. The path running parallel to the aqueduct is in good condition, the vegetation is much as we have already seen and the landscape is rather monotonous.

POMAR and EIRAS

Those who cross the Arco da Calheta and Canhas by car cannot even suspect the beauty and sadness hidden in the most secluded places here. On foot, unhurriedly covering the fourteen kilometres of the aqueduct which begins at the Calheta hydropower station, we discover a world of fascination in Florenças, Cova do Arco,

Time:
A: 4 hours
B: 6 hours

Starting-point:
Calheta
Hydropower
Station

Arrival points:
A - Canhas-Paul da Serra road, in Levada do Poiso, near the football ground.
B - Livramento, Ponta do Sol, near the old cinema.

Length:
A - 12 kilometres
B - 18 kilometres

MF

Cova do Arco and Pico da Bandeira

Pomar, Pinheiro, Eiras, Lombo da Piedade or Pomar de D. João.

More or less one kilometre from the power station, the aqueduct meets a stone path linking Lombo do Doutor with the tunnel which carries water from the slopes of Rabaçal to feed the surge tanks of the electricity generating unit.

The vegetation around the levada here is dominated by the blackwood acacia, which nevertheless leaves the occasional space for small groups of Madeira mahogany trees. The landscape continues in this way until the first cultivated fields appear in the heights of Florencas, the last hamlet on our route within Calheta parish. Behind us lie the lands of Lombo do Atouguia and Lombo das Faias. In the Arco parish, the levada continues through Achada de Cima, above Loreto.

The population is distributed in the lower areas in sites of easier access. The few houses which appear along the aqueduct are abandoned, though many of the terrraces here continue to be cultivated. Those which produce corn and barley in one year are then left fallow ready to be planted again in February or March of the following year with potatoes.

The path running alongside the irrigation channel offers walkers a fine panoramic view of the vast depression of the Arco da Calheta, bordered to the west by the Achada de Cima and to the east by the Achada de Santo Antão. This place is also known as Pico da Bandeira or Facho. Was the elevation over Madalena do Mar once used to give the alert, using *fachos* (torches) at night and some other form of signal, such as *bandeiras* flags, during the day?

This arc-shaped parish lies in the remains of a volcanic crater partially broken up by the erosive action of the sea. Cova do Arco is the name of the hamlet which occupies the most northern part of the old crater. Here, the levada is embedded in the great rock wall marking the northern limits of the concave depression, walnut trees form pretty patches and houses stand close to the aqueduct.

The poverty and lack of hygiene of the people of Cova do Arco contrasts with the grandeur of the natural landscape it occupies. Amidst the profusion of greens, the rude dwellings and unfinished buildings are clearly of poorer quality than the housing of places nearer the coast.

Winding along the Ribeira da Madalena valley, the levada crosses through Pomar, the lower section of Pinheiro, still in the parish of Arco da Calheta. Despite the isolation and poor resources of this village, the inhabitants generally keep their modest houses cleaner, their gardens better-tended, than do the inhabitants of Cova.

In the valley close to the tributary of the Madalena river, which lies to the east of Pomar, we can still see an area of Laurisilva. Here, Madeira mahogany, til and laurel trees flourish alongside fine examples melliferous spurge and shrubby sow thistle.

Even before reaching the village of Eiras in Canhas, the aqueduct winds through a number of deep, narrow valleys and and along mountain ridges. Indigenous species become less common and pine, eucalyptus and acacia more frequent.

Irrigation channel running past the hydroelectric power station

In Eiras, the houses, though their colours are generally unsuited to the landscape and their architecture bizarre, show greater prosperity than in Pinheiro or Cova do Arco.

After crossing the road linking Canhas and Paul da Serra, the aqueduct runs along the slopes of Meio and Piedade, in the Canhas parish and Lombo de São João, in Ponta do Sol. Finally, it reaches Pomoar de D. João, where it fills a great irrigation tank. From Eiras to Pomar de D. João, the landscape presents little in the way of novelty. Nevertheless, those with the strength and desire to carry on walking for another hour can follow the aqueduct through the slopes, ridges and valleys separating the two paths leading to Paul da Serra.

MF

To get to Pomar de D. João, we have to descend along the path through Lombo das Adegas, as the levada ends a little farther, on the slope above the Ponta do Sol River. This is a walk of just over one hour, downhill all the way, which should only be attempted by those reasonably fit.

POMAR AND EIRAS

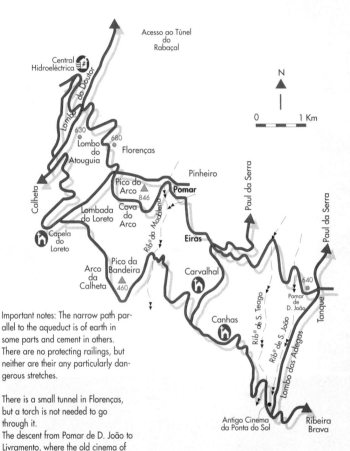

Acesso ao Túnel do Rabaçal

Central Hidroeléctrica

Lombo do Doutor

630
680
Lombo do Atouguia
Florenças

Pinheiro

Calheta

Pico do Arco
846
Pomar

Lombada do Loreto

Cova do Arco

Eiras

Capela do Loreto

Pico da Bandeira
460

Arco da Calheta

Carvalhal

Canhas

Paul da Serra

Paul da Serra

640

Pomar de D. João

Tanque

Ribº de S. Teago

Ribº de S. João

Lombo das Adegas

Ribª da Madalena

Antigo Cinema da Ponta do Sol

Ribeira Brava

N

0   1 Km

Important notes: The narrow path parallel to the aqueduct is of earth in some parts and cement in others. There are no protecting railings, but neither are their any particularly dangerous stretches.

There is a small tunnel in Florenças, but a torch is not needed to go through it.

The descent from Pomar de D. João to Livramento, where the old cinema of Ponta de Sol stands, is around three kilometres. After the long walk along the channel, this final stretch can be fatiguing for the leg muscles and joints of less experienced walkers.

Hikers who are not so fit should end their walk at Eiras, descending from here along the road between Canhas and Paul da Serra to Levada do Poiso, near the football ground, where it is possible to catch a bus.

Road
Footpath
Irrigation channel
Direction of water flow
500 Altitude in metres
Peak
Church

Ribeira do Tristão

Above the Church of Santa do Porto Moniz, at the entrance to Cabo Salão, the old bakery still stands. However, the buildings of the dairy are in ruins, and have almost disappeared. All that remains is a small post for the collection of milk from the few cows that have not yet succumbed to the competition of their European colleagues. Cows fed on grass and kept in barns will soon cease to be represented at farming fairs.

In Santa do Porto Moniz, as in the rest of the island, there is a shortage of labour available to cut grass. The young men emigrate or work on public construction schemes. The elderly and the women, though still working from morn till night, are gradually giving up the harder tasks.

In the past, countryfolk ate almost everything they grew and there were never enough terraces to provide the minimum for a frugal diet. Now, things are much different. Most food now arrives from the city, and the maize and barley grown here goes to feed the cows which live in the barns, now zinc-roofed. When the price of milk no longer makes it worthwhile, which will not be long in happening, more terraced plots will be abandoned if sufficient incentives are not provided

Time:
6 to 7 hours

Starting-point:
Church of Santa
do Porto Moniz

Arrival point:
Church of Santa
do Porto Moniz

Length:
12 kilometres

and a change in mentality brought about so that changes in land use can be made.

The path which begins at Cabo Salão later goes through Pombais, where there are a few houses of shocking construction and colours. Nevertheless, these blots do not take away from the outstanding beauty of the landscape. Pretty, even beautiful, are the little gardens which embellish many of the houses and decorate the path. Here we find large roses of indescribable perfume, densely-flowering primroses, tiny crassulas which the locals call «balões de São João» ("Saint John's globes"), while lilies with their six showy anthers encircling shy little seed capsules.

The road ends a few dozen metres after the last houses in Pombais. From the viewpoint here, we can see below the beach of Achadas da Cruz and part of Quebrada Nova. On the other side of the Tristão River, winding along above us, we can

The coastline between Achadas da Cruz and Ponta da Pargo

see perfectly the path between the beach and Achada da Arruda, which forms part of the plateau known as Achadas da Cruz.

The descent begins right here, close to the viewpoint. The path is narrow and almost disappears completely in some places where the grass grows high. This is a long, steep descent, and the path is slippery in places. It is important to take our time on the way down if we want to avoid mishaps, taking care where we place our feet.

The start of the narrow path runs through carefully-cultivated fields of crops where we find sweet potatoes, beans and vines growing in abundance. Canes and dry heather are used to form screens to protect the crops from the sea wind, which is strong and salty in these lands overlooking Ponta do Tristão.

The further we go from the road, the less frequent are cultivated fields, though the existence of terraces is a clear sign that in the times of abundant labour the entire area was cultivated. In some plots, the vine, which no longer receives the attention of man, competes against species which have returned to occupy the space which was theirs before the coming of agriculture. Fig trees, which someone once planted along the path, continue to produce tasty fruits to delight hikers.

As we draw nearer to the course of the Tristão River, close to its mouth now, we stop before a giant, awe-inspiring monument. Walls of dark, ashy basalt embrace great pot-holes carved by water out of the red tuff and the embedded waste of volcanic bombs. In summer, the water disappears, tired of its labour. In autumn, it returns with redoubled force to carry on with its interminable work on this great sculpture.

The river ends at the beach in the form of a gorge, not far from the point where João Gonçalves Zarco and Tristão Vaz Teixeira terminated their first exploraty expedition along the coast. In Ponta do Tristão, which now forms part of the parish of Porto Moniz, was one of the ends of the line separating the two, administrative halves, into which Madeira was divided during the early days after the colonisation of the island.

MF

To the southeast of the river mouth lies a *fajã* - rocky platform - with a length of almost 1,500 metres. Quebrada Nova and Quebrada do Negro are the names of two areas in that *fajã* which, like all the others, were formed by the fall and break-up - «quebrada» - of the earth and rocks of the cliffs.

Vineyards protected by stone walls and cane fences occupy almost all the fertile soil of the Quebradas. Wine presses and small stores are the only buildings in these almost flat lands near the sea. A cable-car transports wine and other products of the earth to Achada da Arruda.

Quebrada Nova on the
Achadas da Cruz coastline

If, for whatever reason, the cable-car is not working, the sacks full of grain and the baskets of tomatoes or onions are transported up along the path, which winds to the clearing where the motor which drives the cable-car lies, at an altitude of some 640 metres.

Those wishing to go from the coast to Achadas da Cruz need to ascend along that path, the Vereda do Calvário. The path begins by the mouth of the Tristão River, forking off a little further up from the route leading to Santa do Porto Moniz. It is almost two kilometres of constant ascent (640 metres altitude).

It is just over one kilometre from the clearing with the cable-car motor to the centre of the parish. Close to the interesting church is a lovely garden, and the old paths which converge here are bordered by age-old heather and bushes known locally as *verdegaio (Euonymus fortunei)*.

The stage between the churches of Achadas da Cruz and Santa do Porto Moniz is the last and easiest of this route. It is some five kilometres along the regional road which is in some places surrounded by rich and varied vegetation.

Important notes: The path between the viewpoint at Pombais, in Santa do Porto Moniz, and the beach of Achadas da Cruz is narrow, the ground slippery in some places, and great care needs to be taken. A walking stick is recommended.

Just above the mouth of the Tristão River, this path meets the path known as the Vereda do Calvário, which leads to Achada da Arruda, Achadas da Cruz.

Care is needed to ascertain where these paths meet just above the stair-way leading to the sea.

It is some two kilometres as the crow flies to the clearing with the cable-car motor, ascending 640 metres in altitude. The ascent is tiring, particularly on hot summer days, but the path is not dangerous. The ground is sandy in some places.

It is also possible to go up to the church of Achadas da Cruz along the path which begins at Quebrada do Negro, but the route is in poor condition and the steeper parts are dangerous, and it is therefore recommended that this route should not be taken.

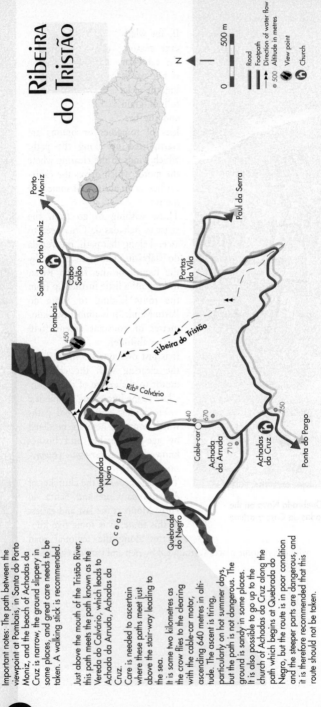

RiBeiRA do TRisTÃo

N

0   500 m

Road
Footpath
Direction of water flow
● 500 Altitude in metres
View point
Church

Porto Moniz

Santa do Porto Moniz

Cabo Salão

Pombais

450

Ribeira do Tristão

Portas da Vila

Paul da Serra

Ribº Calvário

Quebrada Nova

Ocean

Quebrada do Negro

Cable-car

Achada da Arruda

640
670
710
750

Achadas da Cruz

Ponta do Pargo

PESQUEIRO, PONTA do PARGO

Ponta do Pargo is a parish where good apples are produced. Every year, at harvest time, there is a popular celebration here, which attracts people from all over the island.

Time:
3 hours

Fajã Grande   MF

In those high plains at the western end of Madeira, at altitudes between 400 and 600 metres, the apple tree finds reasonable living conditions and people maintain the proud tradition of keeping their own little apple orchards. The distance, both physical and psychological, between Ponta do Pargo and Funchal, is the prime cause of the ignorance of most of the people of the capital with regard to the landscape of this parish at the westernmost point of the island. Many inhabitants of Funchal have

Starting-point:
Chapel of Nossa
Senhora da Boa
Viagem,
Lombadinha

Arrival point:
Church, Salão.

Time:
3 hours

never visited the area, and many more who have been here saw only the scenery in the immediate vicinity of the regional road where the apple festival takes place.

Have you been to the top of tiny Pico das Favas? Have you visited the lighthouse which stands at the most westerly point of Madeira?

If you have never been to the west of the island, take the next opportunity you get to go, and I am sure you will not feel you have wasted your time. Quite the contrary.

If, on the other hand, you belong to the minority which has already visited these lands, I am sure you will have been enchanted by the fine coastline with its high cliffs and narrow plateaux between Achadas da Cruz and Fajã da Ovelha.

And if you took a little time to observe the landscape, you will have seen, almost directly below the viewpoint at the lighthouse, the remains of an old path winding along the mountainside to

Fajã Grande and, some two kilometres to the east, the old Pesqueiro path, another route which coils snake-like towards its destination.

This steep road was in the past used by men loaded down with baskets or sacks weighing as much as 100 kilos. They would sometimes go up and down this path two or three times a day under the scorching sun depending on, a calm sea and the presence of goods to load or unload.

Until just 50 years ago, everything the people here needed and which the land did not produce was brought in this way up the mountainside from the coast.

Sacks of rice, pasta, salt or fertiliser, as well as heavy crates of drinks, all this was carried up by these men. The women and children carted the fish brought to the shore by the boats of Paul or Câmara de Lobos. But then the car arrived, lightening the load of of survival. Not for nothing do the older people of Lambadinha or Amparo invariably stress, when you talk to them that «Ah, sir, these are good times. In the old days, people really suffered just to bring a bit of food home».

Nowadays, the path to Pesqueiro is practically abandoned, like almost all the land below the road. The closer to the sea, the greater the abandonment.

Brambles, grasses, prickly pear, houseleek and fish-stunning spurge grow freely on the slopes where the best *Sercial* wine was once produced. Of the vines which once produced tiny grapes, nothing remains. Of the presses where the must was produced to make that strong, dry wine which became truly a joy to drink ten years after the harvest, all we can see are a few walls, camouflaged by spontaneous vegetation. The only clearly visible mark of the golden days of wine-making is a small house which still remains standing, though now roofless, in Fajã

The Ponta da Pargo coastline

Pequena. Nearby, an age-old, robust palm tree provides gratifying shade for the old priest, the owner of these lands, on hot days.

Just above this house there was a path linking Pesqueiro and Fajã Grande but it is no more. It went the same way as so many, other paths on the island, erased and unrecognisable due to landslides and the invading brambles. It is a pity. It is a pity that elements of our common heritage, which took such great efforts to build, should be buried in this way. If certain stretches are not recovered soon, moreover, the Pesqueiro path will also be lost. And if that happens, in just a few decades, not even the residents of Ponta de Pargo will know or understand anything about the Herculean struggles of their ancestors.

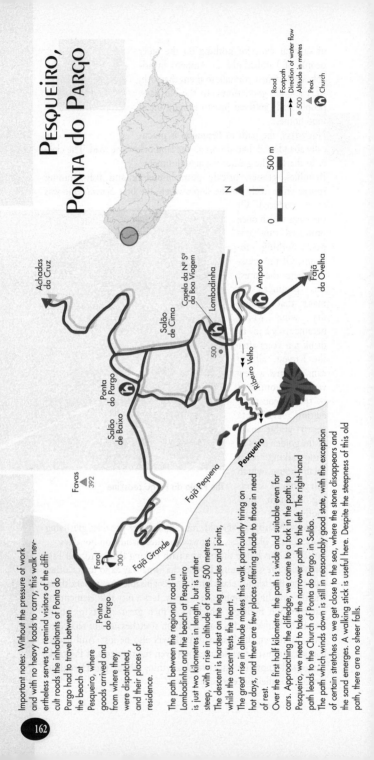

PESQUEIRO, PONTA DO PARGO

Important notes: Without the pressure of work and with no heavy loads to carry, this walk nevertheless serves to remind visitors of the difficult roads the inhabitants of Ponta do Pargo had to travel between the beach at Pesqueiro, where goods arrived and from where they were dispatched, and their places of residence.

The path between the regional road in Lombadinha and the beach at Pesqueiro is just two kilometres in length, but is rather steep, with a rise in altitude of some 500 metres.

The descent is hardest on the leg muscles and joints, whilst the ascent tests the heart.

The great rise in altitude makes this walk particularly tiring on hot days, and there are few places offering shade to those in need of rest.

Over the first half kilometre, the path is wide and suitable even for cars. Approaching the cliffedge, we come to a fork in the path: to Pesqueiro, we need to take the narrower path to the left. The right-hand path leads to the Church of Ponta do Pargo, in Salão.

The path which winds down is still in reasonably good state, with the exception of certain stretches as we get close to the sea, where the stone disappears and the sand emerges. A walking stick is useful here. Despite the steepness of this old path, there are no sheer falls.

Road
Footpath
▲➔ Direction of water flow
●500 Altitude in metres
▲ Peak
Ⓖ Church

0   500 m

Achadas da Cruz

Favas ▲ 392

Farol ▲ 300

Ponta do Pargo

Fajã Grande

Salão de Baixo

Ponta do Pargo

Salão de Cima

Capela da Nª Sª da Boa Viagem

Lombadinha

500

Ribeiro Velho

Amparo

Fajã da Ovelha

Fajã Pequena

Pesqueiro

From Salão to Cabo da Ponta do Pargo

I n Salão de Baixo, beside the parish church of Ponta do Pargo, are many cowsheds and small storehouses where the bracken is kept for the cows to sleep on, and straw to feed the animals.

This landscape is unique in the entire island. Why these cowsheds (many of them no longer used for livestock) beside the houses? Probably because the oxen were used to pull carts and they therefore needed to be kept near the houses.

We can still see the old carts in the storehouses.

MF **Sítio do Salão**

Most of them are no longer used, and many have been severely damaged by time. Some, just a few, still grind their way along the paths carrying maize or bracken. The wheel axles are made from the wood of the *pau branco*. The wheels are made from the wood of the til-tree. The body is made from the wood of the lily-of-the-valley tree, a lighter wood. The goods are tied to the floor and the cart is pulled by the patient animal to the destination determined by the owner.

From Salão, a road starts out for Ponta do Pargo, which gives its name to the parish, and where a lighthouse has stood since 1922. Between the church and this lighthouse is Pico das Favas, a small volcanic cone offering lovely views of the sea and the mountains.

But for now we are not going to the lighthouse. We shall walk without stopping as far as the end of the Ponta do Pargo, to Cabo, a hamlet on the boundary of the districts of Calheta and Porto Moniz. The road to the lighthouse joins the regional road which continues as far as Porto Moniz. Beside the

Time:
5 hours

Starting-point:
Church of Ponta
do Pargo

Arrival point:
Church of Ponta
do Pargo.

Length:
14 kilometres

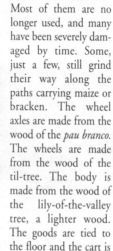

meeting-point of these two roads is where the old path begins, running from the centre of the parish to Pedregal, Serrado, Ribeira da Vaca, Lombada Velha and Cabo.

The road is paved with stones and is in good condition. Beside it are many fig trees, offering succulent fruit in summer.

In Pedregal is a cave excavated into the rock in which there is an interesting wine-cellar. Just one glass won't do us any harm!

This is a zone which has lost many of its inhabitants in recent years, and there are many abandoned houses here. Some of them have elegant cement adornments in windows and doors, vestiges of art nouveau.

Chapel of Boa Morte

In Lombada Velha we see, below the path, a fine old house surrounded by trees, the largest of them a eucalyptus with a tiny altar carved in its trunk.

From Lombada Velha to Cabo, the path is of earth, and runs through a pine forest much damaged by fire.

This route leads to the Chapel of Nossa Senhora da Boa Morte, from where the ascent to Cabo begins.

Between Lombada Velha and the Chapel of Nossa Senhora da Boa Morte, most of the farming lands have been abandoned. The chapel itself is large, with an architectural style which still conserves elements from the original building, which dates to the second half of the 17th century, 1666 to be precise. The interior houses nothing of interest to our cultural heritage. Outside, the negative note is given by the paving tiles in front of the main door.

From Cabo to the regional road, it is uphill all the way, but without particularly steep sections. Close to the road is an irrigation

MF

**Lighthouse at the westernmost
point of Madeira**

tank where the levada which brings water from the Calheta hydropower station ends.

The return journey to the Church of Ponta do Pargo begins here. Our route is along the irrigation channel, through eucalyptus and pine woods. From many points along the way, we can enjoy magnificent views of Ponta do Pargo, from Salão to Cabo.

From Salão to Ponta do Pargo

Important notes: This route is suitable for anyone who enjoys walking. The four-kilometre path from Salão to the Chapel of Nossa Senhora da Boa Morte is almost completely flat.

The ascent to the chapel and the tank where the aqueduct ends is 1.5 kilometres in length, with a rise of 150 metres. This is the most tiring section of the walk.

There is a seven-kilometre walk along the aqueduct, with no particularl difficulties.

From the channel to the church is around 1,500 metres of gentle descent.

Map labels:

Achadas da Cruz

Nª Sª da Boa Morte

420

Cabo

590

600

Lombada Velha

Ribeira da Vaca

Regoara

Rib.ª da Vaca

Serrado

Estrada

630

Rib.ª do Serrado

Pedregal

Salão de Cima

Corujeira

650

Rib.ª do Pedregal

Salão de Baixo

Ponta do Pargo

Fajã da Ovelha

392

Pico das Favas

Fajã Pequena

Farol

Fajã Grande

Ponta do Pargo

Pesqueiro

Fajã Nova

O c e a n o

Legend:

Road
Irrigation channel
Direction of water flow
● 500 Altitude in metres
▲ Peak
Church

0   500 m

N

The Foothills of Paul do Mar

"**I**n the distance, the undulations of the mountains stand out against the blue of the sky, and the winding paths, tracks and trails weave amongst them in different directions. Nearby, the vegetation is a carpet covering the ground all around. The roads are lined by box and

Time:
4 to 5 hours

MF

Paul do Mar

Starting-point:
Church of
Prazeres

Arrival point:
Church of Fajã
da Ovelha

laurel trees, and the air is pure. Nothing can match the breat-htaking beauty of the a view from a mountain overlooking the sea - the Assomadouro. Down below on the left, a village whose dwellings are almost hidden amongst the embracing vegetation: it is the Jardim do Mar. To the right is another parish - Paul do Mar. And how lovely are the houses clustered by the waters at, Paul».

Walking the path from the church built in honour of Our Lady of the Snows to Lombo da Rocha, in Prazeres parish, I remembered these words, written a century ago by Father Fernando Augusto de Pontes in his book «Excursões na Madeira». Not even the tiled houses with their rather strange architecture can mar the beauty of

Length:
8 kilometres

these hills, extending to the cliffs overlooking the sea platforms - *fajãs* - of Jardim and Paul do Mar.

There are still box trees, laurels too. The fields are not cultivated so much, and some of the old houses are abandoned. Nevertheless, it is a joy to see the cabbages and the wheat germinating close to terraces of potatoes or carrots.

Path from Prazeres

After the road was built, the path to Jardim do Mar fell into disuse. Now, only a few tourists come here to climb up and down for exercise and to seek the peace and quiet they need to soothe the torments of urban stress.

Abandoned too, with the arrival of the motorcar, was the path to Paul. But even today it is possible to ascend or descend, without excessive risk, the path between Assomadouro and the quay at Paul. "Assomadouro" - the view point at Lombo da Rocha at 540 meters above the sea - provides magnificent views and it is not surprising that a hotel has been built there. Those who have never gone beyond this point have no idea of how much nature reserves to show those who venture down to Paul.

The slope begins by the hotel. Below are the supporting walls of the terraces, but the plots which once produced cereals and vegetables are now invaded by innumerable wild plants.

Descending quickly, one can get to Paul in less than half an hour. But why run? Unhurriedly, stopping whenever we see an interesting plant or outstanding geological formation, the descent takes one or even two hours. The path goes through a veritable living museum, with the richest flora: willows, pride of Madeira, fish stunning spurge, myrtle, the houseleek, known here as *farrobo,* wallflowers, fennel, globularia, sumach, saxifrage, etc, etc.

The geomorphology is monumental: layers of compact ashy basalt alternate with encrusted ochre-coloured volcanic rock: dikes shoring up the softer rocks and determining the course of streams and torrents.

The waterfalls here are, moreover, a spectacle in themselves. The water leaps down in different stages before and after the Cova and Paul rivers meet. The last fall is over the beach, right beside the quay. The descent is worthwhile just to follow the lines drawn by this hydrographic network.

The slope ends close to the waterfront. This is Quebrada, and a glance up at the cracked rocks above make clear the reasons for which it was given this name.

MF

The descent from Prazeres to Paul

There are 900 inhabitants in Paul. Their houses are distributed in a linear fashion along a road almost 2 kilometres in length. Going west, after Quebrada, is the area where the ugly church of Santo Amaro is situated and where the road widens. What a shame to have destroyed the old church only to build this one, which looks more like a department store than a place of worship!

Between the church and lagoon is the area known as Espanha, a group of dwellings built during the Second World War to house the families of fishermen. Now, most of the people living here are not professional fishermen. That was when Paul was an important fishing centre. The chimneys of the fish processing factories stopped smoking long ago. Nowadays, the people of Paul fish little from the waters of Madeira. The seas which give money are

RQ

Ribeira do Paul

those of the Cape of Good Hope, San Diego and Panama.

The caps of the men, the short culottes worn by the young women, showing off their grace and splendour, and the vocabulary, a mixture of Portuguese, Spanish and English, are all marks of the foreign cultural influence on the way of life of the people of Paul.

After passing through Espanha, we come to the football ground, in Lagoa to be exact. Protected by a wall, this area is flooded when the rough sea sends in great waves from the west or south-west. Before the construction of this protective wall, the area was filled with water in winter, explaining the name of this area and, indeed, of the parish.

"Paul" means marshy terrain, swamps.

To the west of Lagoa, before reaching the slopes to Fajã da Ovelha, we find the hamlets of Serrado da Cruz and Ribeira das Galinha. Here, the houses are less closely grouped together, and there are lovely fields where banana trees and vines grow.

Without wishing to make facile distinctions, I would dare to divide Paul into two socio-geographical areas. The first, from Cais to Espanha, is more a fishing village, apparently less prosperous, its dwellings less salubrious. The second, between Lagoa and Ribeira das Galinhas, is more agricultural, with better housing, signal of a higher standard of living, or at least a better quality of life.

Now we have to climb up the Fajã da Ovelha. The old slope begins on the left-hand bank of the Galinhas river and snakes its way up the hillside through globularia, prickly pear and agave. Of the junipers which once put down their roots here, only the place name remains, Zimbreiros.

Finally, after many twists and turns, we come to Massapez, at an altitude of just over 400 metres, its heavy clay soil producing potatoes for the city. Phew, an hours climb!

The Foothills of Paul do Mar

Important notes: There is a wide, stony path from the Church of Prazeres to Assomadouro in Lombo da Rocha which offers no difficulties.

The path to Paul do Mar begins by the hotel. Rather steep, in certain sections the supporting walls threaten to collapse or have already done so. The ground is very grassy, and can be slippery when it rains, and a walking stick should be used. Though neglected, the path down is not dangerous at any point. The path between the mouth of the Ribeira das Galinhas and Massapez in Fajã da Ovelha is a little longer than that between Paul and Prazeres. Nevertheless, the ascent to Fajã da Ovelha is less tiring because the old path, broken up by a series of sharp bends, is less steep. This path is in a reasonably good state of repair.

From Raposeira do Lugarinho to Paul do Mar

Raposeira do Lugarinho is a small village in the parish of Fajã da Ovelha in the district of Calheta. Beside the Church of Santo Antonio, at an altitude of 670 metres, the regional road crosses the path known as the Caminho da Atalaia. Ascending, this path leads to Fonte do Bispo in Paul da Serrra. Descending, it takes us close to the top of the cliff, then becomes narrower as it winds down to the coast. This is one of the three paths by which it is still possible to go down to Paul do Mar. Less known than the two described in the preceding walk, it is little trodden by visitors to Madeira who explore these old paths as a way of discovering the island.

In the past, all these slopes were trodden daily, but not for fun, but for reasons of subsistence. At around 5 in the morning, the women of Paul went up there with tuna, skipjack tuna or chub and horse mackerel returning home with marrow, potatoes, sweet potatoes, beans and other products of the earth. These were the times of trade by barter.

Men descended the Caminho da Atalaia carrying barrels of wine. Even today we can find old men in Raposeira do Lugarinho who used to take down five cart-loads per day. Hard times indeed!

In Raposeira do Lugarinho, the fields are well tended. In May, the terraces are planted with sweet potato cuttings. Broom and manure from the cowsheds are arranged in alternate layers in furrows along the terrace. All this is covered with a layer of earth. With the soil prepared in this way, the cuttings brought from the warmer lands of Calheta or Câmara de Lobos can be planted in the earth. Now it is just a case of watering the plants well and waiting for the roots to become swollen and sweet. If the weather is favourable, in September or October the farmers will have sweet potatoes to eat and to sell.

But not only sweet potatoes are produced in these little plots. Barley, wheat, potatoes, carrots and beans all go to make up this mosaic of crops.

Time:
1 to 2 hours

Starting-point:
Church of Santo
António,
Raposeira do
Lugarinho

Arrival point:
Serrado da Cruz,
Paul do Mar

Length:
3 kilometres

172

Atalaia - Raposeira do Lugarinho

MF

There still remain a few houses of simple architectural style in this flatter area between the Church of Santo António and the mountainside. Blocks of red tuff and slabs of basalt give form to the walls which support hipped roofs. The same materials are used to build the small gable-roofed cowsheds where one or two cows are kept which, as well as providing milk, also produce manure for fertilising the croplands.

In contrast with the older houses, the larger, newer buildings do not always have forms, colours and materials suited to the landscape. In compensation, however, these houses usually have gardens full of roses, fuchsia, mallows, Busy Lizzies, etc.

The Caminho da Atalaia ends in a small clearing with a geodesic mark in the centre. From this view point, we obtain our first glimpse of Paul do Mar whilst to the east, at the top of the slopes of Prazeres near the Assomadouro (viewpoint), is a hotel.

MF

To descend to Paul we need to retrace our steps some 100 metres. The earthen path begins near a group of laurels. At first, the track is wide, passing through agricultural lands.

Around 100 metres below, we come across a wood of laurel and oak trees. From here on, the path is narrower, with abandoned terraces on either side. Where crops once grew bracken now prospers. On walls, sumach, houseleek, bitumen plant and woodbine grow impregnating the air with agreeable aromas during the flowering season.

Paul do Mar

Raposeira do Lugarinho

Further on, the path reaches a basalt rock outcrop which commands fine views of Paul. To the west we can see perfectly the twists and turns of the Zimbreiros path. Until we reach this natural viewpoint, the path runs through fields which in other times were sown with crops, and the ground is in good condition, without steep falls.

Lower down, though there are still no precipices, the path is not in good condition. In some sections, there is slippery sand underfoot, and care is needed to avoid falls.

Grasses and prickly pears are abundant here, as well as sumach, globularias and houseleeks. But there are also laurels, fish-stunning spurge and wild olive trees. Amongst this xerophilous vegetation, the path finally reaches the road in Serrado da Cruz, a little to the west of the football ground.

FROM RAPOSEIRA TO PAUL

Key:
- Road
- Footpath
- Direction of water flow
- ⊙ 500 Altitude in metres
- 🏛 Church

0 ——— 500 m

N

Labels on map:

Prazeres

Estrada Regional

Faja da Ovelha

Lombada dos Cedros

Maloeira

670

Rib.º do Paul

660

Raposeira do Serrado

610

Raposeira de Lugarinho

590

Rib.º do Cova

Rib.º das Galinhas

Ribeira das Galinhas

Quebrada

Lagoa

Serrado da Cruz

Cais

Paul do Mar

Important notes: This walk is downhill all the way. It begins by the Church of Santo António in Raposeira do Lugarinho, at an altitude of 660 metres above sea level, and ends in Paul do Mar almost at sea level.

It is a good idea to take a walking stick to avoid falls on the slippery ground, particularly in the final stretch of the path, where there is loose sand. There are no precipices or sheer falls along the route.

176

Jardim do Mar

T he sea took many thousands, perhaps millions of years, to build its garden.

Waves without number carved out the foot of the cliffs, forming caverns, leaving the overhanging rocks unsupported. Gravity and the percolating water did the rest.

The scarp is cut back, the ocean level falls and a handful of earth was left to await the arrival of settlers.

It was a long wait.

By the time the first people arrived, in the 15th century, the *fajã* (platform) thus formed was covered by wild flowers. For that reason, they baptised it Jardim, garden.

Time:
A - 4 hours
B - 3 hours

Starting-point:
Lombo dos Reis,
Estreito da
Calheta

Arrival point:
Church of
Prazeres

Length:
A - Lombo dos
Reis - Jardim do
Mar - Paul -
Prazeres:
8 kilometres
B - Lombo dos
Reis - Jardim do
Mar - Prazeres:
6 kilometres

According to tradition, amongst the plants growing spontaneously there, various rose bushes particularly stood out. Filled with wonder at the roses, but hurt by the thorns, many «gardeners» were forced to abandon these fertile but socially hostile lands in search of rands and dollars.

It was with money earned abroad that the housing estate gradually increased in quality. Now, Jardim do Mar is no longer a huddle of small, insalubrious houses surrounding the mansion of the lord of the estate. Despite the poorer architectural quality of some of these constructions, Jardim appears prosperous and clean to our eyes. The settlement grew up on the broader part of the *fajã*. The manor house, with a chapel in honour of Nossa Senhora da Piedade and the tiny church of Nossa Senhora do Rosário are the most important buildings of this small parish.

The church began to be built on 3 May 1906 and was blessed on 19 September 1907. Its architect and works director was Father César Martinho Fernandes, whose mortal remains are buried in the porch at the main entrance. The church was completed quickly due to enormous popular involvement in the project.

MF

Agriculture is the main, practically the exclusive, source of income of the population here, though Jardim lies beside the sea.

In the eastern part of the town, near the cemetery, is the old factory which ceased long ago to produce sugar and rum. Little by little, the memory of bygone times is allowed to decompose.

With the decline in the sugarcane industry, the banana came to dominate these sunny lands, with some terraces left for grapes and others for vegetable crops. And a new agricultural crisis is looming with the abandonment of the banana plantations due to the lack of markets for the Madeiran banana.

A small group of houses with ochre-coloured roofs in the midst of green banana trees, squeezed in between the heights above and

the vast Atlantic. That is how Jardim appears to those emerging from the tunnel which perforates the rocky massif on the right-hand side of the Ribeira Funda - deep river. A river which is deep when seen from the heights of Prazeres, but whose mouth is higher up than the ocean. A suspended valley? An ancient vale formed level with a sea which was once higher than now? Sign of the island's rising?

Only research and study can find answers to really clear up these and other questions about the genesis and geological evolution of Madeira.

Interesting and surprising to those who descend for the first time from Estreito da Calheta to Jardim do Mar is the difference between the vegetation which covers the

The path tot he beach of Jardim do Mar

embankments above the road on either side of the tunnel.

On the Estreito side of the tunnel are pride of Madeira, fish stunning spurge, globularia, brambles and many other species accustomed to long periods of drought.

On the slopes overlooking Jardim do Mar, however, water flows all the year round, and the willows form pretty patches of pale green, set off by the darker canopies of wax myrtle and laurel trees.

In a break with the local agricultural traditions, a new period is beginning to take shape in the economy of Jardim do Mar. The waves here are the delight of the most demanding windsurfers, and tourists are beginning to flock here from all over the world to discover a coast which, according to experts on the subject,

Jardim do Mar

has similar characteristics to the famed surfing paradises of Hawaii.

Walking around the little streets, we can see small hotels, bars and restaurants opened to accommodate and feed these acrobats of the waves. The agricultural village with its ageing population is being rejuvenated by the discovery of the sea. On their light boards, young people defy the fury of the Atlantic, masterfully avoiding the rocky perils of the coastline.

At low tide, it is possible to walk from Jardim to Paul do Mar. The walk along the rocky beach, skirting the cliffs, requires care with regard to the overhanging rocks and to the waves. The quay at Paul gets closer and closer, on a small bay which was, in bygone times, the home of fishermen. Now we must climb up the slopes to Lombo da Rocha at Prazeres.

If the tide is high, it is better to climb the path from Jardim to Prazeres.

JARDIM DO MAR

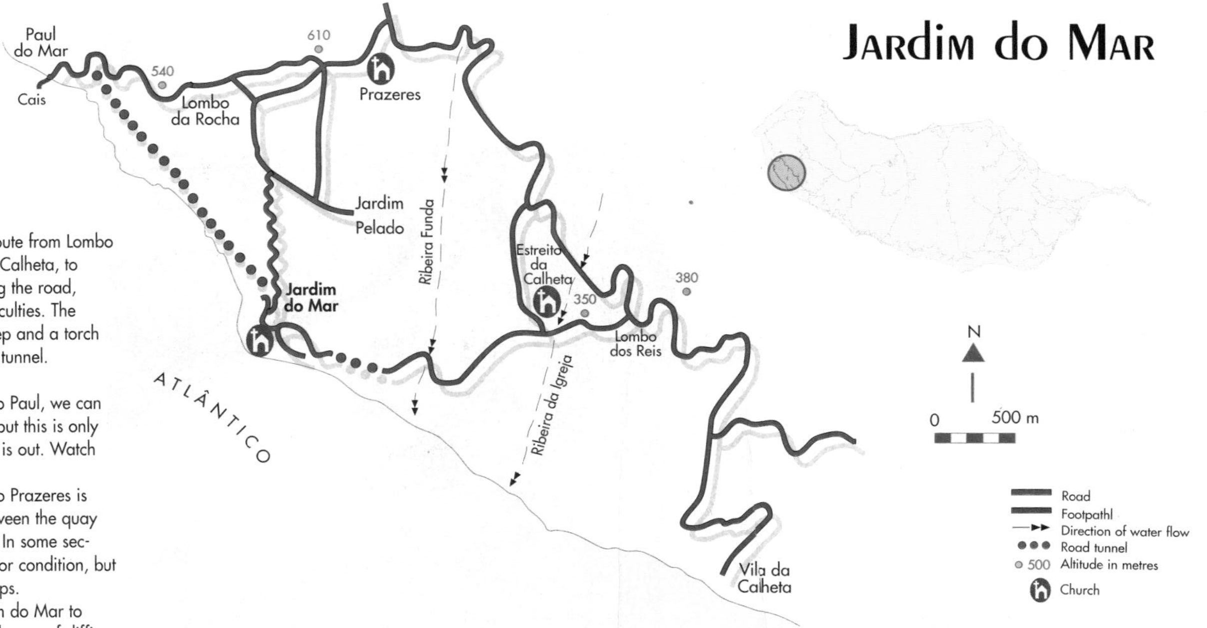

Legend:

Road
Footpath|
Direction of water flow
Road tunnel
○ 500 Altitude in metres
🏛 Church

N ◄—

0 ——— 500 m

Place names on map:

Paul do Mar
Cais
Lombo da Rocha
○ 540
○ 610
Prazeres
Jardim Pelado
Jardim do Mar
ATLÂNTICO
Ribeira Funda
Estreito da Calheta
○ 350
Lombo dos Reis
○ 380
Ribeira da Igreja
Vila da Calheta

Important notes: The route from Lombo dos Reis in Estreito da Calheta, to Jardim do Mar is along the road, which presents no difficulties. The descent is not very steep and a torch is not necessary in the tunnel.

From Jardim do Mar to Paul, we can take the coastal path, but this is only possible when the tide is out. Watch out for rock falls.

The ascent from Paul to Prazeres is steep, particularly between the quay and Lombo da Rocha. In some sections, the path is in poor condition, but there are no sheer drops.

The ascent from Jardim do Mar to Prazeres is similar in degree of difficulty to that from the slopes of Paul.

181

Levada dos Piornais

I t has its source on the left bank of the Socorridos river, more exactly in the spot known as Fajã do Poio. It is known that in 1562 its waters already irrigated the large plantation of sugar cane which covered the lowlands of Santo António, São Martinho and São Pedro. The channel is now one of the oldest in Madeira, continuing to water the croplands which yet resist the encroaching cement and asphalt of the

Time:
3 hours

Starting-point:
Estádio dos
Barreiros

Arrival point:
Lombada, São
Martinho

MF

Length:
10 kilometres

zone of tourist expansion to the west of Funchal. This is, of course, none other than the Levada dos Piornais. Until not so many years ago, this aqueduct fulfilled other functions as well as that of irrigation. There used to be many watermills along the length of the great

The Piornais irrigation channel and the Ribeira dos Socorridos bridge

MF

canal, and there were also many washing-places along it, in Quebradas, Areeiro, Piornais, Casa Branca, Ajuda, Barreiros and Ilhéus. The waters flowed along the channel throughout the year, from March to November for agricultural purposes above all, and during the rest of the year for washing clothes and turning mill-stones.

Though now in disuse, the mill near the village of Ajuda still has all the equipment it used for years to grind maize and wheat into flour for the people who inhabited the houses scattered in the surrounding area, lands which used to be given over to agriculture but which are now occupied by hotels, apartments, restaurants and pubs. Other cultures!

It might be a good thing if this mill began to work once more, for its ethnographic value and for the attraction it would be for the numerous tourists who pass by everyday.

With the distribution of water to the home, the washing-places gradually became abandoned. Those who see them now can scarcely form an idea of how important they were in the past. In those sinks installed below the aqueduct, the clothes were washed both of local people and those from other places, such as city-dwellers who sent their articles to be washed in water from the irrigation channel as there were more guarantees of hygiene than if washed in the rivers. Throughout the day and even at night, by candle-light, the water provided by the water management board for public washing-places was hotly disputed by women who earned their daily bread from washing clothes.

MF

The Ribeira dos Socorridos Valley

I suggest that we start this walk from behind the Estádio dos Barreiros, at the point where the irrigation canal meets the road leading to the village of Nazaré, which commands magnificent views over the Bay of Funchal.

Shortly after beginning the walk, the landscape below the channel is dominated by great apartment blocks and hotels. Skirting around Pico da Cruz, on whose summit is an ugly military building, we are struck by the sensation that cement and chlorophyll are irreconcilable elements in the disorderly zone of tourist expansion. Seen from up here, many of these developments seem even uglier than from the Estrada Monumental. Fortunately, they have not as yet built a pub or nightclub on the Island of Gorgulho!

But, listen. It is not only unpleasant views we can obtain from this levada. If such were the case, I should never have suggested this walk. Besides the interesting things I describe below, I should also like to mention the fine views of the coastline, particularly of Cabo Girão.

Leaving the Caminho do Amparo behind us, in uncultivated lands overlooking Praia Formosa now, interesting nuclei of spontaneous vegetation begin to appear. Side-by-side are indigenous plants and exotic prickly pear. Amongst the first, special mention should be given to the pride of Madeira, which is adorned with lovely blue flowers in winter and early-spring, globularia with their tiny lanceolate leaves, and houseleeks, which do all they can to expose themselves to the rays of the sun.

What we do not see around this area, or indeed anywhere along the entire aqueduct, is the soft broom, *(Genista tenera)* which is called *piorno* in Portuguese. Piornais, lands populated by soft broom, are rare these

days. Formerly, this plant was very common around Funchal and it is for this reason, that this aqueduct and a village in the parish of São Martinho are named after it. This species should not be confused with *Teline maderensis*, also called *piorno* which is abundant in the humid valleys on the north of the island, extending to high alitudes. According to Carlos Azevedo de Menezes, the wood of this bush with its yellow flowers similar to those of the broom *(Cytisus scoparius)*, «is heavy, hard and compact, at first a yellowy-white, later a reddish chestnut colour». It is known, too,

that it was often sought after for use in marquetry, which perhaps explains the enormous recession it has suffered.

After the Estrada da Liberdade, the aqueduct runs parallel to the Ribeira dos Socorridos valley, but rather higher than the river course. It is from here until Engenho Velho that walkers can enjoy the finest views. The course taken by the river is truly surprising and guaranteed to impress any observer.

When the sky is completely clear, the rays of the sun shine down on the steep hillsides, making clearly visible the outcrops of black rocks rising up amongst patches of vegetation. When the north-east winds bring clouds over the valley, the winding valley is filled with wafting fogs.

Whilst above us, it is the elements of nature which are most impressive to the walker's eye, towards the sea it is

MF

the human landscape which dominates. An industrial zone lies along the river banks, which are linked by an elegant bridge.

On reaching the first tunnel, it is not advisable to continue along the course of the levada, because there follow a series of very low tunnels, stretches of canal with no protection on either side and very slippery ground.

To reach the village of Engenho Velho, which lies on the left-hand bank of the Socorridos river a little upstream from the water collection station for Funchal, it is not necessary to con-

MF

**Danger awaits
from this point on**

tinue along the aqueduct. Just before the tunnel, there is a stair-case leading down. During the descent, we can see the arches over which the aqueduct passes, without doubt an interesting engineering work, achieved not without risk.

The land around Engenho Velho is dominated by banana trees, but it was not always so. The name of the tiny village («Old sugar-armill») refers to the existence, long ago, of a factory which crushed sugarcane produced on those floodplains. Of this factory, not a trace remains: what we do find here now is a hydropower station.

For centuries, the inhabitants of Engenho Velho could only escape from their isolation along the staircase leading up to the aqueduct. A few years ago, when drilling began to be used to collect water reserves from underlying geological layers, a path of beaten earth was opened up. Now, though this road is a modest affair, it is along it that persons and goods enter and leave Engenho Velho.

Our walk also continues along this path to Lombada, where we can catch the bus back to the centre of Funchal.

Levada dos Piornais

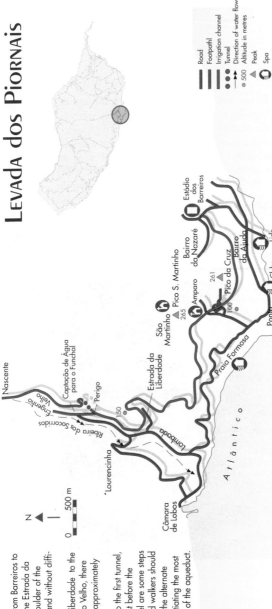

Important notes: From Barreiros to the crossing with the Estrada da Liberdade , the shoulder of the aqueduct is wide and without difficulties or danger.

From Estrada da Liberdade to the descent to Engenho Velho, there are precipices for approximately one kilometre.

When you come to the first tunnel, do not cross it. Just before the mouth of the tunnel are some steps leading down, and walkers should take this path, as the alternate route entails negotiating the most dangerous stretch of the aqueduct.

Road
Footpath
Irrigation channel
Tunnel
Direction of water flow
500 Altitude in metres
Peak
Spa
Church

Nascente
Captação de Água para o Funchal
Perigo
Engenho Velho
Ribeira dos Socorridos
150
Lourencinha
Lombada
Estrada da Liberdade
Câmara de Lobos
Praia Formosa
São Martinho
265
Amparo
Pico S. Martinho
261
100
Pico da Cruz
Bairro da Nazaré
Estádio dos Barreiros
Bairro da Ajuda
Ponta da Cruz
Clube Naval
Lido

Atlântico
Atlântico

0   500 m
N

FROM MONTE TO CAMACHA

Time:
A: 4 hours
B: 4 hours

The sun was just beginning to shine through the branches of the great plane trees which still resist the weather and men of bad will. At the fountain which gave its name to the square, the water still poured forth fresh, working the miracle of sating the thirst of christians and pagans alike. In the valley below the square and in the garden plots around the church, rhododendrons and magnolias stood out amongst the variegated vegetation with their beautiful flowers, even in the heart of winter. The Monte Municipal Park, built towards the end of the 19th cen-

Starting-point:
Largo da Fonte,
Monte

Arrival point:
Largo da
Achada,
Camacha

Park at Monte

Length:
A - Monte -
Choupana -
Carreiras de
Cima - Rochão -
Church of
Camacha:
12 kilometres
B - Monte -
Choupana -
Levada da Serra
- Vale Paraíso -
Church of
Camacha:
13 kilometres

tury and recovered on the occasion of its first centenary, has all the air of a Romantic garden.
Largo da Fonte, in the parish of Nossa Senhora do Monte, starting-point for more than one hike along

old paths and aqueducts. The road to Largo das Babosas, half a kilometre away, runs through old market gardens. Near the start, sheltering under the wall of the old Hotel Belmonte, are the white dressed carters, *carreiros*, with their straw hats, waiting to take tourists on a descent in toboggans *carros de cesto*. Farther on is the entrance to the Berardo Foundation Gardens. These gardens, situated in the area of the old Hotel Monte Palace, are inhabited by many of the species endemic to Madeira, as well as a fine collection of «cycas» from South Africa. In the shade of the leafy trees are fine tiled panels.

From Largo das Babosas, we can enjoy magnificent views over the João Gomes river. Opposite, on a ridge between the main stream and a tributary, is the tiny village of Curral dos Romeiros, half-hidden behind the great trees covering the left-hand slopes of the valley.

After a brief pause at the viewpoint to admire the valley, we continue the descent to the bottom. We cannot get lost here as there is only one path one used quite often by *carreiros* - who live in Curral dos Romeiros.

The water mill at Carreiras

MF

The rocks and walls around the pedestrian path are predominated by one particular plant, originally from Mexico and Central America and known popularly as *abundância* - abundance - and a better name could not be given to this species, so common as to be a pest. Nevertheless, there is still space for hawkweed with its yellow flowers, for the houseleek, and for the periwinkle with its pretty blue petals arranged into the shape of a helix.

Heather, globularia and brambles struggle with acacias and eucalyptus for a place in the sun on these steep banks. Where competition is not so strong, sweet chestnuts manage to prosper.

And all this is repeated on the other side of the charming bridge, which links the two sides of the river in a place where the impetuous waters have carved out enormous potholes into the riverbed.

At the end of the steep climb up, even before we reach the first houses of Curral dos Romeiros, we can see almost all Funchal. In fact, the excellent views are one of the virtues of this little village, with almost 300 inhabitants whose houses are scattered randomly over the sunny hillside.

After Curral dos Romeiros, our walk continues along the Levada dos Tornos, passing amongst the houses. The levada path is wide and presents no difficulties or dangers. From January to March, the woods which surround the canal are embellished by the yellow flowers of acacia and groundsel. When we reach the Caminho do Meio, we have two options: to climb to the Caminho dos Pretos or to continue along the irrigation channel to the Caminho do Terço.

The second is the more interesting of these options. The aqueduct passes behind the chapel and the house of an estate which formerly belonged to the deceased Viscount Cacongo. From the path along the irrigation channel, we can admire the gardens, with their beds of geometric forms limited by trim boxwood hedges.

Even before reaching the Caminho do Terço, a *caixa divisória*, or dividing tank, diverts the water from the channel into various branches or irrigation canals. Once more, we are faced by two choices: to continue along the aqueduct to Palheiro Ferreiro or to go up to the Caminho dos Pretos, passing close to the Choupana football ground.

I suggest the second option.

Some 300 metres above the Caminho dos Pretos appears, on the right, the Levada da Serra do Faial. Here, we can choose either to walk along the aqueduct or to continue ascending along the old stony path which skirts around Pico Infante and passes through Carreiras de Baixo, still in the parish of Santa María Maior, Funchal district. Beside the tiny village, at the point where two old paths meet, is a sign showing the borders of the parishes of Santa Maria, São Gonçalo and Camacha. This is an unusual and attractive area on the boundaries of three parishes and two districts.

In Carreiras de Baixo, the Caminho do Pico do Infante meets the Estrada das Carreiras. Continuing along this road, 500 metres up, is the shop Venda do Vinte e Um, which sells good home-made bread at the weekend. On the other side of the road, near the Levada do Blandy, is an old mill, still standing, which for many years ground the whea produced in the village of Carreiras de Cima. The mill-stone ceased turning almost twenty years ago, when the cultivation of wheat was abandoned. A detour along two pedestrian ways is strongly recommended here. These, skirting the village of Carreiras de Cima, give us an excellent opportunity of observing the plinths, where the corn was threshed, the terraces with their flowers, which the women sell at the weekend at the Lavradores market, craftsmen producing wicker-work articles.

The park at Monte

After a walk around the village, where traditional ways of life are conserved, our route takes us towards the centre of Camacha, passing through Rochão.

It is four kilometres, more or less, at first through untended woods and later through fields of cabbages and oiser. In Rochão, we find many new houses, but the pretty flowers in their gardens successfully distract us from their architectural shortcomings.

Different, and less demanding physically, is the walk along the Levada da Serra Faial, the same aqueduct which passes through Ribeiro Frio and which is dry in this last section. The air is exhilarating here, and we can enjoy fine views over the Quinta do Palheiro Ferreiro and the lands of Caniço.

MF

**Levada da Serra
irrigation channel**

Just before crossing the Estrada das Carreiras, the aqueduct passes close to the Quinta do Vale Paraíso, where the Aldeia do Padre
Américo is found. Here live young orphans and abandoned children. Children as poor as church mice in a *Quinta* with enormous floral wealth. A space with exceptional conditions for a
school of gardening and the training of sensitive nature-lovers.

From Vale Paraíso to the path which descends to the Church of
Camacha, the route is less interesting. Particular mention should
be made, though, of the Quinta das Almas, with its botanical
wealth and interesting landscape. It would be well worth recov-
ering as part of the heritage of Camacha and Madeira.

FROM MONTE TO CAMACHA

Important notes: Route A, though not so long, is a little harder than Route B because of the ascent from the Caminho dos Pretos to the path between Carreiras de Cima and Rochão.

However, both are perfectly suitable for anyone who likes walking, as there are no dangerous points along the aqueducts and paths. These are routes which can even be recommended for those afraid of heights.

Santo da Serra

Camacha
650

Quinta das Almas
730

Rochão
900

Achadinha

Casais D' Além

Vale Paraiso
800

Aldeia do Padre Américo

Levada de Serra

Palheiro Ferreiro

Poiso

Silva
1113

Carreiras de Cima

Carreiras de Baixo

Infante
944

Terreiro da Luta

Choupana

Funchal

Quinta do Pomar

Curral dos Romeiros

Rib.ª de João Gomes

Rib.ª das Cales

Jardim Botânico

Funchal

600

Babosas

Monte

Poiso

Funchal

Santo da Serra

Legend

- Road
- Footpath
- Irrigation channel
- Direction of water flow
- 500 Altitude in metres
- ▲ Peak
- ⛪ Church
- Football ground

N

0   500 m

193

SERRAdo dAS AMEiXiEiRAS

Robert Reid Kalley was born near Glasgow on 6 September 1809. Twenty-nine years later, with a degree in medicine, he disembarked at Funchal with the firm intention of establishing his residence here and of devoting himself to healing the sick. Dr Kalley's fame spread rapidly to the four corners of the island. He achieved extraordinary cures and provided his services free to the needy. The Funchal Council even gave him public homage.

Time:
5 hours

But the Catholic hierarchy began to suspect that the good doctor was not only dealing with the body of his patients. He was also spreading ideas about protestantism, subverting the ancestral beliefs of the people of Madeira. Because in these days no such thing as ecumenical celebrations existed, from being considered a saint, Dr Kalley became tarred as a dangerous protestant. Such was the persecution he suffered that it was only by disguising himself as a woman that he was able to leave Madeira alive, in August 1846

MF

**Eucalyptus
Quinta dos Charcos**

Starting-point:
Church of Santo
da Serra

Arrival point:
Church of Agua
de Pena

Dr Kalley, who received compensation some years later from the Portuguese government, lived for some time in the Quinta do Serrado das Ameixierias, in Santo da Serra. This *quinta* - estate - still retains much of the charm of the times it served as a pulpit for Presbyterian evangelism. Opposite the main house, the little fountain continues to flow and the *carocha* - a tiny tree forming part of the magnolia family - is still adorned with perfumed flowers. With little care from people but with much support from nature, in long avenues box trees prosper, some of them reaching as high as five metres and above. Enormous til-trees, pretty wax myrtles, graceful lily-of-the-valley trees are also to be seen here.

Length:
13 kilometres

These and other indigenous plants, side-by-side with fine rhododendrons from the Himalayas, camellias from Japan and European holly trees, populate another *quinta* lying along the path between the Church of Santo António da Serra and Serrado das Ameixierias. This is the Quinta dos Charcos, where stands what I consider to be the largest eucalyptus on Madeira. The trunk of the giant *Eucalyptus globulus* is so broad that it takes eight men to embrace it. Walk around it and see for yourself!

It is approximately two kilometres from the centre of Santo da Serra to Serrado das Ameixierias along the old stony path. The section between this *quinta* and the source of the Levada do Poiso is that which presents the most difficulties on this walk.

After crossing some 500 metres of cultivated land, below the Quinta, the narrow path meets the Levada dos Tornos, which is normally either dry or carries very little water.

At the junction of the path with the aqueduct, we have three possible routes before us:

- To continue along the path to visit the hamlets of Madre de Água and Roma before reaching the Caminho de D. Mécia, a path which takes us down a deep descent to the town of Santa Cruz.

Serrado das Ameixieiras

MF

- To continue along the aqueduct to the right, crossing the lands of João Frino. This route, walking against the direction of the water, leads to the descent via Gaula or to Camacha.

- Finally, we can turn left, reaching the end of the irrigation channel a few hundred metres ahead. This is the best option but be careful not to loose your way.

The first time I walked around here, I reached the end of the Levada dos Tornos without previously finding the narrow path to the Santa Cruz river, the source of the Levada Nova do Poiso. If this should happen to you too, don't worry, but turn back. The little extra walk will not be time wasted, for the dense woodlands around the canal are full of interest.

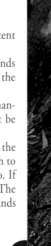

You will, no doubt, find another pipe-line crossing the aqueduct and will, perhaps, wonder about its origin and destination. Well, this great tube carries water from the Levada da Serra do Faial to Lagoa do Santo during months when there is no requirement for irrigation. Let me tell you too, if you did not know, that this depression, situated at the top of an elevation overlooking the golf course, is an old volcanic crater which became flattened. So, the lake is a tiny caldera. Madeira is full of surprises!

Well, all this has almost made me forget to indicate our descent. Don't be impatient, its is just a few dozen metres after turning back to the pipe-line.

MF

Serrado das Ameixieiras

Though the descent is steep and the ground rather slippery, this narrow path is not at all dangerous. Descending amongst til-trees, lily-of-the-valley trees, wax myrtle, bilberry, heather and other indigenous and exotic species, we reach a small bridge in the valley of the Santa Cruz river.

On the other side of this bridge there is an ascent to the Levada Nova do Poiso, which waters the lands of Santa Cruz and Água de Pena. In the lagoon where the aqueduct has its source, two water channels meet amongst dense vegetation. This beautiful natural scene forms part of the Santo da Serra parish.

The source of the Levada Nova, Quinta dos Charcos, Quinta do Serrado das Ameixierias, such beauty in just three kilometres!

After a short pause to take physical and spiritual sustenance, our walk continues along the Levada Nova. It is some 7 kilometres with the lands of Santa Cruz in view, until we arrive at the tiny, simple Chapel of Dos Cardais. Soon, on crossing through Poiso, still in the parish of Santo António da Serra, hikers have the rare felicity of seeing in the Santa Cruz valley a superb waterfall

surrounded by laurel and pine trees partially camouflaged by ivy and other climbing plants.

Little by little, the quality of the vegetative covering on the land around the irrigation channel diminishes. Where formerly were fine pines, now are burnt trunks or invading acacia and eucalyptus. The outstanding aspect of our route now are the landscapes we can see in the distance more than the beauty of the area around the aqueduct.

Beside the Chapel of Cardais is a path by which we can descend to the Church of Agua de Pena. Those preferring to go on to

Chapel of Cardais

MF

Matur should continue for a short way along the channel, which terminates there.

SERRADO DAS AMEIXIEIRAS

Important notes: The path between the Church of Santo da Serra and the Quinta do Serrado das Ameixieiras is signposted. Although its paving has been lost in some sections, the walk to the quinta presents no difficulties.

The descent from Levada dos Tornos to the Santa Cruz riverbed is steep, and a walking stick should be taken.

Between the source of the Levada Nova, in Poiso, and the Chapel of Cardais, the route follows the aqueduct, along a path in good condition and with no precipices. The same is true of the section between the chapel and the end of the irrigation channel in Matur.

From Cardais to the Church of Água de Pena, the path is wide enough even for cars.

Map labels

- Matur
- Água de Pena
- 110
- 480
- Cardais
- Aeroporto
- Campo de Golfe
- Levada Nova do Poiso
- Lagoa do Santo
- 752
- 450
- 550
- Poiso
- Source of Levada Nova do Poiso
- Ribª de Sª Cruz
- Fonte dos Ingleses
- Santo da Serra
- 684
- End of Levada dos Tornos
- 620
- Charco
- Inatel
- Serrado das Ameixieiras
- João Frino
- Camacha
- Poiso

Legend

- Road
- Footpath
- Irrigation channel
- Direction of water flow
- ● 500 Altitude in metres
- ☗ Farmhouse
- ⛪ Church/Chapel

N

0   500 m

Along the old path to Santana

Time:
5 or 6 hours

Ascending and descending slopes, climbing up ridges, crossing *fajãs* and plateaux, all this was what anyone wishing to go to the city from Santana had to do before the arrival of the motor-car in that town in the north of the island. They had to walk and walk, for there was no time to lose. A short stop in Poiso for a coffee and a drop of rum. How many times they must have set out for Monte or Ribeiro Frio in thick fog.

Only strong rain or a hailstorm could force them to take shelter in the house that Governor José Silvestre Ribeiro ordered to be built in 1850 and was finally completed in 1852. According to the order issued by Silvestre, one of the most outstanding governors in the island's history, the house was to be permanently ready "to receive travellers - allowing them to heat water if necessary - to always have a good supply of wood so that during the winter they will have the comfort of a good fire - to give all possible help to those in need".

Starting-point:
Ribeiro Frio
forestry post

Arrival point:
Town of Santana

RQ

The old bridge at Ribeira da Metade

Nowadays, few in Santana and Faial still remember those times when places on the island seemed a long way away, but the old path, though here and there the new road cuts through it, is still in a reasonable state of repair.

Without the worry of arriving on time, loaded down by no goods or obligations, the route between Poiso and Santana along the old path is extremely interesting. A little long, perhaps, mak-

Length:
13 kilometres

MF

ing it advisable to leave the hike from Poiso to Ribeiro Frio for another day. Getting up early is no problem if you go to bed early too, and is not at all bad for the health. That being the case, it is no trouble for us to catch the bus which leaves Funchal at seven fifteen, arriving at the Ribeiro Frio forest park just after eight. A good time to start our walk.

Before starting out along the old path, some 1.5 kilometres after the forestry post, there is a viewpoint from where we can enjoy views of Ribeiro Frio and the valley slopes, carpeted with an infinite range of green hues, descending from Chão das Feiteiras.

The first cultivated fields we find bordering the stony path belong to Carvalho which, like Ribeiro Frio, forms part of the parish of São Roque do Faial, in Santana district. The houses are arranged along the path which runs over a narrow ridge, the cultivated terraces descending down the slopes to the valley floors. In the same plot, potatoes and cabbage grow, giving way three or four months later to maize and beans. Here, as in other places we shall pass through, nothing is left to chance. There is a time for each sowing and each harvest. The position of each type of crop in the cultivated areas is well-defined.

But the people of Carvalho do not only live from this traditional polyculture. For over a decade now, cress, which requires much sunlight and water, has also been grown here.

This is a crop which, in spite of requiring great care, gives a relatively good yield economically. Two months after sowing, transplanting takes place, when the tiny plants which at first grow very closely together are transferred to wider spaces where they can grow freely. To speed up growth, the crop is watered as many as five or six times a day, and the soil is fertilised with hen manure and chemical fertiliser. Some three weeks after transplanting, the first crop is collected, with each sowing yielding three or four harvests. The land is then weeded and a new crop sown immediately. Every year, each plot is sown two or three times. After passing through Carvalho, the path continues to Achada do Pau Bastião. From here, even before we reach the regional road once more in this village in São Roque do Faial, we can enjoy fine views over the Ribeira da Metade valley.

A few dozen metres below the small Chapel of São João Baptista, on the left-hand side of the road, we find the old stony path once

Faial

more, some 3.5 metres wide and in a good state of repair. Descending through lands belonging to the Fajã do Cedro Gordo, we soon see

an old bridge with a round stone arch, over the Metade river.

From this bridge we can see, upstream, the more modern bridge, also with a round arch, over which cars pass. Willows cover the flood plains above and below these bridges.

The ascent to Cruzinhas begins at the old bridge. This is a small village overlooked by a pyramidal rocky outcrop.

Leaving the Ribeira da Metade valley and the parish of São Roque do Faial behind us now, we begin the descent to the bottom of the Ribeira Seca do Faial. Down below, the path runs through the tiny village of Limoeiro and, farther on, at the beginning of an ascent, Fajã da Murta.

Something which always attracts the attention of visitors to this area is the great number of cowsheds scattered amongst the farmlands around the little villages. Most of them now have zinc roofs, usually painted in a colour which imitates tiles in order to minimise impact on the landscape.

From Fajã da Murta to Lombo Galego, the path leads uphill all the way. Thirty minutes at a good pace.

Up here where the views are superb, the branches of dry trees are used to support the ears of corn selected for the next sowing, and the branches of til-trees and lily-of-the-valley trees continue to be the preferred food for cows.

The ascent does not end at Lombo Galego. It is another steep two-kilometre climb to Cova da Roda. Nevertheless, our efforts are rewarded by beautiful views over the profiles of the Seca and Metade valleys, the ridges separating them, and the great Penha da Águia, as well as the landscapes of Porto da Cruz from Terra Baptista to the heights of Larano.

It is well worth pausing for a few minutes at Cova da Roda, on a clear, mist-free day, to allow one's eyes to wander freely from the sea to the mountains, from Ponta de São Lourenço to Ponta do Clérigo.

There are no more ascents on our walk after Cova da Roda. It is just over two kilometres to the Santana football ground, the path, gradually descending, passing amongst neglected gardens, abandoned woods and new apple orchards.

MF

**More modern bridge at
Ribeira da Metade**

On the descent into the town, if you try not to notice certain tiled monstrosities and bizarre architectural styles, you can reach the end of this walk with the feeling that Santana is still a pretty place...

Along the old path to Santana

Santana

Campo de Futebol

Pico das Pedras e Pico Ruivo

615

Cortado de Santana

Cova da Roda — 699

Pico das Pedras

Lombo Galego

Ribeira Seca

450

Ponte do Faial

Fajã da Murta

300

Ribeira da Metade

Limoeiro

São Roque do Faial

Cruzinhas

△ 506

400

Fajã do Cedro Gordo

Achada do Cedro Gordo

620

Achada do Pau Bastião

Carvalho

800

Important notes: Walk without sheer drops. The old path is between 3 and 3.5 metres wide and is, generally speaking, in good condition.

The ascent between Limoeiro (300 metres in altitude) and Cova da Roda (699 metres) is approximately four kilometres, and can be hard work on a hot day for those not prepared for such walks. From Cova da Roda to the Santana football ground, there is a gentle descent and the road is even suitable for cars.

N

0   500 m

850

Casa Florestal

Ribeiro Frio

Poiso

Road
Footpath / old road
Direction of water flow
500   Altitude in metres
△   Peak
⊐⊏   Bridge

203

WANDERING IN SANTANA

Time:
4 to 5 hours

Cortado de Santana, half past nine on a Saturday morning, cloudy sky, mild north-easterly wind and ideal temperature for walking.

We wanted to see Santana, get to know the place better, talk with the people who work from morning till night on those lands, far from the gaze of tourists and locals in their cars. We walked down the earth path and, one hundred metres along it, found the entrance to the tiny tunnel leading to the aqueduct which waters the lands overlooking Ponta do Clérigo. We had hardly stuck our heads out of the tunnel than we saw the most beautiful views of the Bay of Faial, protected by the imposing rocky heights of Penha de Águia, which seems almost glued to the rocks of Larano. Completing the fine view of the escarpments

were, the silhouettes of the isles of Farol and Desembarcadouro in Ponta de São Lourenço. Tired by its titanic struggle with the rocks, the Atlantic frothed and milled.

Stopping here and there, the picture presented to us by nature seems to change completely at every new perspective. And when

MF
Typical house, Santana

the rays of the sun managed to burst through the cloud barrier, then our attention was taken by an illuminated patch of landscape.

We walked up to Pico da Boneca, a volcanic cone with a geodesic mark at the top. Who says our people have no imagination? Only with a strong dose of fantasy is it possible to transform into a *boneca* (doll) the cement prism placed at the mountain top to indicate its 509 metres altitude.

Starting-point:
Cortado de Santana

Arrival point:
Church of Santana

Length:
7 kilometres

Those who have not been to Pico da Boneca cannot say they know Santana. From here, one can see all that nature and people have built in this northern corner of Madeira. Right by the base of the cone, Cova do Centeio is separated from Achada de Santo António by a small river. Beyond the secondary school and the sports pavilion, the Achada de Simão Alves stands out due to its size. In the distance is the Achada do Gramacho, watched over by Pico Tanoeiro with an old mansion in ruins, symbol of the decadence of the formerly wealthy rural areas. Wrapped in the arms of the Ribeira de São Jorge, we see, further into the distance, the parish of Ilha and, up there on high, the crests of the mountains guarding Caldeirão Verde and Caldeirão do Inferno. We descended Pico da Boneca towards Cova do Centeio and after, crossing a small river, reached Achada de Santo António, which has a chapel built in the 16th century but reconstructed various times since. All around is cultivated land: some plots growing wheat just beginning to ripen, others potatoes, cabbage and maize. Next year, to ensure that the soil does not become barren, the crops will be rotated. American vines prosper in the sunniest fields. Bordering the terraces are til-trees and lily-of-the-valley trees, many of them stunted due to continuous pruning for cattle feed. And when anyone asks why they carry out such wicked destruction on these trees, the answer is invariably the same: "If you have a til-tree at hand, you have a supply of food for the cows when there is no grass".

Fajã da Rocha do Navio

Amongst the cultivated fields there are ever-fewer houses and cowsheds whose thatched roofs are in good condition. Straw has been replaced by zinc, a change which impoverishes the quality of the landscape and brings suffering to the animals during hot summer days.

As for the houses, times have changed and even those who think it is very romantic to live in a thatched cottage do not build their homes using the traditional techniques and materials of Santana. Nevertheless, the construction of such new housing with new technologies and materials need not necessarily lead to the degradation of the landscape: the damage is done by the poor

Irrigation channel between
Covas and Parlatório

Sítio das Covas

architectural quality of many new houses, and the colours in which they are painted.

But there still exist thatched houses in good condition and which are still inhabited. They are almost always protected from the prevailing winds by fences of bamboo, box or the Cape honeysuckle, a South African bush species which is covered by red flowers practically all the year round and which is popularly known here as *camarões*.

On this subject, let me mention, too, that there still exists in Santana the salutary custom of planting trees and plants to embellish houses and roads. Fine til-trees and graceful box trees still line the old paths, moreover. It is a pity that the tradition of planting these species was not continued along the new streets of Santana. What is the local council waiting for?

From Achada de Santo António, we went through Achada de Simão Alves along old paths practically all of which are in good condition. After admiring some of the old thatched houses of Covas, many of them well-cared-for, and the spectacular box trees, which grow to height of up to five metres here, we continue on our way beside the aqueduct to the village of Parlatório. The road to the viewpoint begins at Parlatório. From here we can see the Ilhéu da Viúva (Viúva Islet) or Rocha do Navio and a fine platform, painstakingly cultivated, at the foot of the high sea-cliffs.

According to the Elucidário Madeirense, the name of Rocha do Navio ("Ship Rock") derives from the fact that on 24 December 1860 a Dutch ship sailing from England to Haiti came aground here, though all seven crew members were saved.

The scarp, which separates the ridges of the platform, is dotted with handfulls of soil in the fissures and cracks of the basalt rock, inhabited by Canary laurels, wax myrtle, fish stunning spurge, pride of Madeira and a vast range of small spontaneous plants interesting enough to keep students of nature occupied for hours at a time. Lovers of the peace and quiet of the rural landscape, as well as its aesthetic beauty, will find the descent to

Thatched cowshed

Fajã da Rocha do Navio an unforgettable experience. For the ascent, the cable-car is recommended.

WANDERING IN SANTANA

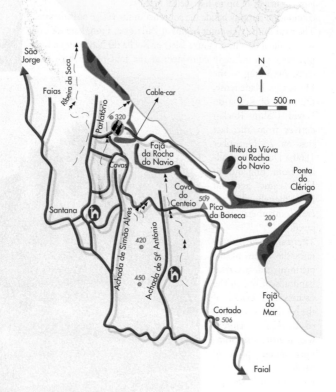

São Jorge

Faias

Ribeira da Soca

Parlatório

320

Cable-car

N

0   500 m

Fajã da Rocha do Navio

Ilhéu da Viúva ou Rocha do Navio

Ponta do Clérigo

Covas

Cova do Centeio

509 Pico da Boneca

200

Santana

Achada de Simão Alves

Achada de Sª António

420

450

Cortado
506

Fajã do Mar

Faial

Important notes: The paths are in good condition and present no danger.

A stick is useful for the descent to Fajã da Rocha do Navio.
A cable-car has operated between the viewpoint and the Fajã da Rocha do Navio, carrying goods and people, since 1997.

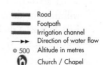

━━━ Road
━━━ Footpath
━━━ Irrigation channel
▸▸ Direction of water flow
◦ 500 Altitude in metres
🏠 Church / Chapel

From Santana to São Jorge

S erafina is still less than 60 years old, but her face shows the marks of a life with more winters than summers. She has eleven living chil-

Time:
4 to 5 hours

Starting-point:
Church of
Santana

Arrival point:
Church of São
Jorge

Achada do Gramacho

**The mouth of
the river
S. Jorge**

dren, and prides herself on having a Seraphim in heaven. A Seraphim? "Ah, sir, you don't know! The people of Santana call a baby who dies before it can drink its mother's milk a *serafim*". The everyday life of this women from Parlatório is the same as that of many women in Santana, São Jorge or any other parish in rural Madeira. Looking after the cows,

Length:
9 to
10 kilometres

tending the little plot of earth near the house and doing the housework. At night, the daily "soap" on the TV and mass on Sunday without fail.

Thanks to the hard work and wisdom of the older men and women, the fertile land all over the plateaux, slopes and hollows of Santana appears to the visitor as a gigantic work of gardening. The earth track between Parlatório and Barreiro runs amid fields planted with potatoes, maize, cabbages and beans. In other terraces, the wheat is ripening. In contrast with the traditional agricultural crops, here and there we find fields of strawberries.

These crops are repeated in Faias to the west of the Ribeira da Soca. The stony path which crosses this ridge is adorned along the way with fine rows of Cape honeysuckle and Japanese privet, with its bunches of white, aromatic flowers.

Farther on, the Casa do Lino dominates the Pico Tanoeiro. This is a great quadrangular construction protected from the prevailing winds by a wood of wax myrtle sweet pittosporum, laurel and oak trees. Abandoned, the gardens have been invaded by brambles, and houseleek and bushes grow freely on the roof.

From this high spot, we can see most of the lands of Santana and São Jorge. The most interesting part of the landscape is perhaps that around Achado do Gramacho, with a hotel and a few houses scattered amongst fields of vines and strawberries.

MF

When the wind is not too strong, it is possible to walk along the aqueduct near the edge which separates the ridge from a narrow coastal *fajã* known as Rocha da Vinha. Opposite the platform, a pretty island can be seen, with different layers of volcanic materials sculpted by the winds and the waves.

Achado do Gramacho and the mouth of the São Jorge river are linked by a broad, steep path constant with twists and turns.

Before the car reached São Jorge, those with business to attend to at the town hall or needing to go to Funchal had to take this route, as did men bearing goods unloaded from boats at the São Jorge quay.

Though little used in recent years, the path remains in a good state of repair, and the descent along it is an interesting part of our excursion. The dark green foliage of the wax myrtle trees and the globularia with their tiny lanceolate leaves of a lighter green dominate the vegetable formation covering the rocks through which the path runs. Here and there, the occasional Canary laurel or fish-stunning spurge. On the sunnier slopes is much *farrobo,* a species of houseleek with yellow flowers

impregnated with a sticky substance. Also yellow are the flowers of the *gnidia,* bushy plants from South Africa, rare in Madeira, but which adorn parts of this path. The mountainside is embellished by broom with its golden petals, and betony with their bunches of purple flowers emerging from amongst silvery-green leaves.

Pausing here to admire the flowers along the way, here to take in the fantastic views of the great valley, the descent to the old bridge at the mouth of the river can take 20 or 30 minutes.

On the left-hand bank, squeezed between the craggy rocks and the sea, is a small *fajã,* partially occupied by struggling banana trees and the odd vine, marking the ruins of the original centre of São Jorge. Here, at Calhau de São Jorge once stood the original parish church and a tiny chapel built in honour of Saint Sebastian. Of the latter, all that remain are a few sections of wall, whilst the church was completely destroyed by tor-

Path between Calhau de São Jorge and Achada do Gramacho

rential floods. After its destruction in the winter of 1660, the present church was built on the flat lands higher up in the mountains, where the population had already begun to establish their residences. The church took over one century to complete, and is now considered the finest example of baroque architecture in rural Madeira.

Calhau was for several centuries one of the most important trading centres in the north of Madeira. Shops and warehouses were the visible signs of an activity which only finally disappeared after the Second World War. There was also a sugar cane mill here, powered by water from the pretty aqueduct, still conserved. The walls which protected the village are still standing, but the stone gateway opening up towards the sea has been lost.

The path through this practically deserted village forks just outside the great quadrangular house whose walls are corroded by the elements. One section runs parallel to the coastline to the quay, whilst the other ascends to São Pedro. I suggest we go up this latter path, because the sea has partially destroyed that to the quay, and there are difficulties in certain sections.

The ascent is steep, but takes no more than 30 minutes even at a slow pace. The path is surrounded once more by wax myrtle, globularia and Canary laurel, which share the space with pride of Madeira and, in the more humid spots, give way to willows, sweet pittosporum and eucalyptus.

MF

Almost at the end of the climb up, in the spot known as Lapa da Areia, is a pretty fairy-tale chimney sculpted by draining water and the damp winds lashing this terrain of volcanic ash and rock. A small tuff with plants stands guard around the top of this natural sculpture.

The path ends in a clearing surrounded by eucalyptus and pine, where lie the parts of the motor which was used for years to winch up goods from Calhau.

From this spot to the lighthouse is just a moment. There are various possible routes, but the nearest is the one which starts out beside the path ascending from Calhau.

The lighthouse is in Farrobo, just above the most salient point of the northern coast of Madeira. From here, on a clear, mistless day, we can see the entire northern coast of the island from Ponta

de São Lourenço to Porto Moniz. The silhouette of Porto Santo, a few miles to the north-east, completes the superb natural picture before us. Having feasted our eyes on these beautiful landscapes, we do not even notice the walk to the Church of São Jorge.

Our walk would be incomplete, however, without a visit to this baroque church, whose high altar is adorned by a fine gilt carving.

S. Jorge lighthouse
at Farrobo

Church of S. Jorge

MF

FROM SANTANA TO SÃO JORGE

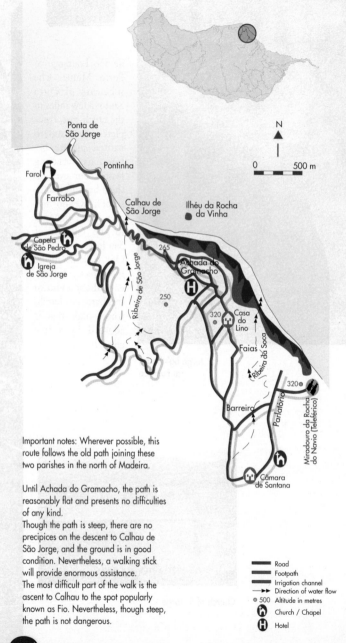

Important notes: Wherever possible, this route follows the old path joining these two parishes in the north of Madeira.

Until Achada do Gramacho, the path is reasonably flat and presents no difficulties of any kind.
Though the path is steep, there are no precipices on the descent to Calhau de São Jorge, and the ground is in good condition. Nevertheless, a walking stick will provide enormous assistance.
The most difficult part of the walk is the ascent to Calhau to the spot popularly known as Fio. Nevertheless, though steep, the path is not dangerous.

▬▬▬	Road
▭▭▭	Footpath
┄┄┄	Irrigation channel
▸▸	Direction of water flow
● 500	Altitude in metres
🛉	Church / Chapel
🅗	Hotel

Ribeiro Bonito

ibeiro Bonito ("Pretty River")? Yes, dear reader. And if it had been my job to name it, I would not have been content with this one. I would have called it Ribeiro Lindo ("Beautiful River"), Ribeiro Maravilhoso ("Marvellous River"), perhaps even Palacio da Naturaleza ("Palace of Nature"). The floors are covered with mosses and selaginellas, the envy of carpet-designers

Time:
6 hours

Starting-point:
Cascalho
Forestry Post,
São Jorge

Arrival point:
Church of Fajã
do Penedo,
Boaventura

RQ

Ribeiro Bonito is surrounded by Laurisilva

Length:
16 kilometres

and manufacturers everywhere, the walls are decorated by ferns from a vast variety of species and the ceilings are formed by the most beautiful canopies of laurel, til-trees and Madeira mahogany. Ribeiro Bonito is not a fairy-tale. Ribeiro Bonito exists.

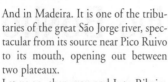

And in Madeira. It is one of the tributaries of the great São Jorge river, spectacular from its source near Pico Ruivo to its mouth, opening out between two plateaux.

Let us go, then, you and I, to Ribeiro Bonito.

To get there, we have to take the old forest path which runs past the São Jorge football ground in Achada da Felpa. Though this is an earth track and the ground in poor condition, it is possible to drive to the Cascalho forestry post. Near the guards' lodge is a path to the Levada do Rei, which has its source in the Ribeiro Bonito and carries water to irrigate the crops of Achada da Felpa, Achadinha, Pico and Achada Grande.

Those not wishing to start out at the forestry post can begin the walk along the levada at a point rather lower down, where this emerges close to the road beside the São Jorge water treatment station.

MF

Our knapsacks filled with the necessary provisions, we start off along the shoulder of the irrigation channel, walking against the flow of the water. Some two kilometres along the aqueduct, we find the path descending to the Cascalho forestry post beside the Ribeiro de Sebastião Vaz.

Continuing along this path parallel to the aqueduct, we reach the point where water is collected to supply the parish of São Jorge. Here, the path narrows rather due to the materials tipped down the hillside.

The first great objective of our excursion is to discover the origin of the aqueduct and to find delight in the vale of Ribeiro Bonito. At a certain moment, we come across a stream and the path continues to the right, leaving the irrigation channel. Here, the correct option is to continue along the aqueduct, which crosses a short tunnel before joining up once more with the path.

Here and there, we are treated to splendid views: the São Jorge river valley, with its network of streams; the village of Ilha, isolated amongst the valleys of the São Jorge and Marques rivers; more distant, the ridges and slopes of the parish of Santana; and, finally, the great Atlantic, patient sculptor of the coast.

Near now to the left-hand slopes of the Ribeiro Bonito, the aqueduct separates from the path once more, this time never to rejoin it. The path leads into the valley bottom, whilst the irrigation channel continues at the same altitude for a few hundred metres more, until we reach its source. How should we set about exploring this marvellous landscape? By continuing along the aqueduct? Or descending towards the stream which flows down below? First, let us go up to the source of the Levada do Rei.

The water channels, the golden flowers of the buttercups, the pinks of geraniums and orchids, the silver of grasses and the greens of ferns blend with the black of the basalt rock and the red volcanic tuffs. All together form varying compositions the length of the aqueduct.

The Levada do Rei irrigation channel near Ribeiro Bonito

The water not collected by the irrigation channel continues its journey down towards the valley floor, broadening out here and there into small lakes. One of these lakes lies close to the path, which at this point is completely carpeted in green.

To observe the many species of trees, bushes, small flowering and cryptogamic plants is a labour of love for students of nature who are blessed with the privilege of descending to the bottom of the Ribeiro Bonito and to continue their journey of discovery as far as Chão das Faias.

From Ribeiro Bonito, our route continues along the path opened up during the construction of the Levada dos Tornos. The vegetation covers the mountain sides here, and the path begins to narrow, though one can travel the length of it easily.

Nonetheless, great care should be taken in some places where there have been landslides. One such rockfall occurred at a point just before a stream from where, looking upstream, we can see a fine cascade.

After crossing the valley, we climb up the slope to rejoin the track used by jeeps during the works. Carrying on straight ahead, some 500 metres later we find the Levada dos Tornos.

This entire walk runs through the Laurisilva , with its large til-trees, Madeira mahogany and laurels dominating amongst the dense green blanket, populated, too, wax by myrtle, *pau branco* and willow, these last particularly where there is abundant water.

The source of Ribeiro Bonito is in these mountains, which are covered by dense forest

The relation between the trees and the rocks is very interesting, a surprising symbiosis between vegetable elements and the mineral world.

It is quite common to see the Madeiran laurel pigeons flitting swiftly from branch to branch in search of laurel berries.

The spot where the path reaches the Levada dos Tornos is known as Chão das Faias, perhaps because of the enormous wax myrtle trees (*faias das ilhas*) found here. But to some the place is known as Caldeirão Verde de Baixo, as it is situated in the Caldeirão Verde, though at a lower altitude.

From here, we can climb up to Caldeirão Verde along a steep path which begins beside the Levada dos Tornos, beginning at an altitude of some 600 metres and terminating 1,000 metres above sea level. At first, the path is easy, but it later becomes more inclined and the ground slippery due to the presence of fine stones. This is an ascent which is hard on the heart, a 45-minute walk at a good pace until we glimpse the irrigation channel between Caldeirão Verde and Caldeirão do Inferno. During the final stretch, the bends of the path provide awesome views of astounding beauty over two valleys which meet upriver of the Ribeira Grande de São Jorge. One stretches from Caldeirão Verde, the other, the more narrower of the two gorges, from Caldeirão do Inferno.

But the objective of this hike is not to visit the Caldeirões, but to reach the village of Fajã do Penedo in the parish of Boaventura. To reach our destination, we have to cross a 2,400-metre tunnel, something only possible with the use of a torch.

Careful, because two tunnels come out at Chão das Faial. The longer, joining up with the Ribeira Seca do Faial, is almost 4,200 metres in length and impossible to pass through. The tunnel beside the source of the irrigation channel is the one we must take.

It takes around 40 minutes to reach the other end of this tunnel. A few metres beyond the tunnel exit is the aqueduct workers' house, with a rest-room for hikers.

The Levada do Rei irrigation channel between Ribeiro de Sebastião Vaz and Ribeiro Bonito

The final stretch of our journey is the descent to the Church of Fajã do Penedo, four kilometres along a narrow road which runs beside agricultural lands practically throughout.

Ribeiro Bonito

Important notes: Various small sections of the path along the aqueduct are obstructed by fallen stones, earth and tree-trunks. At some points close to precipices, the path is without railings, and great precaution is necessary to avoid accidents.

Walkers should take great care during the descent from Ribeiro Bonito, as the ground is usually wet and slippery.
Between Ribeiro Bonito and Ribeira Grande de São Jorge, there are small sections where falls have left the path covered with rocks, and special attention is also required at such points. A torch is needed to pass safely through the tunnel. A walking stick is useful along this route, and waterproofs should also be taken.

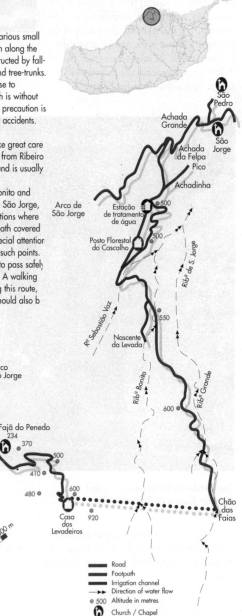

Legend:
Road
Footpath
Irrigation channel
Direction of water flow
● 500 Altitude in metres
Church / Chapel

THE LEVADA dos TORNOS in THE lands of BOAVENTURA

he people of Lombo do Urzal, Achada da Madeira and Falcas make their living almost exclusively from agriculture. They grow vines, cabbages, potatoes and grain. When a purchaser comes along, they sell part of their crops, keeping the rest for themselves. The men seek employment with public works, working in the fields at the weekend, whilst the women combine the housework with turning the earth. The more

Time:
5 hours

Ribeira de João Fernandes

RQ

Starting-point:
Lombo do Urzal,
parish of
Boaventura

Arrival point:
Fajã do Penedo,
Boaventura

adventurous young people emigrate seasonally to find agricultural work in the Channel Islands. They work for six months, bringing back money and new ways of life to their little villages, little by little altering the traditional lifestyle here.

Traditional architecture gives way to houses which are not always built with much thought for the landscape. In just a few years, Lombo do Urzal has been transformed into an agglomerate of poorly-built constructions. Flat roofs placed

Length:
18 kilometres

MF

Fajã do Penedo

anyhow on four walls, supported by pillars skewered onto the
rocks like exquisite mountain palafittes.

With the aim of minimising the negative impact on the landscape and improving housing standards, São Vicente council
launched a programme for the rehabilitation of houses in Lombo
do Urzal, and the effects of this can now be seen. The addition of
tiled roofs and the painting of the walls has significantly
improved the image of this isolated village.

It is four kilometres from the regional road to Lombo do Urzal,
passing through Falca de Baixo and Falca de Cima.

At first, this may appear a difficult walk due to its length, but the
truth is you hardly notice the distance.

Our walk begins at the little clearing at the end of the Lombo do
Urzal road. It is 1,500 metres from here to Levada dos Tornos,
uphill all the way, at first along a cement path between houses,
later along a narrow earth track amidst farmlands.

On reaching the levada, we see that the path continues to the
mountain top. If we carried on upwards, in two hours we would
be in Boca das Torrinhas, having hiked over 5 kilometres along a
path in poor condition, through dense forest. From Boca das
Torrinhas we can continue to Pico Ruivo, Encumeada or Curral
das Freiras.

Sit down by the side of the irrigation channel for a minute, recov-
ering from the fatigue of the ascent, and observe the landscape

down to the sea. Small groups of houses along the left bank of the Ribeira do Porco. Farther upriver, Falca de Baixo, then Falca de Cima and, almost at our feet, Lombo do

Ribeira do Porco Valley at Boaventura

MF

Urzal. Close to Lombo do Urzal but on a plateau somewhat higher up is Achada da Madeira, with a dozen modest houses.

For its part, Achada Grande, high up on the left bank of the river, has fertile land but just a few houses.

On the right is the little village of Serra de Agua, its houses huddled around the rocks overlooking the river.

Having recovered our strength during this reading of the landscape, we continue on our way, against the direction of the water. The source of the irrigation channel is some three kilometres away, the path is flat and there are no precipices. On either side of the aqueduct are great trees providing the shade needed by the many species of ferns and mosses which carpet the ground. This is fully-fledged Laurisilva. Here and there, the waters of the aqueduct are increased by the flow of tiny streams.

Finally, we come to the source of the irrigation channel. Still small at this point, it is fed by a beautiful waterfall. Rest and revive your spirit here.

Now returning back, we have the strange but agreeable sensation of taking a different route, with new perspectives of the forest and the agricultural landscape in the lower regions.

Arriving once more at the crossroads with the path to Lombo do Urzal, we continue to walk along the levada. It is around seven kilometres from here to the house of the levada workers, at times amidst dense forest, at others enjoying splendid views over the sea. Lovers of plants, botanists and students of biogeography will find ample material here to occupy their time. Just along the side of the irrigation channel it is possible to identity scores of plants endemic to Madeira, some of them rare.

The channel crosses various rivers, receiving the water the city so badly needs. Rising and falling along these watercourses, we find spots of extraordinary beauty and many species of indigenous plants.

The João Fernandes river flows amidst tall trees. A dense til-tree can no longer remain standing, and falls into the riverbed, dragging along with

it earth and stones caught in the embrace of its roots. In the riverbed sleep great blocks of rock, torn out and carried downstream by the water on days of great kinetic energy.

Some 50 metres after the João Fernandes river, a short section of the irrigation channel is covered by rock and earth, and particular care should be taken at this point. A little farther on, its course overlooks a deep vale, and attention is also required here.

Around 500 metres after crossing the João Fernandes, the aqueduct follows a basalt dike of rare beauty, with fine prismatic columns.

Along the stream near the house of the aqueduct workers, the water flows gently, tripping over basalt blocks and small depressions excavated into the reddish tuffs. This stream lovingly deliv-

ers up its water to the irrigation channel to quench the thirst of the people in the city . Along its banks flourish elder, deciduous trees which produce tasty fruit in summer.

Near the source of the
Levada dos Tornos

The house of the aqueduct workers stands by the first of a series of tunnels this water has to cross before reaching the heights above Funchal. This house has a small room where walkers can rest.

In the mountains overhead, an enormous basalt dike, known popularly as the *chaminé* (chimney), emerges from the thick green of the landscape. To the east, Pico do Arco de São Jorge is easily identified due to the television tower on its peak. To the north, in the background is the Atlantic, in the foreground are fields of crops enveloping the houses of Fajã do Penedo.

Swallows fly low over the waters of the irrigation channel.

The final section of our walk leads us to the Church of Fajã do Penedo, a four-kilometre path in good condition and with no dangers. Terraces growing maize, beans and potatoes predominate this agricultural landscape, in which apple and walnut trees are also common.

The irrigation channel is surrounded by vegetation

The Levada dos Tornos in the lands of Boaventura

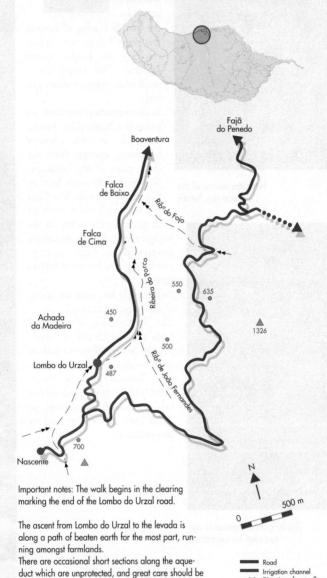

Fajã do Penedo

Boaventura

Falca de Baixo

Falca de Cima

Rib.º do Fojo

Achada da Madeira

Ribeira do Porco

450

550

635

1326

500

Rib.º de João Fernandes

Lombo do Urzal

487

700

Nascente

N

Important notes: The walk begins in the clearing marking the end of the Lombo do Urzal road.

The ascent from Lombo do Urzal to the levada is along a path of beaten earth for the most part, running amongst farmlands.

There are occasional short sections along the aqueduct which are unprotected, and great care should be taken to avoid accidents.

The descent to Fajã do Penedo is some four kilometres along a path in good condition, suitable for cars.

0   500 m

Road
Irrigation channel
Direction of water flow
500 Altitude in metres
Peak

From Ribeira Funda to Fajã do Penedo

T he village of Ribeira Funda forms part of the parish of São Jorge in the district of Santana. It occupies a flat area at altitudes of around 500 metres above sea level, cut through by a river, the Funda. The town is built on a plateau.

It is still possible to see a few quadrangular thatched houses in Ribeira Funda. Close observa-

Time:
3 hours

Starting-point:
Ribeira Funda, in the parish of São Jorge

Arrival point:
Fajã do Penedo, below the church

Round House ("Casa Redonda") - Ribeira Funda, S. Jorge

MF

Length:
6 kilometres

tion reveals that these dwellings are different from those of the neighbouring parish of Santana, rectangular in shape.

From the distance, the quadrangular roofs of the thatched houses appear to be rounded, and the traditional dwellings of Ribeira Funda are in fact known as roundhouses. Due to the expense of maintaining these houses and the lack of straw, few of these typical dwellings are in a good state of conservation. Those remaining are precious. Rows of Japense privet or Cape honeysuckle protect the little gardens from the rigours of the wind. In the gardens grow winter-flowering camellias, house-leeks, pelargoniums, roses and fuchsias.

The path which runs through Ribeira Funda continues towards Pico do Arco de São Jorge. This is a forest track of beaten earth, with not a very steep ascent to the peak, which lies at an altitude of 825 metres above sea level.

At a certain point, the path divides into two, a short section leading to Pico do Arco de São Jorge, easily identified due to the television broadcasting tower on its peak, the other continuing towards Miradouro das Voltas. A visit to the peak is rewarded by simply fantastic views. The central ridge, with Pico Jorge and Boca das Torrinhas, overlooks the Ribeira do Porco Valley, which separates Fajã do Penedo from the villages of Falcas. Over to the west is the Fajã do Seixal and in the north-west corner of Madeira is Porto Moniz with its islet.

The more or less 2.5 kilometres of ascent from Ribeira Funda to Pico do Arco de São Jorge take around three quarters of an hour to cover.

Returning to the fork in the path, our route continues towards Miradouro das Voltas on the border between the districts of Santana and São Vicente. We reach Cabeço das Voltas, with a fine viewpoint and picnic area, in less than 30 minutes.

Before we come to the viewpoint, we come to a conifer wood, its species dominated by *Chamaecyparis lawsoniana*, originally from

Typical house in S. Jorge

**Farmlands
Ribeira Funda, S. Jorge**

the state of Oregon in the United States, for which reason it is known as the Oregon cedar. In this area we can also see the *Sequoia sempervirens*, the redwood, a native of California. Groups of European beech trees (*Fagus sylvatica*), with light green trees in summer and golden foliage in autumn, contrast with the dark green of the dense conifer wood. Where this is particularly dense, there is no ground cover, whilst in areas with clearings, bilberry, laurels, Madeira cedar and lily-of-the-valley trees begin to prosper. From Miradouro das Voltas, when the Ribeira do Porco Valley is not hidden by mist, we can enjoy beautiful views over Achada da Madeira, Lombo do Urzal, Achada Grande, Falca de Cima, Falca de Baixo and Fajã do Penedo.

The forest trail which ascends from Ribeira Funda continues towards the Cascalho forestry post, after which it leads on to Achada da Felpa.

The path down to Fajã do Penedo and Fajã Grande starts out from beside the fireplace at the viewpoint. The path, some two kilometres in length, is downhill all the way, with many twists and turns, amongst dense indigenous forest. Here are many laurel and til-trees, as well as dogwood, not to mention an extraordinary variety of ferns.

The path is not dangerous, and is enveloped almost throughout by trees and bushes. From the few openings, the views are breathtaking.

The final section of the path, in the almost-flat lands of Fajã Grande, runs through fields where potatoes and cabbages grow.

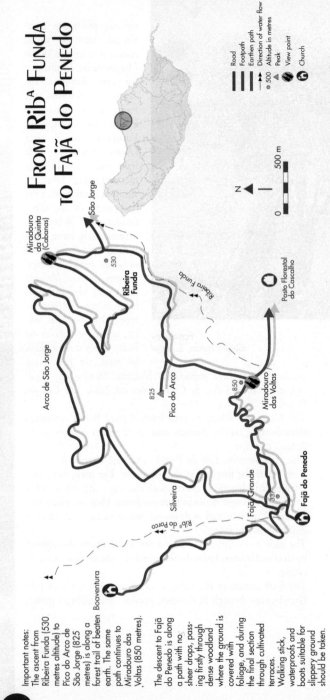

FROM RIBᴬ FUNDA TO FAJÃ DO PENEDO

Important notes:
The ascent from Ribeira Funda (530 metres altitude) to Pico do Arco de São Jorge (825 metres) is along a forest trail of beaten earth. The same path continues to Miradouro das Voltas (850 metres).

The descent to Fajã do Penedo is along a path with no sheer drops, passing firstly through dense woodland where the ground is covered with foliage, and during the final section through cultivated terraces.

Walking stick, waterproofs and boots suitable for slippery ground should be taken.

Miradouro da Quinta (Cabanas)

São Jorge

Ribeira Funda

Arco de São Jorge

Ribeira Funda

Pico do Arco

● 530

825

Posto Florestal do Cascalho

850

Miradouro das Voltas

Silveira

Fajã Grande

337

Ribª do Porco

Boaventura

Fajã do Penedo

N

0   500 m

Road
Footpath
Earthen path
Direction of water flow
● 500 Altitude in metres
▲ Peak
  View point
  Church

230

LARANO

arano is the name of a small hamlet in the parish of Porto da Cruz with some six dozen houses, mostly modest, scattered amongst the fields whose principal crop is the vine, but where potatoes, cabbages, carrots, maize and beans are also grown.

Near the rock overlooking Fajã do Mar, are fig trees of varying quality, and a few surviving junipers (*Juniperus phoenicea*), small trees once common on the coast of Madeira and Porto Santo but now practically extinct.

Larano is the village in Porto da Cruz closest to the city of Machico, capital of the district since October 1852.

Time:
5 hours

Starting-point:
Levada do
Caniçal, beside
the tunnel
entrance

Arrival point:
Church of Porto
da Cruz

MF

View of Porto da Cruz from Larano

Length:
12 kilometres

This parish in the north-east of Madeira has formed part of the *Capitania* of Machico since its foundation, except for a short period, from 1835 to 1852 to be precise, when it was integrated into the district of Santana.

Though close in terms of kilometres, Larano was for centuries over three hours from what was then the village of Machico. A path, cutting through the reddish volcanic waste and dark basalt dikes near a peak rising over 300 metres above sea level, was the only access. It was this path that the people of Porto da Cruz had to take when reasons of bureaucracy made it necessary for them to visit the offices of local government or the income tax department. Not a few of these, victims of one over the nine or of a strong gust of wind, perished on the rocky slopes along the way.

This route being as frequently-trodden as it was dangerous, a succession of projects were put forward from the 18th century onwards for a road between Casas Próximas in Porto da Cruz and the town of Machico, passing through the Maiata River Valley and Larano. But these projects never became reality, and only recently did the nearly 300 inhabitants of Larano finally see the realisation of their historic aspiration to have a road giving them access to the civic centre of the parish.

It is now much easier to visit the doctor or to attend mass. Vans have replaced the men transporting wine in great skins. The vans of sellers of fish, shoes, clothes, electrical appliances and goodness knows what else are no longer exhausted by the effort of attending to customers in Maiata de Baixo and Larano.

From Larano to Ribeira Seca, in Machico, the path has been the same for centuries. And it is just as well, since, once the problem of the isolation of the people of Larano was resolved the opening of a road to Machico cannot be justified. Such a work, as well as extremely expensive, would cause the destruction of one of the most beautiful stretches of the Madeiran coastline. What is recommended is the preservation of the path, widening it a little and fencing the most dangerous sections.

This is one of those walks that it is possible to undertake at any time of the year, being inadvisable only on days of heavy rain or strong winds.

For those setting out from Machico, the best starting-point is beside the tunnel to Caniçal. The first three kilometres are along the irrigation channel to Pastel. The name of this village in the parish of Ribeira Seca refers to the plant of the same name (dyer's woad) which once grew abundantly here. This herbaceous plant, whose scientific name is *Isatis tinctoria*, is embellished with tiny yellow flowers in summer, and belongs to the mustard family, that is to say, that it is a relative of the cabbage and the wild rape.

Pass between Boca do Risco and Larano

Spontaneous patches of dyer's woad can still be admired around here during the flowering season.

The leaves of the woad plant used to be boiled to extract blue dye, much used in the dye-shops of Madeira. During the time of Zarco, it was even exported to the capital of the kingdom. Nevertheless, in Madeira the cultivation of woad never achieved the economic importance it attained in the Azores.

As we were saying, it is in Pastel that the irrigation channel crosses the path which ascends to Boca do Risco. A certain amount of care is needed to find it, as the path is not signposted and it is not the only one which branches off from the levada. The correct path is the one which passes near two small houses with tiled roofs, separated by a kitchen with a terraced roof. These buildings are below the aqueduct, and there is a washing-place beside the channel as well as the remains of a thatched cowshed above it.

Having found the right path, we have to ascend for one and a half kilometres. At first amongst acacias, wax myrtle and brambles, which produce tasty fruit in August and September. Higher up is a small pine forest and, finally, wax myrtle and heather dominate the vegetation covering the area around the source of the Ribeira Seca.

Boca do Risco ("Risk Mouth"), what a strange name! We cease to be puzzled when, passing through this narrow opening between two sparsely-vegetated hills, we see that the path carved along the mountainside must have been built at great risk, that that we too run a certain risk by walking along it.

But, let us not overdramatise things, because, with care, suitable footwear and a stick it is less dangerous to walk to Larano than it is to cross a busy street in Funchal or in any other city. The risk is not so great, believe me!

Reaching Boca do Risco, below us we can see the clear, blue, restless sea to the north, lapping at the base of the cliffs. We cannot see Porto da Cruz, though, as it is hidden behind Ponta do Espigão Amarelo.

It is over five kilometres from Boca do Risco to the first houses of Larano, our path leading over bare rocks, then through small

MF

Beach of Maiata

woods with wax myrtle, heather, acacia, and indigenous holly trees covered with tiny red fruit at each year's end.

Little by little, we come across abandoned farmlands, vines growing up the trees.

In Larano, things are different, and the fields around the houses are carefully cultivated.

From here, we follow the road which crosses the Ribeira da Maiata, passing through Maiata de Baixo, ending our journey beside the Church of Porto da Cruz.

LARANO

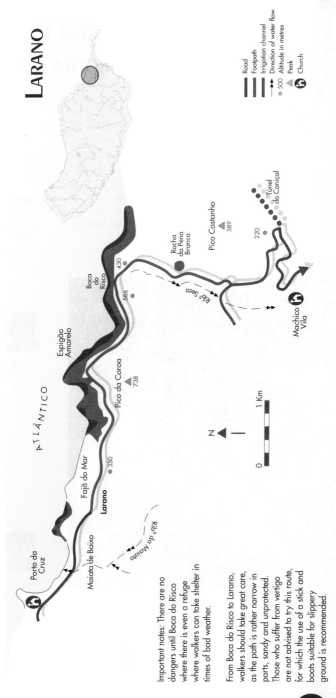

Legend:
- Road
- Footpath
- Irrigation channel
- → Direction of water flow
- ● 500 Altitude in metres
- ▲ Peak
- ⛪ Church

ATLÂNTICO

Porto da Cruz

Maiata de Baixo

Faiã do Mar
● 350

Larano

Pico da Coroa
▲ 738

Espigão Amarelo

Ribª do Maiata

Boca do Risco
● 586
430

Rocha da Pena Branca

Pico Castanho
▲ 589

Ribª Seca

220

Túnel do Caniçal

Machico Vila ⛪

N ↑

0   1 Km

Important notes: There are no dangers until Boca do Risco where there is even a refuge where walkers can take shelter in times of bad weather.

From Boca do Risco to Larano, walkers should take great care, as the path is rather narrow in parts, sandy and unprotected. Those who suffer from vertigo are not advised to try this route, for which the use of a stick and boots suitable for slippery ground is recommended.

235

FROM POISO
TO PORTO dA CRUZ

T hose who visit Porto da Cruz today can have no idea how difficult it was to go to Funchal 60 years ago. Now many of those who live there have their own car and even those who depend on the bus take less than two hours to reach the city. But time has not wiped away the memory of those who laboured along the mountain paths, carrying wine for the city and returning with maize, white or yellow to feed the people who worked the fields of American vines.

Time:
5 a 6 hours

MF

Starting-point:
Poiso

Arrival point:
Porto da Cruz

Length:
14 Km

They started out in groups at three in the morning and only reached Funchal by around midday. In the afternoon, having bought and sold, visited the doctor or a sick relative in hospital, they returned by the same route, arriving home late at night, tired and hungry.

To attend to some administrative matter or to pay taxes in Machico, the path was through Larano. To get to Funchal city, the people of Porto da Cruz could take one or other of two old paths. One began in Terra Baptista and ran along the ridge separating the collection basins of São Roque do Faial and Tem-te-não-caias. The other passed close to where the Lamaceiros forestry post now stands, and was used by folk from Vila, Serrado, Cova do Til, Gambão and Referta.

The two old paths, now rather abandoned, converged near Pico do Suna, a small elevation lying at an altitude of 1,028 metres around one kilometre from the Levada da Serra do Faial.

From here, a single path, seven kilometres of near-flat terrain, led to Carreiras de Cima. Here began a long descent to Choupana, passing through Carreiras de Baixo. At Choupana, there was a choice of descending along either the paths through Meio and Rochinha or those of Terço and Palheiro.

It was always so, carrying goods or the sick. With sweat running in rivers during the heat of the summer, with aching bones and muscles when the wind blew bitter or during rainstorms. And if the outward journey to the city was hard, the return home was no easier.

The opening of new roads and forest trails led to the disappearance of some sections of the old paths to Porto da Cruz, to the point where it is not possible nowadays to exactly reproduce the routes the inhabitants of Porto da Cruz - some of them still alive - used to take. Nevertheless, it is possible to walk from Poiso to this northern parish of Madeira along those stretches of the paths which have withstood the erosion of time and the neglect of men.

With good health and just a rucksack on our backs, suitable equipment, with no hurry and good weather, we can take a pleasant walk from Poiso to Porto da Cruz. There are various possible routes, and I shall describe one here.

The first part of the walk is along the Poios-Santo da Serra forest road. From time to time, to break the monotony of the tarmac and to glimpse a wider panoramic view, we can take short detours, walking along sections of the old paths cut through by the new road.

Soon after starting out, if the mist has not decided to join our expedition, we can begin to enjoy fine views of the central ridge, which give us the impression that Pico do Areeiro is higher than Pico Ruivo.

From one of the hills on the left of the road, we see, lower down, the tiny plateau of Chão das Feiteiras, its rows of young trees contrasting with the patches of the bracken and the foxgloves which surround the sheep pen from which hungry animals set forth each day to look for food in the meagre pastures.

Lower down, in the Terreiros and Pico do Suna area, the scene is repeated: hundreds of sheep, some white, others brown, almost black, are scattered all over in search of food, of necessi-

View from Pico do Suna

ty a frugal meal, amidst the sound of tinkling bells.

It is approximately seven kilometres from Poiso to Pico do Suna, four along the forest road and three more along a track of beaten earth. This section is not signposted, but is the first turning on the left after passing through a small pine forest.

In Pico do Suna, the viewpoint by the forest fire watchtower offers one of the most spectacular views of Madeira: Ponta do Clérigo sheltering the Bay of Faial to the west, the great Penha de Águia to the east; houses embellishing the slopes of Faial and São Roque do Faial; the tiny bay of Proto da Cruz, huddling between the slopes of Penha de Águia and Ponta de São Lourenço and, in the distance, the silhouettes of Porto Santo and the Desertas; finally, the broad Machico valley, houses occupying its concave slopes.

After the visit to the viewpoint, we must turn back to the little clearing beside the fountain. Here, the correct path is that leading off to the left. For a kilometre, more or less, the path is surrounded by laurels, lily-of-the-valley trees - adorned by lovely aromatic white flowers in August - bilberry - loaded with fruits rich in vitamins A and C in September - heather and a huge variety of ferns. In some sections, the bracken makeo passage difficult and in Cabeço Furadao they even conceal the two narrow paths leading to the Levada da Serra do Faial.

In Cabeço do Pedreiro, the path emerges from the dense vegetation to offer the walker another helping of delicious landscape, from

MF

Ribeira de São Roque do Faial to Cortado de Santana.

It is some four kilometres from Cabeço do Pedreiro to the regional road in Terra Baptista, downhill all the way, with steep descents in certain places, as well as sections where the path is in poor condition. Little by little, the forest gives way to fields of cereals and vines, and the state of the path improves greatly once we reach the cultivated zone.

Those who reach Terra Baptista with sufficient strength remaining may like to try the ascent to Penha de Águia, for the path to the peak of this imposing rock formation begins close to this point.

Terra Baptista

MF

But the walk to Penha de Águia is best left for another day, and we shall descend slowly to Porto da Cruz.

FROM POISO TO PORTO dA CRUZ

Important notes: It is four kilometres of forest road from Poiso to Meia Serra. It is possible to take short detours to break the monotony of the tarmac, using stretches of the old path which cross the road.

The path of Pico do Suna is of earth, and is the first on the left as we descend.
Pico do Suna is three kilometres along the Santo-Poiso forest road. Close to the peak is a fountain, beside which the road forks: the wider section leads to the forest fire watchtower, the other, to the left, descends into Porto da Cruz.
The old path to Terra Baptista passes over Levada da Serra do Faial in Cabeço Furado.
After Cabeço do Pedreiro, some sections of the path are in poor condition, and a stick and suitable footwear are required to cross the slippery terrain.

Faial

Penha
de Águia
● 589

Porto
da
Cruz

Terra
Baptista

Cabeço
do
Pedreiro
● 430

Rib.º de São Roque do Faial

Cabeço
Furado

Rib.º Tem te não caias

Ribeiro Frio

Levada da Serra do Faial

Ribeiro Frio

Casa
Florestal

Chão
das
Feiteiras

● 1028
Pico
do
Suna

Ribeiro do Arrochete

● 1306

Santo
da
Serra

Areeiro

● 1410   Casa
do
Poiso

Funchal

Camacha

N

0   1 Km

	Road
	Footpath
	Irrigation channel
	Earthen path
►►►	Direction of water flow
● 500	Altitude in metres
▲	Peak
⊐⊏	Bridge

240

Penha de Águia

T he sky was overcast when we began to ascend on the Porto da Cruz side, in the spot known as La Cruz, in Terra Baptista. The peak of Penha de Águia flew flags of ragged cloud.

The temperature on that December day was pleasant for the climb up to the summit of the promontory. In a few moments, the mist descended the rocks and we could see practically nothing of the sea or the land around.

Time:
2 to 3 hours

RQ

Path near the summit of Penha de Águia

Starting-point:
The road between Porto da Cruz and Faial, at Cruz in Terra Baptista

Arrival point:
Village of Penha de Águia de Baixo

Length:
3 kilometres

Nevertheless, the ascent of the steep slopes to Porto da Cruz is not dangerous, and until the mist dispersed we spent our time examining the plants along the path-side.

Soon after starting out, the path is enveloped by fields of American vines, which disappear once we cross the aqueduct. Above the channel, there are still a few terraces producing dry-farming crops.

Still at low altitude, there are patches of eucalyptus, acacias and pines, species which in the not so remote past produced wood for the people of the surrounding areas.

Many of the terraces which were formerly cultivated are now the scene of an interesting competition between the indigenous species which are spontaneously attempting to return to a space which was once theirs.

Here are many Canary holly trees (*Ilex canariensis*) and wax myrtle (*Myrica faya*). Also dwelling here, forcing their roots amongst the rocks, are globularia (*Globularia salicina*), myrtle *(Myrtus communis)*, laurel (*Laurus azorica*), Canary Laurel (*Apollonias barbujana*), pride of Madeira (*Echium nervosum*), betony (*Teucrium betonicum*) and houseleeks (*Aeonium glandulosum* and *Aeonium glutinosum*).

The end of the year sees the holly adorned with round red fruit which, thanks to the inaccessibility of these rocks, escape being cut for Christmas decorations. Almost at the top now, we find patches of eucalyptus (*Eucalyptus globulus*) competing with wax myrtle, pines heather (*Erica scoparia ssp. platycodon*) and tree heath (*Erica arborea*).

Seen from the distance, Penha de Águia gives the impression that its peak is almost flat. Nothing is further from the truth, however. The morphology of the summit is characterised by the existence of two valleys and three ridges or *lombos*. Lombo de António Dias is in the centre, Lombo da Carqueja to the east and Lombo da Cruz on the Faial side.

The valleys of Penha de Águia terminate at the summit. When it rains, the water cascades down to the sea.

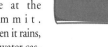

A geodesic mark stands on the highest point of Penha de Águia (589 metres). From here, we can enjoy magnificent views all around, including Faial, Cortado de Santana and Portela and the merging of the Metade and São Roque do Faial rivers, which further down join Ribeira Seca.

The path to the village of Penha de Águia de Baixo starts out beside the geodesic mark. It is less than two kilometres, but the path has practically disappeared in some places, obliging us to descend cross-country through bracken and pines.

Skirting around the Lombo da Cruz, the path then leads almost to the summit. Leaving the path and walking towards the rocks for a little way, we can see the *fajã* and Rocha da Galé from above.

On the night of 1 February 1992, Madeira's youngest *fajã* (platform) was born in Penha de Águia.

Due to the erosive action of the sea, a concavity or abrasion chamber was formed in the base of the mountain. This cave was enlarged by the attack of the waves, particularly in winter and during gales.

The coastline between Ponta de S. Lourenço and Porto da Cruz, seen from Penha de Águia

The fissured rock structure, subject to great infiltration from rain and with no exterior support, finally succumbed to the force of gravity.

With the collapse of a first section, the cliff fell back a little, and an accumulation platform was formed at its base. The submerged part of this platform rests on the bed, extending some twenty metres below sea level, whilst the exposed section forms the *fajã*.

The *fajã* (platform) of
Penha de Águia was
formed in February 1992

Thanks to the wind and birds *Fajã* de Penha de Águia quickly
turned into a fine garden by the sea.

PENHA DE ÁGUIA

Important notes: The ascent, about one kilometre, can be completed in 45-60 minutes. It begins at an altitude of 240 metres and ends 560 metres above sea level, beside the anchorage point of a cable once used to transport wood to Porto da Cruz.

Two paths start out at this point. One, on the right as we ascend, leads to the viewpoint, or Assomadouro, commanding views of Porto da Cruz and Ponta de São Lourenço. The other, on the left, leads to the geodesic mark indicating the highest point of Penha de Águia (589 metres).

The correct path to Faial is the one which runs past the geodesic mark. From here it is downhill all the way, the path, less steep than the one on the Porto da Cruz side, though in certain sections it is necessary to walk cross-country.

The path ends at the tiny village of Penha de Águia de Baixo, in the parish of Faial.

Sturdy boots are recommended for this walk, as is a stick, water, rucksack with calorie-rich food and waterproofs.

In the area of Porto da Cruz (1)

H ow pleasant to look out over the landscape around Porto da Cruz from the viewpoint at Portela: the old paths running straight along the ridges, flanked by houses; the Massapez and Tem-te-não-caias, the Junçal and Maiata rivers separating the small vil-

Time: 3
or 4 hours

Starting-point:
Portela

Arrival point:
Porto da Cruz

Lombo dos Leais

lages; the great Penha de Águia with the black hand of the devil imprinted into the colossal wall surrounded by the town where the old factory chimneys remind us of bygone times of economic boom.

The viewpoint gives us an image of the whole, but it is impossible to hold in the eye the entire range of natural and cultural elements making up this rural landscape. Nothing better than a walk along the paths, old roads and levadas of this area to get to know the heritage it contains.

Length:
9 kilometres

Let us begin, then, by descending from Portela to Cruz da Guarda. The path is easy, and we cannot miss it. Right by the restaurant, we find a forest track from which a path branches off down the hillside after a few metres. This path is signposted and the stony ground is in reasonably good condition.

At first, this route is surrounded on either side by laurels, holly, wax myrtle, bilberry and many ferns. Little by little, the slopes between the path and the valleys on either side become populat-

Serrado

MF

ed with terraces where cabbages, potatoes and sweet potatoes grow. Almost without realising it, we reach the road which links Cruz da Guarda with the regional road. At a good pace, this is a half-hour walk, but those who wish to observe carefully the many species of flora or the beautiful landscapes we pass through will require hours. It is a question of taste...

Farther to the west, separated from Cruz da Guarda by a tributary of the Junçal, more vegetables than vines continue to be cultivated at Lombo do Folhadal. The manor house of the leais, now property of the diocese, and the Chapel of S. João Nepomuceno, built in 1776 by the Leais family, are familiar landmarks embellishing the ridge, which forms part of Gambão. To see these two interesting pieces of local architecture, we have to ascend along a path crossing the Cruz da Guarda road.

Continuing along the Cruz da Guarda road, or along the aqueduct running at a lower level, we reach the main road just below the path to Referta and Achada. Near the entrance to this path are steps leading to the Levada do Castelejo. Here we have two choices: to continue along the aqueduct, skirting deep, narrow valleys and ridges until we come to the path to Achada, near a great reservoir, or to take the Referta path.

Those taking the second option will have the opportunity of observing, soon after beginning the descent, on the right, a beautiful great til-tree which was once a source of food for cattle and which is now a landmark in the Referta area due to its high position. Descending a little more, we come to a chapel adjoining an old house which shows evident signs of ruin. In this simple chapel, built in 1712 in honour of Our Lady of Bethlehem, is the tomb of its founder, Captain Manuel Telles de Menezes. It is a pity this architectural site is on its way to ruin with no one to help conserve it. And this feeling is aggravated when we see that recent constructions in the area are characterised by their poor taste and damage the harmony of the landscape.

Continuing along the road to Achada, we see that this place is rather different in appearance from the other villages of Porto da Cruz. In fact, this is a small plateau surrounded by the deep, narrow valleys of the Massapez and Junçal rivers. Here the land is almost exclusively given over to the cultivation of the vine, and despite talk of change the American vine "Isabella" continues to be

Porto da Cruz

favoured for both, eating and table wine. Between Achada and the church of Porto da Cruz the path goes through a place known to the residents as Cal. This name derives from the fact that an ashen coloured rock is exposed here which those less versed in geology might think is limestone ("cal" in Portuguese).

Various geological studies in this area have shown, however, that this rock, eroded by the physical and chemical action of the winds is not calcareous. It is of volcanic origin, like basalt, though softer, and is known as mugearite.

This is a rock of the same type of which lovely examples of columnar disjunction can be seen on the banks of the Junçal, close to the village. Over this group of columns, which remind us of the old organs of churches, lives a group of lovely Canary laurels whose roots search for nutrition amongst the fissures of the rocks. The pale ashy colour of the great prisms of those magmatic rocks forms, with the dark green of the Canary laurels, a natural sanctuary worth visiting and helping conserve.

Our walk is winding towards its end, and from the road we can see the last bends of the Junçal River. Junçal or Juncal?

If the reader will accompany me on the next walk around the lands of Porto da Cruz, then he or she will find out the answer to this question.

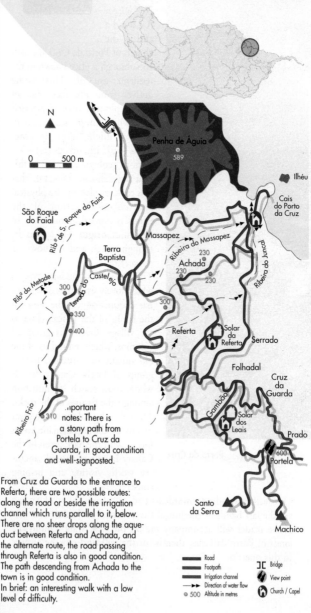

important notes: There is a stony path from Portela to Cruz da Guarda, in good condition and well-signposted.

From Cruz da Guarda to the entrance to Referta, there are two possible routes: along the road or beside the irrigation channel which runs parallel to it, below. There are no sheer drops along the aqueduct between Referta and Achada, and the alternate route, the road passing through Referta is also in good condition. The path descending from Achada to the town is in good condition.
In brief: an interesting walk with a low level of difficulty.

Road	Bridge
Footpath	View point
Irrigation channel	Church / Capel
Direction of water flow	
⊙ 500 Altitude in metres	

In the area of Porto da Cruz (2)

T he previous walk around Porto da Cruz ended in the town of the same name after passing through Cruz da Guarda, Folhadal, Reperta, Achada, Cal and Ribeira do Junçal.

Time:
5 to 6 hours

Starting-point:
Achada

Arrival point:
The quay of
Porto da Cruz

**Achada, Fajã do Milho,
Terra Baptista...**

MF

Length:
12 kilometres

Junçal or Juncal? We left this question unresolved and I promised to give an answer when I wrote about the second and final walk around this parish in north-east Madeira. Being a man of my word, I shall here and now give my own opinion about this problem, which is really no problem at all.

For many years, I called that watercourse which has its mouth near the church after twisting and winding amongst basalt, trachytes and mugearytes, the Juncal River. Later, however, corrected by friends from Porto da Cruz, I became used to calling it the Junçal. Aware that the name I had formerly called this pleasant river was by no means ugly, and because I am that sort of person, I began to look into the origin of the two words. Let me say, in truth, that I did not have to think very hard to realise that JUN-CAL is related to the presence of plants of the *Juncus* family, whilst JUNÇAL refers to *Junça* or, more scientifically, the plant of the Cyperaceas family known by the Latin name of *Cyperus longus*.

Pardon me, but what grows around here are *juncos* more than *junças*, and the river should therefore be called Juncal, not Junçal.

Ah, how relieved I am after arriving at this conclusion! Now, with a lighter step, I am just in the mood to take the path up to Cal.

If you like, you can come with me, and in a quarter of an hour we shall be in Achada, and from there it is just a moment to the Levada do Castelejo.

RQ

This is where the new walk really begins, for if you recall we visited Achada as part of our last excursion. We now walk towards the source of the aqueduct in Ribeiro Frio, 310 metres above sea level. From Achada to the source of the levada is just over four kilometres. We shall allow two hours for this walk in order to give us time to enjoy the landscape to the full. Even before passing through Terra Baptista - thus known because these lands belonged to the estate founded in the late-15th century by a Genoan known as Misser Baptista - the aqueduct skirts around the valleys of two tributaries of the Massapez River. The land around the aqueduct is cultivated right up until the final houses of Terra Baptista, vineyards alternating with vegetable plots and the occasional terrace where cereals are grown.

As we get farther from the village, wild plants gradually take over from cultivated crops. Here and there laurels, two or three holly trees, a wax myrtle. Winding around the tree trunks are the vines of the sarsaparilla family with their heartshaped leaves and also the climbing butcher's broom.

The surface of the path beside the aqueduct is in good condition and we only need to slacken our pace when crossing parts where water runs down from the rocks above. But it is precisely in these

Ribeiro Frio near the source
of Levada do Castelejo

damp places where the vegetation is richest, and we can see the tiny ferns whose leaves remind us of the kidneys, selaginella, liverworts and mosses in company with the lovely yellow flowers of St John's wort. In slightly less humid environments grow balm-of-gilead and shrubby mint, aromatic plants which those who know about such things say can be used to make medicinal infusions.

Meanwhile, the aqueduct comes closer to the bed of the Ribeiro Frio. In a densely-wooded environment dominated by wax myrtle, laurel and lily-of-the-valley trees, the river descends the hills to pour its crystal waters into the channel which irrigates the lowlands of Porto da Cruz. This place is known as Poio do Canto, I know not why. What I do know, is that words cannot describe the incredible beauty of that place where the singing of the waters blends harmoniously into the chorus of birdsong.

In the riverbed, a little upstream from the aqueduct source, a round basalt block attracts the attention due to its size and perfect form. The rock above bears the clear mark of a landslide caused by the physical and chemical action of the infiltrating waters, combined with the force of gravity.

Returning to Terra Baptista along the same irrigation channel, but with a different perspective of the landscape, it is worth making a few stops to appreciate the lovely group of prismatic columns in the rocks on the left bank of the Ribeira Frio, as well as the carefully-cultivated platform at the bottom of the valley.

From Terra Baptista to the town, we can take either the road or the old path. In any case, we pass through Massapez, an area whose soil contains a large proportion of clay which, when it is not well-irrigated, opens up in huge cracks. But do not think this land is barren. Now that water is not lacking, custardapple and papaya grow and give fruit that is a joy to see.

These walks around the lands of Porto da Cruz would be incomplete without a visit to the quay. Even the observer least interested in geology can see that the hill overlooking the tiny harbour has an interesting structure.

Part of Porto da Cruz and quay

MF

It certainly has. Over the basalt substrate emerge fine layers of tuffs, the result of the ejection of loose material. According to the German geologist C. Gagel, these stratified tuffs were deposited below the water. Finally, covering the clayey tuffs with fossilised vegetation, a light-coloured volcanic rock known as mugearyte emerges. This presents spheroid forms separated by a ferruginous material which is the result of weathering.

A small fort was built in the early-18th century on the mountain peak to provide the town with protection. But what the corsairs did not achieve has now been done by time. Fort and town alike are falling into ruin, and the forces of salvation of our heritage are nowhere in sight.

In the area of Porto da Cruz (2)

Important notes: The route from Terra Baptista to the source of the Levada do Castelejo is, without doubt, the most beautiful section, and that which brings us closest into contact with nature.

The aqueduct path is always at least half a metre wide, and there are just two or three sections along it which are a little hair-raising for those afraid of heights.

Map labels: Penha de Águia 589, Ilhéu, Cais do Porto da Cruz, São Roque do Faial, Rib.ª de S. Roque do Faial, Massapez, Ribeira do Massapez, Terra Baptista, Achada 230, 230, 230, Ribeira do Juncal, Rib.ª do Metade, Levada do Castelejo, 300, 350, 400, 300, Referta, Solar da Referta, Serrado, Folhadal, Cruz da Guarda, Gambão, Solar dos Leais, Prado, Ribeiro Frio, 310, 600 Portela, Santo da Serra, Machico

Legend:
Road
Footpath
Irrigation channel
→► Direction of water flow
◉ 500 Altitude in metres
⊐⊏ Bridge
View point
Church / Chapel

N
0   500 m

To Fonte Vermelha

For five centuries, the parish of Caniçal suffered from both isolation and lack of water. In the long, dry summers, every drop of water which trickled from the rocks was eagerly collected for drinking or cooking. People bathed in seawater, and agriculture had to make do with the scarce rainfall in autumn and winter.

In 1949, everything changed, and for the better. The Madeira Administrative Commission for Water Resources that year completed work on the opening of an aqueduct which allowed the irrigation of 500 hectares of farmland in the parishes of Machico and Caniçal. Before the water could reach Caniçal, however, it was necessary to drill a 740-metre-long tunnel, which was widened later to take cars.

Walking along this irrigation channel between the Caniçal tunnel and its source in Fonte Vermelha, we see surprising and beautiful views, rather different from what we are accustomed to see in the Machico valley. Below are a few notes on what we may expect to observe along the ten kilometres of this route.

Time:
5 hours

Starting-point:
Caniçal tunnel

Arrival point:
Machico

RQ

Prismatic columns, Ribeira Grande

Walking unhurriedly, stopping to examine natural or man-made elements, taking a photo here and there, the hike to the souce of the levada takes around four hours.

Length:
14 kilometres

Four hours of skirting valleys and ridges, now hiding in the skirts of the Seca, Nóia, Grande and Cales rivers, now emerging along the sunny ridges between them. Now crossing cultivated lands, now penetrating woods of acacia and eucalyptus, their roots digging into the cracks of the rocks above the canal to find water to slake their insatiable thirst.

Along this path, we can detect microenvironments, which find their expression in the diversity of plants

The Valley of Machico

which grow in them and in the composition of the woods. Where the sun provides longer hours of light and heat, bananas, vines, sugarcane and custard apples are cultivated. Where there is less sunlight and temperatures are not so high, mixed crops dominate, with potatoes, sweet potatoes, cabbage, beans, carrots.

If this variety of plants of such different origins and climatic requirements we find in the lands below the aqueduct is curious, nonetheless interesting is the difference between the system of cultivation between the irrigated lands and some of the terraces situated above the irrigation channel. Here, wheat and potatoes are the main dry-farming crops subject to the rhythm of the rainfall.

Those who think the construction of the irrigation channels of Madeira belongs to another age will find their ideas changed by a walk along this aqueduct. As recently as 1985, I saw the construction of some of the small terraces which today lie side by side with

Source of the irrigation channel

others hundreds of years old. And this Herculean task is not over! Here, the cowsheds, as in the rest of the island, are losing their thatched roofs, and the frequent presence of zinc impoverishes the landscape. Moreover, the aberrant colours and design of many of the new houses are a blot on the landscape of this, the widest valley in Madeira. But in spite of everything, Machico is still a pretty place.

For those with a particular love of plants and who get pleasure in finding out about them, a walk along the Levada do Caniçal is a true delight. Just to whet the appetite, I can say that, amongst other species, we can find here the small fern with kidney-shaped leaves, globularia, wax myrtle, laurel, til-trees and Canary laurel. These are all species indigenous to Madeira and, as well as their individual interest, form associations of great ecological value.

Many other plants grow spontaneously near the aqueduct, some indigenous and others exotic. Amongst these, special reference should be given, for their frequency and decorative effect, to the kalanchoe or, for the more erudite in matters botanical, *Bryophyllum pinnatum*, small fleshy plants with reddish-green bell-shaped flowers.

Of the geological formations which can be seen from the side of the aqueduct, what stands out due to their imposing beauty are the basalt columns of Corujeira, opposite the Chapel of Ribeira

Grande. Though partially covered by vegetation, the mouth of the Furnas do Cavalum can also be observed on the scarped slope on the right-hand banks of the Machico river, some 500 metres upstream from its confluence with the Seca. These are four cavities of volcanic origin which, whilst not as spectacular as calcareous grottoes, are still of interest to potholers. Just one piece of advice. These caves should only be visited in the company of an experienced guide and with suitable equipment.

The irrigation channel near the Caniçal tunnel

Our walk along the levada terminates at its source, that is, Fonte Vermelha. "Red Fountain" is thus known because its waters spring forth from amongst fissured basalt and underlying layers of reddish, impermeable volcanic tuffs.

There is now a gentle four-kilometre descent to Machico, along the road built on the right-hand bank of the river on land reclaimed from the watercourse.

This last hour of walking gives us the opportunity of passing close by and appreciating the details of the basalt columns we saw from the aqueduct. If you are not content with admiring their beauty and want to know also how they were formed, here is an answer which will perhaps satisfy your curiosity. The formation of these enormous vertical prisms was due to the development of contraction fissures during the cooling of the lava, more precisely during the period when the volcanic lava was transformed from its pasty liquid form to the rigid state.

FONTE VERMELHA

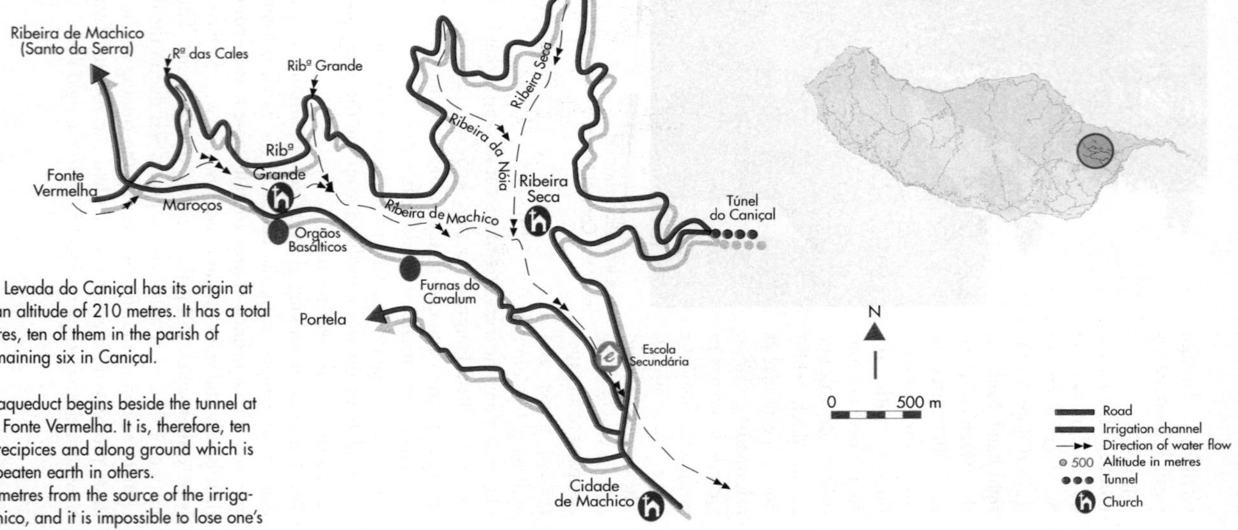

Road
Irrigation channel
Direction of water flow
○ 500 Altitude in metres
Tunnel
Church

N

0   500 m

Labels on map: Ribeira de Machico (Santo da Serra), Rª das Cales, Fonte Vermelha, Ribₐ Grande, Marocos, Ribⁿ Grande, Rib do Nóia, Ribeira do Nóia, Ribeira Seca, Túnel do Caniçal, Ribeira de Machico, Ribeira Seca, Orgãos Basálticos, Furnas do Cavalum, Escola Secundária, Portela, Cidade de Machico

Important notes: The Levada do Caniçal has its origin at Fonte Vermelha, at an altitude of 210 metres. It has a total length of 16 kilometres, ten of them in the parish of Machico and the remaining six in Caniçal.

This walk along the aqueduct begins beside the tunnel at Caniçal and ends at Fonte Vermelha. It is, therefore, ten kilometres without precipices and along ground which is cement in part and beaten earth in others.

It is around four kilometres from the source of the irrigation channel to Machico, and it is impossible to lose one's way, as this entire section is along the road.

A walk suitable for all those who enjoy walking.

260

Caniçal

O ne day not so long ago, I climbed up Pico do Facho, not to keep a lookout for pirates, but to enjoy the views of the landscape all around.

MF

Ribeiro do Natal

Time:
4 hours

Starting-point:
Pico do Facho

Arrival point:
Dunes of Praínha

From the peak, at an altitude of 323 metres above sea level, you can see the entire Machico valley, with houses scattered on the slopes descending steeply to lands once washed by floodwater, and Ponta de São Lourenço, stretching out to the east.

My stay on the peak overlooking Machico was longer than I had initially planned. As well as careful observation of the farms around me, I also lost myself in examination of the tiny flowers of the globularia and heather which adorn the rocky soil around, and the great yellow inflorescence of the *farrobos*. Yes, that's right, *farrobos*. Ah, didn't you know *farrobo* is the name of a plant? It is a kind of houseleek, indigenous to Madeira, which was once widely-used for dyeing and strengthening fishing lines.

Length:
10 kilometres

Known to botanists as *Aeonium glutinosum*, the *farrobo* is the most common of the houseleeks which populate this area, distinguished from other species of the same genus by the sticky substance with which the flower stalks are covered. Natural, efficacious flypaper.

Houseleeks, globularia and the occasional pride of Madeira embellish the sides of the old path which links Pico do Facho with the village of Caniçal. On the terraces once given over to dry-farming, grasses now rule, fending off invading armies of brambles.

Until the opening of the tunnel some 50 years ago, those who could not or would not go to Machico by sea had to take this path. When the sun was high and the ground parched and cracked, this was a laborious journey, and people had neither the time nor the inclination to admire the caprices of nature. But, as the saying goes, if you run for fun you don't get tired, and a walk along this old path is a true pleasure.

From a rocky peak, before the start of the descent to Ribeiro do Natal, I enjoyed another view of Ponta de São Lourenço from a different per-

MF

spective from that I had enjoyed from the summit of Pico do Facho. Before my eyes stretched almost nine kilometres of small bays and headlands, ravines and peaks, pyroclastic material and basalt. At the widest part of the tiny peninsula, the randomly-scattered houses contrasted in their density of population with the practically uninhabited territory all around.

Passing through the lands of Dragoal,where, alas, dragon trees no longer remain, here, I descended in the direction of Ribeiro do Natal, crossing a small bridge with a round stone arch, joining the two banks of the river at a point close to its mouth. How much longer would it resist the destructive action of time? Perhaps not long, to judge by the evident signs of decay.

Near the sea, to the sound of the breaking of the waves and football commentary, groups of men resting from their fishing played cards or dominoes. Carpenters and shipwrights were doing all they could to make two beached vessels seaworthy once more, whilst others for which there was no hope lay on the pebbly beach, slowing disintegrating under the sun and the rain.

Over two hours after setting out from Pico do Facho, I decided to pay a visit to the northern area of Caniçal. In contrast with the dryness of the lowlands, the highlands and the upper part of the drainage canals of the Serrado and Palmeira rivers are covered in the green of acacias, planted there some 40 years ago to combat the erosive action of wind and rain.

In the eastern part of the Palmeira valley, the rocks are bare once more and only a few hardy plants, resistant to drought and wind, manage to survive in the more sheltered enclaves.

In this area, north of the industrial Zona Franca, we find basalt with spheroid forms and in many sizes. These rounded blocks, which give off "scales" and fine particles removed by the draining water,

"Branqueiros" - petrified roots and stems - Praínha dunes

were formed more or less as follows. Lava of submarine origin became consolidated in the form of cushions placed one over the other. The higher cushions fit over the lower ones, indicating that these characteristics were acquired during a period when the lava still had a degree of viscosity. Amongst these pillows, curved joints were developed which constituted the parts most vulnerable to alteration and desegregation caused by water.

From this extraordinary geological park and with the awesome cliffs of the north of the island always in view, I descended towards the Pico da Cancela. This peak and Pico da Piedade are small cones of volcanic waste formed during the final eruptive phases which caused the genesis of the island.

I continued my journey on foot along the narrow aqueduct which skirts Pico da Cancel, where I enjoyed fresh and interest-

Pico da Piedade

MF

ing views of the landscape, from the Island of Farol to the elevations which separate Caniçal from the Machico valley. From the water tank at the end of the irrigation channel, I began my descent to the dunes above Praínha. I shall describe the visit to this natural sanctuary, in danger of extinction, as part of the next walk.

CANIÇAL

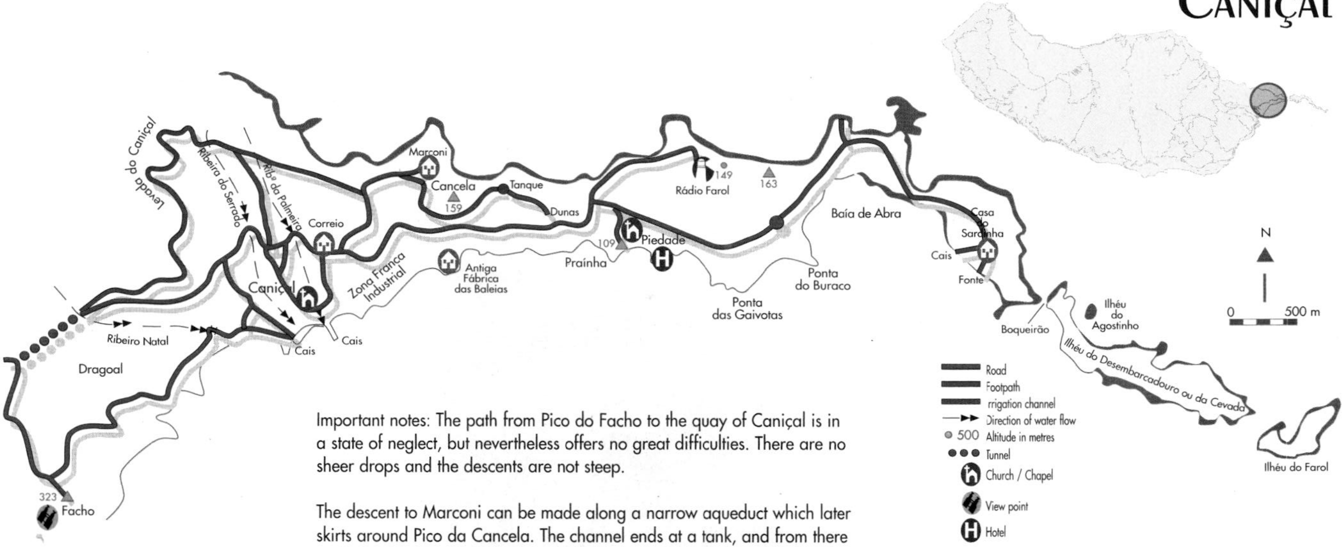

Legend:
- Road
- Footpath
- Irrigation channel
- → Direction of water flow
- ● 500 Altitude in metres
-)(Tunnel
- 🏛 Church / Chapel
- ▲ View point
- 🅗 Hotel

Map labels:
Ilhéu do Farol · Ilhéu do Agostinho · Ilhéu do Desembarcadouro ou do Cevado · Boqueirão · Casa Sardinha · Fonte · Cais · Baía de Abra · Ponta do Buraco · Ponta das Gaivotas · 163 · Rádio Farol · 149 · Piedade 🅗 · 100 · Prainha · Dunas · Tanque · Cancela · 159 · Marconi · Antiga Fábrica das Baleias · 2ndª Túnel Industrial · Cais · Correio · Rib.ª da Palmeira · Caniçal · Cais · Ribeiro do Serrado · Levada do Caniçal · Ribeiro Natal · Dragoal · 322 Facho

Important notes: The path from Pico do Facho to the quay of Caniçal is in a state of neglect, but nevertheless offers no great difficulties. There are no sheer drops and the descents are not steep.

The descent to Marconi can be made along a narrow aqueduct which later skirts around Pico da Cancela. The channel ends at a tank, and from there to the road above Prainha there is no marked path. The descent has to be made by walking cross-country over the dunes.

265

Bay of Abra

Approximately fifty thousand years ago, the Northern Temperate Zone began to feel the symptoms of the Würm glaciation, the fourth and last one in Europe. Large expanses of Europe, Asia and North America were covered by ice, animals emigrated south, many species of plants were not able to withstand the low temperatures and, as had happened during earlier ice ages during this Quaternary Era, the ocean level fell.

During this period of the general cooling of the planet, which lasted until around 15,000 years ago, Madeira was at a periglacial stage. In the upper alti-

Starting-points: A
- Caniçal; B -
End of road, Bay
of Abra

Arrival points: A
- Caniçal; B -
End of road, Bay
of Abra

MF

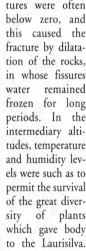

tudes temperatures were often below zero, and this caused the fracture by dilatation of the rocks, in whose fissures water remained frozen for long periods. In the intermediary altitudes, temperature and humidity levels were such as to permit the survival of the great diversity of plants which gave body to the Laurisilva.

At the lower levels, the weather became cooler, with less rainfall than at present.

During this period of greater aridity and lower ocean levels, a beach must have been formed whose sands, carried along by the north winds, were deposited at Ponta de São Lourenço, in a depressed area between the peaks of Cancela and Piedade. In this way, the dunes of Praínha came into being. The ashy sands of the dunes are of volcanic origin, but contain calcareous fractions caused by ground seashells which were also carried here by the wind. The fossil fauna of this

Length:
A: From the end of the road to the Casa do Sardinha and back: 5 kilometres;
B: Caniçal - Casa do Sardinha - Caniçal: 14 kilometres

area is made up of some three dozen species of landsnails which have been studied by scientists since the mid-19th century.

As well as a rich collection of gastropods, the dunes of Praínha also contain a great density of petrified roots and stalks, known popularly as *branqueiros*. Some of these have concentric structures similar to the forms of trunks and roots, but most have no clear-

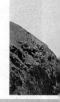

MF

The Bay of Abra, looking east

ly-defined structure due, in my opinion, to the fact that many of the vegetable species which existed then in Ponta de São Lourenço did not have a woody stalk. Take, for example, the dragon tree, possibly one of the dominant species in the area when the dunes were formed. This is of tree size but has a fibrous trunk.

It was with a visit to the dunes of Praínha that I began the second stage of my tour of the São Lourenço peninsula.

MF

I stopped to observe the unusual beauty of the forest of *branqueiros* in the sands which had not as yet gone to make cement or lawns.

Many of those I paused to admire perhaps no longer exist, for sand is a raw material and gives good money, with or without *branqueiros*.

I left the dunes and climbed up Pico da Piedade, an ancient volcanic cone partially destroyed by the abrasive action of the Atlantic waves. At the top is a little chapel, and the views from this point fully justify the effort of making the ascent.

Returning to the road, I started off towards the Bay of Abra, the largest and most spectacular of the little bays of Ponta de São Lourenço. I made a good pace because I wanted to visit the area around the little house at the eastern end of the bay.

At first, the path is easy and well sign-posted. About a kilometre after the clearing marking the end of the road for cars, there is a short detour to the left from where we can appreciate the differences in wave patterns in the sea to the north and south. The sea is usually rougher in the north, and the consequences are clearly visible in the scarps and tiny islets.

Not far after the detour, the path fades away and we have to beat our way along the rocky ground until we find it once more a few hundred metres ahead. It is around this section of our walk that we find, amongst the waste and fissures of the basalt dikes, Madeira sea stock, *barrilha* (species of ice plant) and many other tiny plants which manage to grow in windswept areas with high salinity.

Three species are known as *barrilha* here: two belong to the *Mesembryanthemum* botanical genus in the Aizoaceae family, the third to the *Suaeda* genus in the Chenopodiaceae family. These were once cultivated in Madeira and Porto Santo to extract soda to make soap. Once dried in the sun, the plants were burned in holes in the ground. As they cooled, the ashes formed a hard, alkaline substance known as *pedra de barrilha* or "stone for making soap".

During the Second World War, this age-old technique began to be used once more at the soap factory in Madeira. The soda extracted from the *barrilha* was used as the alkaline base, whilst tallow supplied the fat acid.

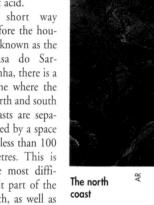

The north coast

AR

A short way before the house known as the Casa do Sardinha, there is a zone where the north and south coasts are separated by a space of less than 100 metres. This is the most difficult part of the path, as well as the spot commanding the finest views of Ponta de São Lourenço. Subsequently, the terrain broadens out once more, and the path is almost lost amongst grasses and thistles.

The little house, surrounded by palms and tamarisks, is used by the Madeira Natural Park guards, who are responsible for safeguarding animal and vegetable species forming part of the ecosystems of the easternmost corner of the island.

The Bay of Abra, looking west

Bay of Abra

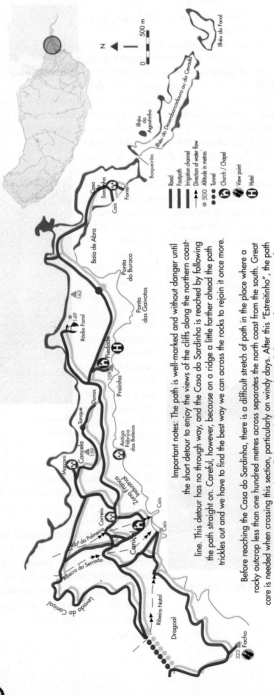

Important notes: The path is well-marked and without danger until the short detour to enjoy the views of the cliffs along the northern coast-line. This detour has no through way, and the Casa do Sardinha is reached by following the path straight on. Careful, however, because on a ridge a little farther ahead the path trickles out and we have to find the best way we can across the rocks to rejoin it once more.

Before reaching the Casa do Sardinha, there is a difficult stretch of path in the place where a rocky outcrop less than one hundred metres across separates the north coast from the south. Great care is needed when crossing this section, particularly on windy days. After this "Estreitinho", the path crosses terrain which is almost perfectly flat to reach the Casa do Sardinha. Here there are two trails, one leading to the little quay, the other to the freshwater spring at the base of a scarp by the sea. The access to this spring is very difficult.

Porto Santo: The North-east Peaks

Who says there are no interesting walks on Porto Santo? Only those who have never trodden the old paths which criss-cross the 41 square kilometres of the island could make such a light statement.

On a fresh summer day or a weekend in mid-winter, it is well worth - believe me - going to discover the beauty of a landscape formed by successive submarine eruptions which began in the Tertiary, even before the Miocene period, and which continued until the Quaternary Era.

Time:
A: 3 hours
B: 5 hours

Starting-point:
Viewpoint at the south of Pico Castelo

Arrival points:
Clearing between Pico Castelo and Pico do Facho:
Largo do Pelourinho, near the town hall.

MF

Vineyards with the peaks of Castelo and Facho

Length:
A - Ascent to Pico Castelo and circuit around Pico do Facho and Gandaia: 5 kilometres
B - Ascent to Pico Castelo - Facho, Gandaia and Juliana - Serra de Dentro - Serra de Fora - Largo do Pelourinho: 11 kilometres

To get our bearings, we shall start by ascending to the top of Pico Castelo, which seems to be, though in fact is not, the highest on the island. Higher than Pico Castelo, which stands scarcely 437 metres above sea level, is nearby Pico do Facho, which reaches an altitude of 517 metres above sea level.

From the summit of Pico Castelo, we can enjoy a broad panorama which allows us to learn some-

MF

thing of the island's morphology: two volcanic groups separated by a low area where the airport lies. Pico Castelo forms part of the principal group of volcanic mountains which occupies the north-eastern and eastern sections of the island. It is here that we find the highest altitudes and the deepest valleys, even though this is the oldest unit. The group includes, besides Pico Castelo and Pico do Facho, Pico Gandaia (449 m), Pico Juliana (441 m), Pico da Cabrita (267 m), Pico Branco (450 m), Pico do Concelho (324 m) and Pico Maçarico (285 m).

Over to the south-west rises Pico de Ana Ferreira (283 m) and Pico do Espigão (270 m).

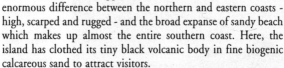

From our vantage-point at the top of Pico Castelo, we can appreciate the enormous difference between the northern and eastern coasts - high, scarped and rugged - and the broad expanse of sandy beach which makes up almost the entire southern coast. Here, the island has clothed its tiny black volcanic body in fine biogenic calcareous sand to attract visitors.

From up here we can also see some of the islets which surround the island: that of Baixo or Cal and that of Ferro to the south-west; Fonte de Areia to the north; Cenouras, Fora and Baixa do Meio to the north-east; and, finally, Cima or Farol to the south-east.

In the early times of settlement, the Isle of Cima was known as Ilhéu dos Dragoeiros - Island of the Dragon Trees. This name, like that of Dragoal which still persists in the toponymy of Porto Santo, refers to the abundance in bygone times of trees producing the much-sought-after dragon's blood.

According to Valentim Fernandes (15th century), the extraction of the red sap from the dragon tree began even before the arrival of the Portuguese: "João Gonçalves Zarco was engaged in a race against the Spanish when it was suggested through a Castilian companion that they should go to Porto Santo, where the Spanish used to hunt and seek dragon's blood on the return journey from the Canaries; on reaching the island, the other boats had already departed, so they stayed there for a few days, and Zarco saw that the place could well be settled, returning to the kingdom to ask the king's permission". Vitorino Magalhães Godinho, in the first volume of the "Documentos sobre a

The path between Pico do Castelo and Pico do Facho

Expansão Portuguesa", opines that "the information Valentim Fernandes gives about Porto Santo suggests a hypothesis: that the king (John 1) undertook the colonisation of the island on the one hand due to its direct economic value - cattle-raising, dragon's blood, agricultural crops - and on the other due to its strategic value - controlling the return voyage from the Canaries, it gave us a pirate base against Castile and for attacking the archipelago".

The extraction of dragon's blood, the proliferation of rabbits - according to the chronicles, introduced here by Bartolomeu Perestrelo - cattle-breeding and wood-cutting, combined to cause the desertification of Porto Santo. Dragon trees and Juniper, which dominated the vegetation of the island during the early colonial period, were decimated. Happily, though, on Pico Castelo and other points of the island, dragon trees have since been replanted, enlivening the landscape with their presence.

Juniper (*Juniperus phoenicea*) and other indigenous species need to be planted year after year and in large numbers until the danger of desertification is finally vanquished. This reforestation was defended as long ago as 1908 by the great Madeiran botanist Carlos Azevedo de Menezes: "In our opinion, the Madeiran species most suitable for the reforestation of the mountains of Porto Santo are Canary laurel, til-tree and bay. This last species already existed here in the past, as can be seen from a diploma registered in the books of the Funchal Municipal Council, dating to the year 1571, prohibiting the collection of bay-leaf both in Madeira and in Porto Santo. Beside Pico do Facho, there is a small fountain known as that of the Louro, which also leads us to believe that in bygone times a good specimen of *Laurus canariensis* grew here".

In this same work, entitled "Vegetacão e Clima do Porto Santo", Carlos Menezes also spoke of "the process of increasing the volume of waters in the fountains and springs of Porto Santo and of creating new water sources entails covering with forest the mountains and coasts of the island, presently bare. Cattle-breeding being, however, one of the island's main sources of income,

273

Beach and harbour

and in view of the fact that this activity cannot exist without
pastures, which are found to a large extent in the mountainous
region, it is clear that any attempt at reforestation there will be
received with hostility by the people, the main enemy everywhere of trees, whose utility they do not recognise".

This excerpt shows us how difficult it must have been to transform Pico Castelo into a veritable oasis soon after Carlos
Menezes wrote the book from which it is taken. This Herculean
task was achieved, above all, thanks to the work of forestry man-
ager António Schiapa de Azevedo, whose memory is perpetuat-
ed by a bust installed on the Pico Castelo and by many of the
trees which he lovingly planted and watered and which still pop-

ulate the slopes, vigorous and full of life.
Now, then, we shall finally leave the peak
of Pico Castelo to descend along the path
to the north side. Until we reach the clearing where the road ends, the most common trees are Aleppo pines and cupressus,
as well as a few holm-oaks and cork-oaks.

The El-Rei path begins just at the end of the road, skirting
around the south side of Pico do Facho. We soon come to a section where care is necessary not to lose the way. The path forks,
and it is more interesting to take the route leading upwards.
Even on the edge of Pico do Facho, on the peak of which is a
telecommunications tower, the path allows us a series of spectacular views over the central and western parts of the island.

On the slopes of Gandaia now, we see the village of Serra de Fora
between Cabeço da Graça and Pico do Concelho. Later, we catch
sight of the tiny bay of Serra de Fora between the hills of
Maçarico and Concelho.

Skirting around the southern slopes of Gandaia, we pass along a
headland buffeted by the north winds. From here, in Matos de
Dentro now, we begin to glimpse the tiny village of Serra de
Dentro and the river whose mouth lies in the bay between the
hills Branco and Concelho. Little by little, Pico Juliana comes
closer, the prismatic columns of its basalt rock powerfully
attracting our attention.

Reaching the divide between the Gandaia-Facho and Juliana systems, the path forks, leading off two ways: one track completes
the circuit around Gandaia and Facho, ending close to our starting-point; the other descends towards the foot of Pico Juliana.

Those who plump for the circuit around the two peaks will have
the opportunity of crossing through a fine wood of *Cupressus*
and Aleppo pines and of enjoying interesting views over Fonte
da Areia opposite the island of the same name.

Those opting for the descent to Serra de Dentro should bear in
mind that there is no path from Pico Juliana, and that the route
is of necessity cross-country, though the terrain is not difficult.

Now it is road all the way into the town, passing through Serra
de Dentro and Serra de Fora, which we saw from the mountain
top. This walk would not be complete without a stop at the
Portela viewpoint, which offers spectacular views over the town
centre, harbour and the beach.

PORTO SANTO:
THE NORTH-EAST PEAKS

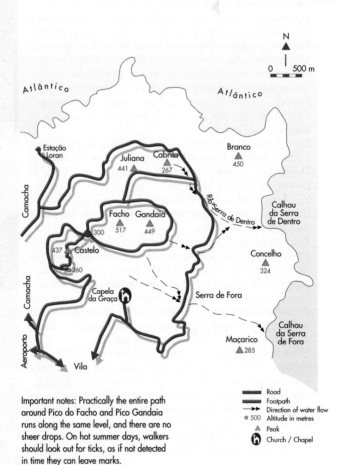

Important notes: Practically the entire path around Pico do Facho and Pico Gandaia runs along the same level, and there are no sheer drops. On hot summer days, walkers should look out for ticks, as if not detected in time they can leave marks.

The major difficulty of this walk is the section running through the foothills of Pico Juliana to the Serra de Dentro road, but the descent, even though cross-country, is not complicated.

Porto Santo: From Fonte da Areia to Zimbralinho

We begin by visiting Fonte da Areia. Here, by paying a little attention and without the need to be experts in the subject, we can see that various layers of sand alternate with clay sediments. How were these formed?

The calcareous sand is a whitish-yellow colour, and its origins are very probably related to a coral reef formed north of Porto Santo during the

Time:
5 hours

Prismatic columns - Pico Ana Ferreira

MF

Starting-point:
Fonte da Areia

Arrival point:
Calheta

Tertiary Era, when the climate was hotter and more humid than at present, and the temperature of the water was higher. During the glaciations of the Quaternary, sea temperature and level fell. The wind began to carry away particles from these coral formations which, meanwhile, became submerged under water, the deposition of this sand leading to the formation of the Fonte da Areia dunes.

This expression, Fonte da Areia ("Fountain of Sand"), has a more profound meaning than may appear. Do you know why?

Length:
12 kilometres

Central plains

MF

Because it was from here that, later, the prevailing north-easterly winds and draining waters carried most of the sand which now forms the long, lovely beach. Funny, isn't it?

And now, before continuing with our walk, we shall see how it all ties in.

The beach is nothing more than a dune formed by the accumulation of this sand carried here by the north-east winds. And this dune is mobile: when the wind blows from the north-east or north, the sands are driven towards the sea and the beach becomes narrower; when they blow from the south, the sands are pushed inland. This instability is limited by the row of tamarisks parallel to the sea, and which plays a key role in fixing the sand. To destroy these bushes and to allow the spread of building on the dune would be to sign the beach's death certificate. Prevention is better than cure...

Continuing our walk, we ascend Cabeço de Bárbara Gomes (227 m) which, along with Cabeço das Eiras (170 m) form the only two elevations in the central part of Porto Santo. To ensure that there is no confusion in identifying these two summits, Cabeço de Bárbara Gomes is easily recognised due to the various telecommunications towers on the summit.

In the wind corridor between these two peaks and Pico de Ana Ferreira are installed various wind turbines, which use wind power to produce electricity.

Cabeço do Zimbralinho and the Islet of Ferro

From Cabeço das Eiras, the surrounding landscape which comes into view differs little from that observed from Cabeço de Bárbara Gomes. Another five kilometres and we reach Pico de Ana Ferreira, leaving behind us the central section of the island, the lowest part, where calcarenite sediments predominate.

Pico de Ana Ferreira (283 m), Pico do Espigão (270 m) and Cabeço do Zimbralinho (183 m) are the principal and most outstanding landmarks in the eastern corner of Porto Santo. Though not as high as those in the eastern zone, these volcanic peaks are younger.

Pico de Ana Ferreira boasts a monumental group of prismatic columns. The enormous columns were formed by the development of retraction fissures during the cooling of the magma which brought into being an extensive dike oriented NE-SW. The more curious, those who are not content merely to appreciate the aesthetic beauty of these columns, may like to know that these volcanic rocks have the exquisite name of trachyandesites. To now, we have come across but few trees on our walk. Apart from vineyards and a few plots where cereals are grown through dry farming techniques, the vegetative covering is made up of creeping plants which awaken with the autumn rains and return to sleep once more under the drought and heat of summer.

Skirting Pico de Ana Ferreira from the north, we glimpse the first wooded slopes. The most westerly of these, Cabeço do

279

Cove at Zimbralinho

MF

Zimbralinho, catches our eye due to the lush green of its young woods of Aleppo pines.

It is a joy to see them, from the distance or close-up. Here, Man was able to remedy his mistakes. Yes, because at Zimbralinho juniper used to grow, giving up its wood to the carpenter and the cabinet-maker. It only ceased to be exploited when it had completely disappeared.

What a wonderful thing if, amongst the Aleppo pine, should also begin to grow juniper, pride of Madeira, Canary laurel and iron-wood. There are already a few dragon trees here, struggling against the wind and the impoverished soil, close to Porto dos Porcos.

What a marvel, this tiny bay! Dikes, sills. Some of basalt, or andesite. Hard rock injected amongst pyroclastic materials.

This is a tiny island with so much to get to know. To end in beauty, a dip in the clear, clean waters of Calheta, followed by a refreshing picnic by the sea.

PORTO SANTO
FROM FONTE dA AREÍA
TO ZImbRALINHO

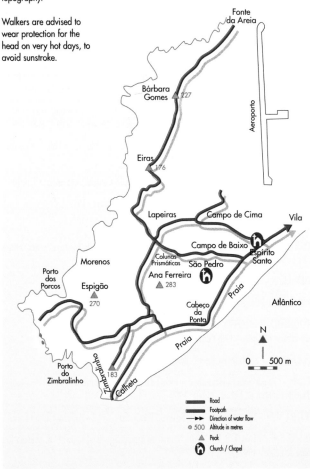

Important notes: A walk with no difficulties regarding the terrain and the topography.

Walkers are advised to wear protection for the head on very hot days, to avoid sunstroke.

Fonte da Areia

Bárbara Gomes ▲ 227

Eiras ▲ 176

Aeroporto

Lapeiras

Campo de Cima

Vila

Campo de Baixo

Espírito Santo

Morenos

Colunas Prismáticas

São Pedro

Porto dos Porcos

Espigão ▲ 270

Ana Ferreira ▲ 283

Cabeço da Ponta

Praia

Atlântico

Zimbralinho

183

Catheta

Porto do Zimbralinho

Praia

N ▲

0 — 500 m

Road
Footpath
Direction of water flow
⊙ 500 Altitude in metres
▲ Peak
🄷 Church / Chapel

Bibliography

ABELLA, I. – "La Magia de los Árboles" • Oasis S. L. – Barcelona – 1996

ATTENBOROUGH, D. – "A vida privada das plantas" • Gradiva – Lisboa – 1995

BELLOT, F. - "El tapiz vegetal de la península ibérica" • H. Blume Ediciones • Madrid - 1978

BILLINGS, W. D. - "Plants, Man and the Ecossistem" • Macmillan Press Lda. • 2ª ed. London - 1972

BOSSER, E.W. - "Esboço sobre o endemismo e a colocação fitogeográfica da flora madeirense" - 1ª Conferência da Liga para a Protecção da Natureza - Funchal - 1950

BRAMWELL, D. e BRAMWELL, Z. - "Flores Silvestres de las Islas Canarias" • Editorial Rueda – Madrid – 1990

CADAMOSTO, L. - In "A Madeira vista por estrangeiros" • Coordenação e notas de António Aragão Ed. DRAC - Funchal - 1981

CÂMARA, D. B. – "Guia de Campo das Aves do Parque Ecológico do Funchal e do Arquipélago da Madeira" • Edição da Associação dos Amigos do Parque Ecológico do Funchal - Funchal - 1997

CARVALHO, A. M. GALOPIM DE e BRANDÃO, J. M. – "Geologia do Arquipélago da Madeira" Museu Nacional de História Natural (Mineralogia e Geologia) da Universidade de Lisboa - 1991

CAUFIELD, C. - "A destruição das florestas - uma ameaça para o Mundo" • Pub. Europa-América Lisboa - 1988

CEBALLOS, L. e ORTUÑO, F. - "Vegetacion y Fora Florestal de las Canarias Ocidentales" • Tenerife - 1976

DUVIGNEAUD, P. - "A Síntese Ecológica" • Ed. Sociocultur • Lisboa - 1977

ELHAI, H. - "Biogéographie" • Paris, 1968

FERREIRA, A. B. - "Manifestações periglaciárias de altitude na Ilha da Madeira" • Rev. Finisterra, XVI,32 • Lisboa - 1981

FISCHESSER, B. - "Conhecer as árvores" • Pub. Europa-América • Lisboa - 1986

FITTER, A. - "Wild flowers of Britain and North of Europe" • Collins Ed. • London - 1987

FRANQUINHO, L. e COSTA, A. - "Madeira - Plants and Flowers" Editions Francisco Ribeiro - 17th Edition - Funchal - 1999

FRUTUOSO, G. - "Saudades da Terra" - livro segundo • Ed. Ponta Delgada - 1968

GAGEL, C. - "Estudo sobre a estrutura e as rochas da Madeira" • Centro de Estudos de Geologia da Faculdade de Ciências de Lisboa - Lisboa -1969

GODINHO, V. M. - "Documentos sobre a Expansão Portuguesa" - Vol. I • Editorial Gleba • Lisboa, s. d.

GOMES, C. S. F. e SILVA, J. B. P. – "Pedra Natural do Arquipélago da Madeira" • Ed. Madeira Rochas – Câmara de Lobos - 1997

HANSEN e SUNDING - "Flora of Macaronesia - checklist of vascular plants" • Sommerfeltia nº 1; Oslo - 1985.

HUXLEY, A. - "Mountain flowers of Europe" • Blandford Press - 1986

KUNKEL, G. - "Flora de Gran Canaria" - Vols. I,II,III e IV • Col. Naturaleza Canaria Las Palmas - 1974 / 1979

LAMAS, M. - "Arquipélago da Madeira - maravilha atlântica" • Editorial Eco do Funchal • Funchal, s.d.

LAMB, H. - "Climate present, past and future" - Vols. I e II • Methuen & Co Lda. London - 1977

LEMPS, A. H. - "La Végétation de la Terre" • Masson - Paris - 1970

MEDEIROS, C. A. - "Portugal, esboço de geografia humana" • Ed. Terra Livre • Lisboa - 1976

MENEZES, C. A. - "Flora do Arquipélago da Madeira" • Ed. Junta Agrícola da Madeira • Funchal - 1914

MENEZES, C. A. - "Vegetação e clima do Porto Santo" • Rev. Portugal Agrícola - Vol. XIX - nº6 - 1908

MORAIS, J. C. - "A Ilha do Porto Santo e as suas rochas" • Publicações do Museu Mineralógico da Universidade de Coimbra, nº 12 • Coimbra - 1943

MORAIS, J. C. - "O Arquipélago da Madeira" • Publicações do Museu Mineralógico da Universidade de Coimbra, nº 15 • Coimbra - 1945

MOREIRA, M. E. e DANTAS, M. G. - "A praia do Porto Santo" • Separata da Revista Islenha, nº 5 Funchal - 1989

NEVES, H. C. e VALENTE A. V. – "Conheça o Parque Natural da Madeira" • Ed. Parque Natural da Madeira – Funchal - 1992

ORTUÑO, F. - "Los Parques Nacionales de las Islas Canarias" • Madrid - 1980

QUAMMEN, D. – "The Song of the Dodo – Island Biogeography in an Age of Extinctions" • Ed. Scribner – New York - 1996

QUINTAL, R. e VIEIRA, M. - "Ilha da Madeira - Esboço de Geografia Física" • SRTC - Funchal - 1985

QUINTAL, R. -"Laurissilva a floresta da Madeira" – 2ª Edição • Editorial Correio da Madeira • Funchal - 1996

RIBEIRO, O. - "A Ilha da Madeira até meados do Séc. XX" • Instituto de Cultura e Língua Portuguesa Lisboa - 1985

ROSE, F. - "Clave de las plantas silvestres" • Ed. Omega • Barcelona - 1983

ROSNAY, J. - "O Macroscópio - para uma visão global" • Ed. Arcádia • Lisboa - 1977

SANTOS, A. - "Vegetación y Flora de La Palma" • Tenerife - 1983

SARMENTO, A. - "Vertebrados da Madeira" - 1º Vol. • Ed. J.G.D.A.F. • Funchal - 1948

SILVA, F.A. e MENEZES, C. A. - "Elucidário Madeirense" - 3ª edição • Ed. Junta Geral do Distrito Autónomo do Funchal • Funchal - 1965

SJÖGREN, E. - "Vascular plant communities of Madeira" • Bol. do Museu Municipal do Funchal Funchal - Novembro de 1972

STRAHLER, A. - "Physical Geography" - 4ª Edição • Wiley International edition • New York - 1975

TAVARES, C. N. - "Ilha da Madeira - o meio e a flora" • Separata da Revista da Faculdade de Ciências de Lisboa • 2ª Série - n - Vol. XIII • Lisboa - 1965.

TOMÉ, A. V. - "Alguns aspectos do cadastro geométrico da propriedade rústica na Ilha da Madeira" Revista do Instituto Geográfico e Cadastral, nº 4 • Lisboa - Dezembro - 1984

VIEIRA, R. - "Álbum Florístico da Madeira" • Funchal, 1974

VIEIRA, R. – "Flora da Madeira – o interesse das plantas endémicas macaronésicas" • Colecção Natutreza e Paisagem nº 11 • Serviço Nacional de Parques, Reservas e Conservação da Natureza • Lisboa - 1992

"Comunicações apresentadas ao 2º Congresso Internacional pró Flora Macaronésica" - Funchal - Junho de 1977

"The Oxford Encyclopedia of Trees of the World" • Peerage Books • London - 1980

"O aproveitamento da água na ilha da Madeira" • C.A.A.H. da Madeira - 1969

"Região Autónoma da Madeira - Censos 91" • Serviço Regional de Estatística da Madeira

"Estudo global dos recursos hídricos da Ilha do Porto Santo" • Laboratório Nacional de Engenharia Civil • Lisboa - Dezembro - 1981

"Plano energético da Região Autónoma da Madeira" - Relatório Base Centro de Estudos em Economia da Energia, dos Transportes e do Ambiente - Junho 1989

"Anais do Município do Porto Santo" - introdução e notas de Alberto Vieira e João Ribeiro • Ed. Câmara do Porto Santo - 1989

"Actas do Primeiro Colóquio Internacional de História da Madeira" - Vols. I e II • Governo Regional da Madeira - 1986

"Roteiro do Arquipélago da Madeira e Ilhas Selvagens" – 2ª Edição • Instituto Hidrográfico • Lisboa - 1979

Carta Militar da Madeira - escala 1:25000

Carta Geológica da Madeira e notícia explicativa – Serviços Geológicos de Portugal • Lisboa -1985

CONTENTS